PENGUIN BOOKS

FROM BRAINS TO CONSCIOUSNESS?

Steven Rose is Professor of Biology and Director of the Brain and Behaviour Research Group at the Open University. A biochemist by training, his research centres on the molecular and cellular mechanisms of memory formation, although he has also written and worked extensively on issues concerning the social framework and consequences of science. He is author of many books, including, in Penguin, *The Chemistry of Life* (first published in 1966 and now approaching its fourth edition), *Lifelines* (1997) and, with Richard Lewontin and Leon Kamin, *Not in Our Genes* (1984). Steven Rose won the 1993 Rhône-Poulenc Science Book Prize for *The Making of Memory*. *From Brains to Consciousness?* is the result of an open symposium convened by Steven Rose for the 1996 meeting of the British Association for the Advancement of Science.

From Brains
to Consciousness?

ESSAYS ON THE NEW SCIENCES
OF THE MIND

Edited by Steven Rose

PENGUIN BOOKS

PENGUIN BOOKS

Published by the Penguin Group
Penguin Books Ltd, 27 Wrights Lane, London w8 5tz, England
Penguin Putnam Inc., 375 Hudson Street, New York, New York 10014, USA
Penguin Books Australia Ltd, Ringwood, Victoria, Australia
Penguin Books Canada Ltd, 10 Alcorn Avenue, Toronto, Ontario, Canada m4v 3b2
Penguin Books (NZ) Ltd, Private Bag 102902, NSMC, Auckland, New Zealand

Penguin Books Ltd, Registered Offices: Harmondsworth, Middlesex, England

First published by Allen Lane The Penguin Press 1998
Published in Penguin Books 1999
3 5 7 9 10 8 6 4 2

Printed in England by Clays Ltd, St Ives plc

Contents

Acknowledgements

'Brains, Minds and the World' copyright © Steven Rose, 1997
'The Human Brain: 100 Billion Connected Cells' copyright © John Parnavelas, 1997
'The Pharmacology of Thought and Emotion' copyright © Trevor Robbins, 1997
'Memory and Brain Systems' copyright © Larry R. Squire, 1997
'The Physiological Basis of Memory' copyright © Tim Bliss, 1997
'Ageing of the Brain: Is Mental Decline Inevitable?' copyright © A. David Smith, 1997
'Why There Will Never Be a Convincing Theory of Schizophrenia' copyright © Richard Bentall, 1997
'Nuclear Schizophrenic Symptoms as the Key to the Evolution of Modern *Homo sapiens*' copyright © Tim J. Crow, 1997
'Can a Computer Understand?' copyright © Roger Penrose, 1997
'A Neurocomputational View of Consciousness' copyright © Igor Aleksander, 1997
'Flagging the Present with Qualia' copyright © Richard Gregory, 1997
'How Might the Brain Generate Consciousness' copyright © Susan Greenfield, 1997
'Consciousness from a Neurobiological Perspective' copyright © Wolf Singer, 1997
'One World, but a Big One' copyright © Mary Midgley, 1997

Preface

To my surprise and pleasure, I was invited to serve as the President of the Biology Section of the British Association for the Advancement of Science for 1996. On inquiry, I discovered that the sole function of the President, who serves for but a single year, is to prepare, in discussion with his Committee, a programme for the Section's participation in the BA's annual meeting. As a reward for this activity, he is permitted during the week that the meeting (these days renamed a Festival) lasts to wear pinned to his chest a medal labelled 'President', rather as in some schools one was allocated badges labelled 'Prefect'. (I never was, incidentally, being a less than virtuous adolescent.) Other than this the President is a sort of puppet in the hands of the real organizer of BA events, the Section Recorder, in the case of Biology, Gary Cleland. When Gary faxed me to ask if I would serve as President, he kindly also enclosed a summary of the sort of programme, on the brain, that he thought I might like to organize. Thus put to work, I did what he told me to do, and the result was a two-day symposium, entitled 'Minds, Brains and Consciousness', held before packed audiences in Birmingham in September 1996.

As I began to put the meeting together, it struck me that despite the enormous interest there is today in the findings of neuroscience and their philosophical and social implications, there is no readily accessible collection of the many voices and tendencies within our subject, and that, almost inadvertently, we had succeeded in assembling in Birmingham an astonishing array of leading players in the field. I felt it would be a pity, therefore, if I didn't try to persuade the distinguished neuroscientists and philosophers who took part to also prepare their talks in the form of chapters to a book. Normally when this demand is made of a seminar speaker, the response is an audible groan. 'Not another chapter to write – I hadn't bargained for *this* when I agreed to talk at your poxy meeting!' To my delight, this was *not* the response of most of the speakers at our meeting. They responded gamely to the challenge to write about their subject in an accessible way with minimal benefit of the usual paraphernalia of coloured slides and videos, and indeed to a relatively tight time-table. I am most grateful to them all, both for meeting the constraints of writing and accepting my sometimes severe editorial torturing of their texts.

The result is the book that follows. In the event four speakers – Anders Bjorklund, Daniel Dennett, Richard Frakowiak and Semir Zeki – were unable to provide chapters, in all cases for honourable and quite understandable reasons. However, we were able to include one fine chapter – that by Mary Midgley – not based on a contribution to the meeting itself. Thus the coverage of the book not only reflects the themes of our meeting but, much more significantly, raises a number of highly important and sometimes controversial themes in contemporary thinking about the brain and its functions. For this reason, several of the topics, e.g. the origins and meaning of schizo-phrenia and the brain/computer controversy, are presented in the form of debate between contrasting viewpoints from engaged protag-onists.

The British Association is chronically short of money. Our Sym-posium, and hence the publication of this book, was made possible by generous financial support from the Biochemical Society, the Brain Research Association, Glaxo-Wellcome, Penguin Books and the Wellcome Trust, and I am most grateful to them all. My thanks too to the indefatigable Dianne Stillwell of the Biochemical Society, without whose wise advice and organizational skills our efforts would have submerged without trace, to John Newbury, who acted as local organizer for the meeting, to Gary Cleland, and to Brian Gamble and his staff at the BA, who helped to make the whole thing possible.

I

Brains, Minds and the World

STEVEN ROSE

We are well past the halfway mark of what the US has designated the Decade of the Brain. Admittedly, here in Europe we do things slightly differently; our Decade didn't start until 1994 and, at least in terms of European Union rhetoric and funding, seems destined to fade away ignominiously by 1998. Never mind: the sheer scale and speed of the dramatic advances in neuroscience – the collective sciences of brain and behaviour – are unchecked and apparently uncheckable. The annual jamboree of the American Society for Neuroscience attracts some 25,000 participants – many from Europe – and bids fair to be one of the largest specialist gatherings of its type on earth. The number of academic journals with some permutation of the words *neuro, brain* or *behaviour* in their titles runs into the hundreds, and the research papers they publish each year into the hundreds of thousands. Their topics range from the cloning of one of the brain's many proteins, through computer models of neural nets 'capable of learning', to attempts to create brain images of consciousness itself. The vast sweep of advances in biological knowledge of the past half century has made the brain, and its ambiguous relationship to mind, sciences's last frontier. Questions which for most of humanity's existence have been the province of philosophy and religion are now the stuff of day-to-day laboratory experiment.

Furthermore the new knowledge, like so much of the new biology, is far from merely contemplative. It carries with it an action imperative. To uncover the secrets of brain function offers the prospect of treating brain dysfunction, from the seemingly irreversible mental decline of Huntington's or Alzheimer's disease to the existential despair of schizophrenia. And if these conditions yield to molecular explanation, why should not also an even greater swathe of problems in which there seems to be an uneasy fit between the individual mind and the society in which it is embedded? Unhappy at school, unsuccessful in love, stressed at work, violent in the home or on the streets . . . , the neurosciences offer to explain, and the emerging neurotechnologies to treat, the condition. There will be a pill for every ill. If this does not take the form of Aldous Huxley's universal soma, the drug that made life bearable in his 1930s vision of a 'brave new world', then it might be a specifically tailored molecule, designed by computer and synthesized by molecular genetics, to fit every disorder catalogued in the ever-expanding and refined psychiatrist's manual, the famous *Diagnostic and Statistical Manual of Mental Disorders* of the American Psychiatric Association (the fourth version of which, DSM-IV, was published in 1994). No wonder too that, with the World Health Organization's predictions that by early in the next millennium psychiatric distress will be the worst scourge of humanity across the entire globe, the pharmaceutical and biotechnology industries view the brain and its travails as a site for major investment in drug development.

As a neuroscientist whose working life in the laboratory has spanned much of this neuroscientific revolution (the very word didn't exist in the early 1960s; before then we were merely neurochemists or neurophysiologists or behavioural scientists), I view this drama with a certain *schadenfreude*. The prospect of the new knowledge that I and my colleagues can gain in our labs with the help of the new technologies fills me with fascination and excitement, even, to be honest, also sometimes with the fear of simply not being able to keep up intellectually or experimentally, or, indeed, financially, because of the continued need to raise funds to keep our research on the cellular and molecular mechanisms of memory afloat and relevant in such a highly competitive environment. At the same time, some of the claims being made for the power and potential of our science not only to understand but also to manipulate the human mind and behaviour strike me as at best arrogant and at worst positively dangerous.

There have always been such prophets, of course. Back in the 1970s, José Delgado, one of the pioneers studying the role of various regions of the brain in the control and expression of emotion, wrote of the prospects of attaining what he called a 'psychocivilized society', in which individual brains would have regions excised or electrically stimulated through implanted electrodes so as to tailor each individual's thoughts and emotions to fit satisfactorily into the society in which they found themselves. No more square pins in round holes; each of us would have our edges chamfered to fit our niches. And even before Delgado held out the electrophysiologist's approach to such psychocivilization, J. B. Skinner had offered to achieve the same ends by appropriate behavioural therapies and conditioning techniques. Both, of course, were premature, but with neuroscience now very much come of age, what are the prospects that their successors might achieve what the pioneers merely promised?

In this chapter, and partly by way of introducing what follows, I want to review what seem to me to be some of the most salient of the new neurotechnologies and the prospects they bring with them, and then to turn to their potential implications. As John Parnavelas and Trevor Robbins describe in the next two chapters, brains are probably the most complex structures in the universe. Each human brain contains some hundred billion nerve cells (neurons) – more than ten times the earth's human population – interconnected through more than ten thousand times that number of junction points, or synapses. If this phenomenal organ developed – largely over the nine months from conception to birth – at an even rate (which it doesn't of course), this would mean some 4000 nerve cells per second being formed throughout the entire gestational period. And if this seems dramatic enough, it is worth contemplating the fact that over the first few years of life some 30,000 new synapses are being created every second under each square centimetre of the brain's surface!

This huge array develops with impressive orderliness, wiring up the brain so as to perform its manifold functions through the process of ontogenesis – that is, development understood as the product of a continuous exquisite interplay between genes and environment.

Because brains must perform routine functions – such as analysing images falling on the retina and transmitted to the brain's visual regions – in as error-free way as possible, while also being able to modify performance as a result of experience, this creation of cells and their interconnections can best be envisaged as a dialogue between specificity and plasticity. On the one hand, we have the relatively unmodifiable connections that enable sense data to be decoded, motor actions to be performed and even the multiple functions outside normal aware control, such as standing upright, breathing, sleeping and waking. On the other, the subtle changes in cellular connections that form the brain representations of learning and memory enable us to modify our thoughts and actions as a result of experience.

But this is merely neuroanatomy. The language of the nervous system is primarily electrical, the province of neurophysiology. Messages, or information, arrive at and are transmitted by a neuron in the form of fluctuating electrical signals carried by the flux of positively and negatively charged ions – sodium, potassium, calcium, chloride – across its cell membranes. Arriving at the cell's synapses, they trigger the release of chemical neurotransmitters which can cross the gap to the surface of an adjacent cell and, by binding to proteins (receptors) on that membrane, in turn cause a flux of ions across it and hence a signal to be propagated in the neuron. These electrical signals can be detected both at the gross level, by placing electrodes on the scalp and recording the summed activity of many millions of cells, or in individual cells, by penetrating the cell membrane with a microscopically fine electrically conducting wire. The complexity apparent at the cellular level is mirrored and magnified at the biochemical. The variety of different proteins expressed in different brain cells (perhaps 30,000) is greater than in any other body organ and includes a substantial proportion of all those (some hundred thousand in all) coded for by the DNA which comprises the human genome. Each nerve cell is bathed in a continually changing chemical environment of neurotransmitters, neuromodulators, hormones and growth factors that orchestrate its activity.

Thus, studying the brain and its activity is possible at many levels, from that of the output of the entire system to that of the molecular properties of isolated receptor proteins, and hence neuroscience represents the convergence of many technologies. I say convergence, yet the truth is that, despite the unification implied by the word neuroscience, many of its subdisciplines continue to churn out results relatively uninfluenced by – if not unaware of – those working in adjacent parts of the field. It is as if we have available to us a vast array of survey maps all at a scale of 5 centimetres to the kilometre, but no way of putting the whole ensemble together to obtain a satellite's eye view of the country as a whole. We have masses of data and lots of limited theories at different levels, for instance about how nerve cells propagate information or which of the regions of the brain are responsible for encoding speech, but we still lack any grand unified conception of what it means to be a brain, and how it does what it does.

This is at least in part because of the extent to which, despite the power of modern science, we remain very much trapped within conceptual approaches shaped by its history. As I've argued elsewhere, perhaps because the scientific discipline of biology developed later than, and somewhat in awe of, those of the simpler and more obviously technological sciences such as chemistry and physics, biologists have constantly attempted to understand living processes by analogizing them to the most technologically advanced machine of the period. Thus the history of neuroscience is the history of analogies, of brains as wax writing tablets, as hydraulic systems of pipes and valves, as telegraph and telephone systems, until we arrive at today's most seductive of metaphors, that of the brain as a computer.

To me, this analogy is powerful but ultimately flawed. This is not for some metaphysical reason of belief in a non-material mind or soul but because of how I understand the evolutionary processes which have driven the emergence of brains with powerful emotional and cognitive powers as adjuncts to the survival of large mammals such as ourselves. I have argued that brains and minds deal with meanings imposed by their 'hard-wired' ontogenesis, and by the historical personal development of the individual and the society and culture in which that individual is embedded. By contrast, computers deal not with meaning but with dead 'information'. That's why ultimately Deep Blue was able to beat Gary Kasparov at chess, a purely cognitive game, whereas the day has yet to dawn when anyone thinks it will be interesting to play a computer at an emotionally driven game such as poker. However, this is not for one moment to dispute that the computer has become an essential tool of the new neuroscience, not merely to program our instruments and store and manipulate our data, but also to help model brain processes. Models aid understanding – perhaps especially when their predictions are refuted by experiment! Indeed, there is even a way in which the development of computers has been aided by a greater biological understanding of brains. The early generations of computers, and current desktop PCs, deal very rapidly and sequentially with one item at a time. Thus their computing power is ultimately limited by the linear bottleneck. By contrast, brains deal with multiple inputs and outputs by parallel processing, and the more advanced 'neural net' type of computing of the eighties and nineties is designed around such massive parallel processing – even if what the computer buffs call 'neural nets' bear little relationship to real neurons and the networks of connections in which they are embedded.

But such modest statements of the relationships between computers and brains are flanked by more extreme positions on both sides of the debate. We are privileged in this book to have chapters by two of the most articulate exponents of these positions. The mathematician Roger Penrose in Chapter 9 explains why in his view computers must lack understanding (and goes on to offer his own speculation as to how consciousness might emerge from the quantal properties offered by a particular subcellular structure – microtubules – found within neurons, as indeed in all other living cells). By contrast, Igor Aleksander (Chapter 10) describes why he believes that his own computer, 'MAGNUS', is well on the way to becoming conscious.

But in the last analysis, to understand the brain, we must study the brain, and not even the most seductive of technological metaphors for it. Of course, the reason why the study of the workings of the brain has proceeded so much by analogy and metaphor is that it has been extremely difficult. Until relatively recently the techniques available to neuroscience were incredibly limited. One could study experimental animals, and much of our fundamental understanding of the biochemistry and physiology of neurons and their functioning has come from the use of such 'animal models'. Under the microscope, the neurons in the human brain are indistinguishable from those of most other vertebrates. The electrical properties of nerve conduction were worked out in exquisite detail from the 1930s to the 1950s by analysing them in the giant nerves of the squid. The mechanisms and molecules involved in nerve transmission have most effectively been analysed in slices of brain tissue derived from rats. The complexity of visual processing has depended on microelectrode studies in cats, and of complex behaviours in monkeys. Within broad limits, such findings have proved directly applicable to the workings of the human brain as well. Even today, and despite the vociferous arguments of the animal liberation lobby, this remains the case. There is no way that we can investigate the biochemical, cellular and physiological mechanisms of such complex behaviours as, for instance, memory, my own field of research, without recourse to working with experimental animals. In my own case, these are young chicks. The neurophysiologist Tim Bliss describes in Chapter 5 how his pioneering analysis of the physiological properties of slices of tissue taken from one region of the rat brain, the hippocampus, has provided fundamental understandings of the mechanisms of synaptic plasticity underlying memory formation.

However, confronting the human brain itself directly has been harder. Dead brains, since the Renaissance lifted the taboo on the dissection of human bodies, have not been in short supply. Generations of neuroanatomists have explored their convoluted complexities, first with scalpels and later with light and electron microscopes. Unable to interpret the functions of the parts they observed, they gave them the fanciful dog Latin and Greek names we still use for their assumed shapes, as relevant scientifically as those given to the astrological constellations. *Pons, amygdala, mamillary bodies* and *hippocampus* may resemble bridges, almonds, breasts and seahorses respectively, but as clues to function such terms are scarcely instructive. In the late nineteenth century the German chemist Thudicum, working in London, began the biochemical study of the brain by boiling, acidifying and extracting its various long-dead chemicals. Accurate, tedious and necessary work – but still far from function. In the 1920s a Swiss amateur, Hans Berger, placed recording electrodes on a volunteer's scalp and described the appearance of characteristic complex rhythmic waves of electrical activity pulsing across the brain. He wasn't believed until 'genuine' neurophysiologists confirmed that indeed the human brain was in ceaseless electrical flux and that placing an array of electrodes across the head could record these patterns. Great excitement ensued; the electroencephalogram might provide the key to understanding the brain. It was not to be. The patterns and rhythms – alpha, theta and so on – were there sure enough, but as to what they might mean, no-one knew.

So what other techniques were available? To study human brain metabolism, biochemists took to analysing urine in the hope of finding abnormal chemicals excreted by people suffering from mental disorders. All sorts of odd substances were found, but they mainly turned out to be the consequence of the equally odd diets that psychiatric patients were eating in hospital or the drugs they were being prescribed. A sort of empirical psychopharmacology proved an alternative approach to understanding. If a drug turned out to be effective in alleviating the symptoms of schizophrenia, one might argue that the 'cause' of the condition was in some way related to the biochemical processes affected by the drug – and indeed the literature of biochemical psychiatry is full of such claims. The problem with this though is that the fact that a drug 'works' doesn't necessarily explain the origins or function of the condition it treats. To take an example, the fact that aspirin can alleviate the pain of toothache doesn't explain the origins of the pain or what must ultimately be done to treat it. Toothache is not caused by too little aspirin in the brain, even if some biochemical psychiatrists argue that the fact that depression can be alleviated by Prozac does mean that there is a fault in the serotonin reuptake mechanisms in the brains of depressive people!

A final approach has been to study the effects of brain damage on behaviour. Stroke or accident (and sometimes, it must be confessed, inappropriate medical intervention, the so-called iatrogenic disorders) may destroy particular regions of the brain and leave others intact. Back in the 1870s Paul Broca in Paris was confronted by a patient who had essentially lost the power of speech; on post-mortem, he was discovered to have a lesion to a circumscribed region of the left side of his cortex, known subsequently as Broca's area and considered to be part of the brain's system for recognizing and using words. In the subsequent century many other such regions have been discovered; lesions which prevent the person from using or recognizing verbs as opposed to nouns, or names for human artefacts such as 'spades' as opposed to those for animals, for instance. Similarly the visual region of the cortex at the rear of the brain has been shown to be partitioned into fifty or more distinct regions concerned with the analysis of colour, motion, shape and so forth. Lesions to one region may leave the others unimpaired so that, for instance, an otherwise blind individual may still be able to recognize motion if that particular region of the brain is spared. The brain, it turns out, is modular in its functional architecture, just as it appears to be in its anatomy. This type of analysis of accidents of nature has been most ingeniously and illuminatingly extended by Larry Squire and his colleagues in developing a taxonomy of human memory and its brain correlates, an approach he discusses in Chapter 4.

However expertly they are performed, however, such analyses suffer from one unanswerable criticism, well described in a famous analogy offered by Richard Gregory. If one removes the transistor from a radio and, as a consequence, the radio emits a howl instead of a symphony, one cannot therefore infer that the function of the transistor is as a howl-suppressor. Lesion studies – whether the lesions are made by actual brain injury, by drugs which block particular pathways in the brain, or by genetic abnormalities in brain development – speak to us of the function of the system that remains in the absence of the brain region, pathway or biochemical process, not about the piece of the jigsaw that has been removed. Moreover, because in living systems both brain and behaviour are organized towards survival, the residual system, unlike the radio minus its transistor, will always attempt to repair itself or to find other ways, other pathways and strategies, to compensate for loss.

Hence the excitement felt throughout the entire neuroscience community over the development during the last couple of decades of relatively non-invasive imaging techniques which allow one for the first time to obtain, as it were, windows into the living, functioning human brain, to explore the dynamics of its blood flow and energy utilization. These techniques, of positron emission tomography (PET scanning) and functional magnetic resonance imaging (fMRI), have begun to yield results of great fascination and significance. Originally developed to help neurologists locate regions of brain damage after stroke or as a result of tumours, they have now been employed to reveal brain regions active when a person solves a mathematical problem, listens to or recalls music, and many other such tasks. These are the imaging techniques used for instance in David Smith's OPTIMA project, to map the brain changes occurring during ageing and the onset of Alzheimer's disease and to correlate them with changes in cognitive performance – the project he describes in Chapter 6.

With PET or fMRI one now sees the brain not as an orderly fixed pattern of cells and their connections, but in constant dynamic flux, with different areas 'lighting up' at different times depending on the mental challenges being faced. No-one can see such patterns, illuminated as they are by computer enhancement, false colour and all the tricks of the imaging trade, without being entranced and awestruck by the beauty and complexity they reveal. Yet awestruck is, so far, all we can be. There is still no general explanation which can link the dynamics shown by such PET studies with the biochemistry and cell physiology and allow one to say: now, at last, I have an all-embracing empirically based theory of mind, or even of brain. (To gain this some neuroscientists would surely accept the Faustian pact, and on the achievement at last of the grand theory would say with Goethe's Faust – even if they would not phrase it quite thus – Now I can surrender my soul willingly to the devil!)

There are yet further even less invasive approaches under development. One I have been exploring myself is called magnetoencephalography, which exploits the fact that, as every physics student knows, wherever there is an electric current, there is a magnetic field at right angles to it. The brain's language of communication is electric, and so every region of the brain is surrounded by a fluctuating magnetic field – tiny indeed, being only some millionths of the Earth's magnetic field, but measurable using the high technology provided by super-conductivity. One sits rigidly in a chair, one's head in a helmet containing liquid helium and the array of detectors, and gigabytes of data flow into the computers wired up to the helmet. Can we make sense of such a mass of information? It is too early to tell, but not too early to predict that wholly new understandings of brain processes and dynamics are going to cascade out of the imaging laboratories of the twenty-first century. Science fiction writers like William Gibson, with his neuromancers and virtual light, are already there. British Telecom engineers have a twenty-first-century project they call, ominously or romantically, depending on taste, a 'Soul Catcher', destined to download the information stored in the brain on to a chip.

What will such a process tell us? Will it enable us to recreate the mind of the individual from whom the information has been thus extracted? I have the gravest doubts. This is in part because of my lack of confidence in the computer metaphor for brain. Even more, however, it stems from the recognition that being able to map mental processes into physiological, anatomical and biochemical mechanisms, while it may – I would say will – tell us *how* the brain/mind works, will not be able to tell us *what* the mind is doing and *why*. These questions will have to be answered at a higher level of analysis, and using a different language, than that offered by the best of neuroscientific technology.

Within the traditions of Western religion, philosophy and thought, the language of 'mind' has been kept distinct from that of 'brain'. Back in the seventeenth century Descartes expressed this dualism clearly, when he described the brain as a machine animated by a mind or soul which interacted with it via a small gland at its centre: the pineal. The rise of materialism in the nineteenth century was scornful of the Cartesian split, regarding minds as mere epiphenomena – in Thomas Huxley's words, as the whistle to the steam train, or as the Dutch physiologist Jacob Moleschott put it: 'the brain secretes thoughts as the kidney secretes urine . . . genius is a matter of phosphorus . . .'. Of course, these were mere slogans, and psychology and its related sciences were able to continue for many years by either ignoring the brain entirely or at best treating it as a black box whose rules of operation could be understood without reference to its internal contents and composition.

This type of psychology, represented in science by the sterile traditions of Pavlovian reflexology and Skinnerian behaviourism, and in clinical practice by the distinction between 'organic' neurological brain diseases like Alzheimer's and 'psychiatric' ones such as schizophrenia, has largely run itself into the ground. Its questions are replaced by those in which we must ask at what level is it appropriate to understand how the 'mind' is mapped on to the 'brain'. Is such mapping one-to-one or many-to-many? Is the task, as some reductionists within the neuroscience community would claim, following Moleschott, to eliminate mind language entirely and replace it with discussions about biochemical processes or even quantum states? Or is it, more modestly, to understand the translation rules by which the two languages of mind and brain are related? This tension is reflected in, for instance, the debates between Richard Bentall and Tim Crow in Chapters 7 and 8 on how and on what level we should understand schizophrenia. For Crow, it is a unitary disorder of unequivocal genetic and biochemical origin, therefore a disease of the brain. For Bentall, the concept of schizophrenia itself is under question, a diffuse aggregate of different symptoms, to be explored and treated in their own right. For him, whatever the brain correlates of these symptoms might be, their expression can best be interpreted as an aspect of mind rather than of brain processes.

That neuroscience should attempt to explain the mechanisms of visual processing or memory, of neurological disease, or even of psychiatric disorder is perhaps not surprising. These after all have been our goals for decades now. That we might approach the question of consciousness itself would have been out of the question until recently. The mere fact that there are now regular conferences on consciousness, that books with such titles as *Consciousness Explained* (Daniel Dennett) can become relative best sellers, and that there is even a *Journal of Consciousness Studies* indicates how far things have come. Philosophers of mind, especially in the USA, find themselves regularly in conversation with physiologists and molecular biologists, and even enter their laboratories to help interpret their findings. Molecular biologists and immunologists (albeit with the licence that comes to Nobel prizewinners to be listened to when they speak about any subject they like) tell us that consciousness is a function of neuronal ensembles (Gerald Edelman), or that free will is located in a deep fold in the cerebral cortex called the anterior cingulate sulcus (Francis Crick). To achieve this simplification, they assume that consciousness, whatever this may mean, is little more than a synonym for awareness, and that its antithesis is unconsciousness as manifest in sleep, anaesthesia or brain processing below the cortical level. Thus an exploration of the neurophysiology of phenomena such as visual perception and sleep/wakefulness will illuminate the mechanisms of consciousness itself.

Two neuroscientists, the pharmacologist Susan Greenfield and the neurophysiologist Wolf Singer, approach the question in Chapters 12 and 13. Singer's own work on vision was heavily drawn on by Crick in his own book, *The Astonishing Hypothesis*, so it is appropriate that he should here describe how visual awareness may be generated. For Greenfield, drawing somewhat on Edelman's arguments, consciousness is a torch playing across the brain, illuminating now one set, now another, of neurons. The degree of consciousness, she proposes, is roughly equivalent to the number of neurons illuminated at any one moment. Both Greenfield and Singer, of course, see consciousness, however defined, as a property of the brain as a system, rather than of individual cells, molecules or subcellular structures. One of the keys to the functioning of the brain as a system, and indeed of the paradoxes of consciousness, is to understand how it is that the disparate functions of the modular brain are welded together to achieve our own individual unitary sense of personhood, of thought and experience.

Older views of the brain saw its organization as hierarchical. For example, information arriving at the visual cortex from the retina and intermediate staging posts within the brain would first be disassembled and analysed for its various features, such as those described above, of shape, motion, colour, and so forth. Each of these feature analysers would then report upwards, to some 'centre' in the brain which reassembled the whole picture. In such a centre there would be specific neurons which recognized, for instance, one's grandmother and only one's grandmother. However, it is now abundantly clear that this isn't how the brain works. There are no grandmother cells, in that sense. There is no overall coordinating centre to the brain's activity, in which a homunculus sits in what Dennett has called a 'Cartesian theatre', analysing, interpreting and then commanding action. Indeed the brain isn't such a Stalinist command economy at all. Instead it is a smoothly functioning ideal anarchic community in which each group of cells, or module, acts relatively autonomously but with plenty of intercommunication between them to provide the sense of coherent unity. What is unclear is just how this intercommunication occurs – a key question described in the trade as the 'binding problem'. Part of it is certainly achieved by direct anatomical, synaptic connection between cells. But part too also arises as a result of linking the activity of groups of anatomically distant cells together in time, providing a meaning embedded in the system just as a sequence of dots and dashes in Morse code conveys a signal which is not apparent in any individual dot or dash. It is Singer's research which has provided some of the best evidence for this property of coherence, and his chapter hints at its implications.

Even for the orthodox philosophy of mind, personal subjective consciousness means something more than simply awareness. There is the little matter of *qualia* – the actual individual experience of seeing red, feeling pain, or whatever – to consider. Richard Gregory, playing his habitual role midway between sage and neuroscientific mischief-maker, offers a speculation as to the role of qualia in acting as a bridge between present and past (Chapter 11). My own view, however, is that the issue of consciousness lies beyond mere neuroscience, or even psychology and philosophy. The point about brains is that they are open, not closed, systems, in continued interaction with their environments. And for humans, that environment is both the immediate present constituted by the society in which we are embedded, and the past, expressed in our individual and social histories. Consciousness is fundamentally a social phenomenon, not the property of an individual brain or mind. Of course, Marx said something similar back in the nineteenth century, and so, as I was recently reminded, did Nietzsche. So it is appropriate that Singer ends his chapter by pointing beyond neurophysiology to this social context.

And this is the point that Mary Midgley, a philosopher with a deep respect for natural science, but a considerable sense that it needs to understand its limited place in the scheme of understanding, takes up in the final chapter: 'One World, but a Big One', she calls it. It is essentially a plea for ontological unity – one world – and epistemological diversity – many ways of knowing and explaining it. Some concepts, she argues, are irreducibly those belonging to society – money, justice, elections. Others relate both to minds/brains and to the society in which they occur. And still others, while affected by the social order, are to be understood usefully only by exploring the inside of brains. For instance, whilst the energy supply to the brain in terms of glucose depends on a person obtaining adequate food, and this is indeed contingent on the social order, usually harder for a victim of landlord expropriation, war or famine than for a city financier or politician in power, how the brain utilizes that glucose is a question for brain imagers, physiologists and biochemists. For some types of understanding, a reductionist explanation is the most appropriate; for others, it simply confuses.

Which leads me to the final theme I wish to take up in this introductory chapter. Science, as is so frequently pointed out, is about both knowledge and power. The new neuroscience is not merely about understanding but also about changing the world. Further, it is so far not those neurotechnologies which address the brain as a system, informatics and imaging techniques, which claim this power, but the much more reductionist ones which offer the potential of psychopharmacology to adjust our minds to suit the world. Anxiety, depression, anger at social injustice are all now potentially to be explained in terms of disordered biochemistry, itself more often than not the result of disordered genes. The claims that there are specific genes which 'cause' poor learning and attentiveness in school or, among adults, violence, antisocial and criminal behaviour, alcoholism, drug dependency, impulsiveness, compulsive shopping, risk-taking, sexual orientation, and so on, litter the pages of respectable scientific journals and make headlines in the broadsheet press. These genes, it is claimed, affect the way the brain develops, altering its pattern of connectivity or spreading discord into the harmony of its orchestra of neurotransmitters and neuromodulators. My recent book *Lifelines* explains why I would find these claims ludicrously inappropriate were they not power-charged in their potential effects, and I am not going to replay those arguments here. Suffice it to say that aspects of human behaviour such as aggression are portmanteau terms embracing many different types of social behaviour, and indeed social judgements about such behaviour, which do not map onto or reflect unitary brain processes. Still less are they embedded in individual genes or biochemical mechanisms.

But the explanatory failure of such reductionism does not prevent its technological power. We may dismiss as an example of crude victim-blaming the claim that 10 per cent of all US boys between the ages of eight and thirteen suffer from a clinically diagnosable condition called attention deficit hyperactivity disorder (ADHD) due to some fault in their genetic make-up, as a result of which they do badly at school and are a nuisance to their teachers and parents. However, we cannot dismiss the fact that this proportion of American schoolboys are currently being prescribed the potentially hazardous amphetamine-like drug Ritalin to 'treat' this assumed condition. There is no doubt that putting children onto such a drug will affect their behaviour. It may well make them more tractable at home and at school. In this sense the neurotechnology 'works'. But it is also true that, once he had been hung, a sheep-stealer in eighteenth-century England would certainly steal no more sheep. Hanging worked too, though few then had the audacity to claim that the cause of sheep-stealing was too little hanging. Treating bad behaviour at school or in the home by drugging the child who evinces it obscures the fact that being inattentive or naughty may have many other causes, from poor schoolteaching or home abuse to simply the rotten social conditions of derelict schools, large class sizes and sheer poverty.

The technological thrust to generate a psychocivilized society by brain manipulation, from psychosurgery to tailored drugs, is thus very strong. Nor is it merely a matter of adjusting those who fit poorly into society. Psychopharmacology offers to 'improve' already well-adjusted individuals. Listen to the claims for Prozac, one of a newish class of drugs which interact with the neurotransmitter serotonin, that it can turn otherwise 'normal' individuals into super-normal performers, their real personas bursting out of their day-to-day mundaneness like Superman from Clark Kent. Or the purveyors of so-called smart drugs, now universally available via the Internet, to enhance your memory, improve cognition and provide a drug-induced superintelligence. It doesn't matter that these hyped claims are at best wildly exaggerated and largely invalid. The power of the drug enhanced by the magic appeal of technology, and the ideological role of the claims themselves, all serve to turn our attention inwards, away from worrying about the complex problems of the social order in which we live, and towards our own selves, in the search for personal happiness. Back in 1968, a graffito on an Oxford college wall read: 'Do not adjust your mind, the fault is in reality.' Well, the fault remains in reality, but all too often the new neurotechnologies pretend to permit us to ignore it, and to adjust our minds instead.

As Huxley put it, in *Brave New World*: 'Hug me till you drug me honey, Love's as good as soma.'

Further reading

Dennett, D. C. (1991). *Consciousness Explained*. Allen Lane.

Rose, S. (1992). *The Making of Memory*. Bantam.

Rose, S. (1997). *Lifelines*. Allen Lane.

2

The Human Brain:
100 Billion Connected Cells

JOHN PARNAVELAS

Neurons and glia, the units of brain function

The brain is an immensely complicated, intricately woven tissue composed of two general types of highly specialized cells, nerve cells (neurons) and glial cells (glia), the supporting and nourishing elements of the brain. The number of neurons that make up the human brain is of the order of 100 billion, give or take a few hundred million, with a similarly high number of glia. A typical neuron consists of a cell body (or soma), ranging from about 10 to 100 micrometres in diameter, from which emanate a number of fibrous branches, the dendrites, and one fibre, the axon. The cell body contains the nucleus of the neuron and the biochemical machinery for synthesizing molecules essential to the life of the cell. The dendrites, together with the soma, provide the main receptive area for incoming signals, whereas the axon extends away from the cell body and transmits the outgoing signals to local or distant parts of the brain. Neurons vary significantly in appearance, and each part of the brain is characterized by a set of morphologically distinct neuronal types (Fig. 1).

The functioning of the brain involves the flow of information through elaborate circuits consisting of networks of neurons. Information is transferred from one neuron to another at specialized points of contact, the synapses (discussed in more detail in the following chapter). Each of the 100 billion neurons in the brain may have anywhere from a few thousand up to 100,000 synapses impinging on it, and through these synapses can receive information

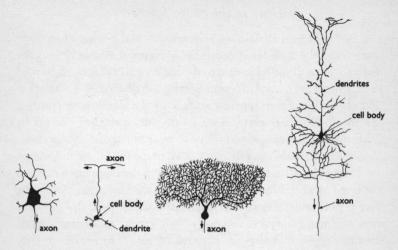

Figure 1. Neurons of many different characteristic shapes.

from hundreds or thousands of other neurons. This means that the brain contains as many as 100 trillion synapses making possible the vast and hugely complex computations we carry out through every moment of our lives.

Communication between neurons involves both chemical and electrical signalling. The signal generated by a neuron and transported along its axon takes the form of an electrical impulse carried by the charged ions of sodium and potassium, but it is transmitted from cell to cell across the synapse chemically, in the form of molecules called neurotransmitters, discussed in more detail by Robbins in the following chapter. There are in addition electrical junctions (called gap junctions) allowing communication not only between neurons, but also between glia or between neurons and glia.

How is the brain formed?

One of the biggest challenges in developmental neurobiology is to understand the molecular and cellular events that give rise to the different parts of the brain and to the cell diversity that characterizes each part. The central nervous system originates as a flat sheet of cells on the upper (dorsal) surface of the developing embryo, the so-called neural plate. This tissue subsequently folds on its front-to-back (antero-posterior) axis into an elongated hollow structure, the neural tube, and from the head of the tube three prominent swellings emerge that eventually give rise to the three main parts of the brain (the forebrain, the midbrain and the hindbrain), while the rear region will form the spinal cord. Exactly how the different regions emerge remains unknown, but recent molecular genetic studies suggest that varying patterns of gene expression in early development might be responsible for creating boundaries between brain regions.

Once the neural tube has been closed off, cell proliferation proceeds at a brisk pace, and before long the simple sheet of cells that formed the neural plate is transformed into a layer several cells thick. Information about the origin of neurons and glial cells in the developing brain was extremely difficult to obtain before the advent in the 1960s of the technique of autoradiography. DNA is synthesized in the cell body from precursor molecules, including the substance thymidine. If radioactively labelled thymidine is injected, it becomes incorporated into the DNA in the cell's nucleus, and as the cells divide and multiply the labelled material becomes distributed through each of the daughter cells. If the brain is then removed, cut into thin sections and placed next to a sheet of photographic film, the radioactive sites in the brain will blacken the film they touch, thus creating a map of the distribution of the radioactivity. Depending on when during foetal development the radioactive thymidine is injected into a pregnant animal, therefore, the birthdays of individual cells can be mapped.

This method has shown that all cells in the wall of the neural tube are capable of proliferation. The daughter cells may both re-enter the mitotic cycle, or one or both may withdraw from the cycle (i.e. become postmitotic) and begin to differentiate. Mature neurons, unlike any other cell type in the body, form a non-dividing population. When they die they cannot be replaced by other neurons, and the space they leave becomes filled either with dendrites and axons from other cells, or by glia, which, unlike neurons, do continue to divide even when in the mature brain. Although it is not known what turns the proliferative mechanism of a cell on and off, what is clear is that the times at which populations of cells cease to divide must be rigidly controlled to create the ordered patterns that constitute the developed brain. It has been estimated that for the human brain to generate its 100 billion neurons, virtually all of which

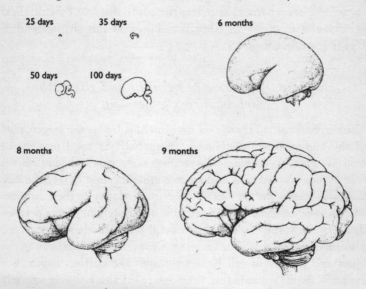

Figure 2. The developing human brain in a series of embryonic and foetal stages seen in a sequence of drawings reproduced at the same scale. The three main parts of the brain (forebrain, midbrain and hindbrain) originate as prominent swellings at the head end of the neural tube. The cerebral cortex eventually overgrows the midbrain and hindbrain. Its characteristic convolutions and invaginations do not appear until after the sixth month of pregnancy.

are present by birth, proliferating cells must generate on average more than 250,000 neurons per minute during the entire period of pregnancy (Fig. 2).

The seemingly homogeneous population of proliferating cells of the neural tube gives rise to the variety of neuronal and glial cell types that will populate each region of the adult brain. Within each region a variety of neuronal cell types is generated, each with distinct identities in terms of shape, precise pattern of connections, neurotransmitter content and so on. The neural tube uses different strategies to generate the cellular diversity that characterizes each area of the brain. I will focus here on the cellular strategies used to generate the diverse array of neurons and glia that forms the cerebral cortex, the brain tissue that covers the entire surface of the cerebral hemispheres in mammals (shown in Fig. 2 of this chapter and in Figs. 1 and 2 in Chapter 4).

How are the billions of neurons and glia of the cerebral cortex generated?

The cerebral cortex, some 2–4 mm thick, is by far the largest part of the human brain, containing about half the total number of neurons. During embryonic development, the cerebral hemispheres fold as they grow in size, leading to a great increase in their surface area and thus in the amount of the cortex relative to their volume. Microscopic examination of a section cut through the cortex perpendicular to the surface shows that the neuronal cell bodies are arranged into six layers (Fig. 3). The layering is produced by variation in the types and density of cell bodies through the cortical depth. For example, layer 1 located at the surface of the brain is sparsely populated by neurons, whereas layer 4 near the middle of the cortex contains numerous small neurons. Each layer contains a complement of pyramidal (so-called for the shape of their somas, shown in Fig. 1) and non-pyramidal neurons. Pyramidal neurons, which make up approximately 75 per cent of all neurons in the cortex, are the projection cells that send axons to distant parts of the brain. Non-pyramidal cells are interneurons – that is, their connections are

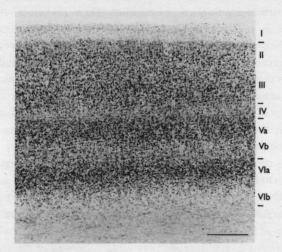

I
—
II

III

—
IV
—
Va

Vb
—
VIa

VIb
—

Figure 3. Low magnification micrograph illustrating the arrangement of neurons in the human neocortex into six distinct layers. The micrograph is of a section, cut perpendicular to the surface, through one of the association areas of the cortex, and stained for Nissl substance. Scale bar: 1 mm. (Micrograph provided by Dr Eva Braak, Anatomical Institute, Frankfurt.)

all made locally. There are variations in size between pyramidal neurons and even some differences in form, although all have a main dendrite oriented upwards, towards the surface of the brain. There are many more varieties of non-pyramidal cells based on differences in size and form of their dendrites and patterns of axonal branching. The two major types of glial cells, the astrocytes and the oligodendrocytes, are found in all layers, but they are outnumbered by the neurons.

Some layers are particularly well developed in certain regions of the cortex, for example layer 4 in the cortical areas that receive sensory information such as visual and somatosensory. Many more differences become apparent when the different layers throughout the cortex are systematically compared. Such cytoarchitectonic differences (that is, differences in cell body size, shape and packing density) form the basis for classifying the cortex into distinct regions with fairly sharp boundaries between them. The most widely used map of the cortex showing the positions of the various regions was published by the German anatomist Brodmann around the turn of the century. His map divided the cortex into approximately fifty areas which were later shown also to differ with regard to connections and functional specialization. The question of how the precise organization of this enormously complicated part of the brain is achieved has been the subject of intensive investigations for more than a hundred years.

The creation of such intricate and highly ordered structures as the cerebral hemispheres from a single sheet of cells is necessarily complex, requiring as it does a sequence of detailed topological transformations. The cerebral hemispheres develop from the front portion of the neural tube. As the progenitor cells which will eventually give rise to the neurons proliferate, the wall of the tube bulges out to form the cerebral vesicles (by the fifth week in the human foetus). Cells close to the ventricular lining of the neural tube, the so-called ventricular zone, are destined to give rise to the neurons and some of the glial cells. During the development of the human embryo the majority of cortical neurons will be born in this zone during the next hundred days of foetal life. The vast majority of glia are produced by cells in a second proliferative layer further from the ventricles, the subventricular zone. The new-born neurons migrate from the ventricular zone towards the surface of the cerebral vesicles. There, the young neurons meet axons, growing in from regions of the developing brainstem, and establish the first horizontal layer, the marginal zone (layer 1 of the adult cortex). Between the ventricular zone and the marginal zone, a thickening layer of fibres appears next; this layer is called the intermediate zone (the subcortical white matter of the adult brain). The later-born neurons have to pass through this region, eventually to form layers 2–6 of the adult cortex. (Fig. 4).

Migrating neurons assemble in the developing cortex in an 'inside-out' order – that is, the deepest cellular layers are assembled first and those closest to the surface last. The process of neuronal

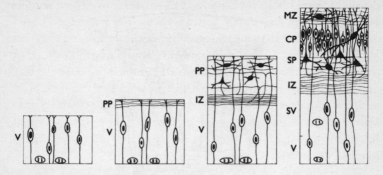

Figure 4. Four panels illustrate cross-sections of the cerebral wall at different stages in the formation of the cortex. V, ventricular zone; PP, preplate; IZ, intermediate zone; MZ, marginal zone; CP, cortical plate; SP, subplate; SV, subventricular zone. The horizontally oriented cell in the MZ is a Cajal–Retzius cell. (Drawing by Dr H. B. M. Uylings, Brain Research Institute, Amsterdam.)

migration must involve a number of steps. First, young neurons must recognize their migratory path; second, there must be a mechanism for moving their cell bodies along the pathway; and third, they must at some point recognize when to stop migrating and instead begin to aggregate with other neurons of the same kind. It has been known for some time that there are specialized glial cells within the developing cortex whose cell bodies lie in the subventricular zone and whose fibres extend radially to the surface of the cortex. These cells, called radial glia, persist until migration has ceased, and provide part of the scaffolding along which cortical neurons migrate. They have specific biochemical properties that may facilitate their initial recognition by young neurons so as to guide them during the phase of migration (Fig. 5). However, a proportion of young neurons (approximately 20 per cent) appears to move horizontally without the support of the radial glia. Very recent research suggests that Cajal–Retzius cells, a unique group of neurons present in layer 1 only at the early stages of cortical development, are involved with the process of radial migration. These early-born neurons secrete a

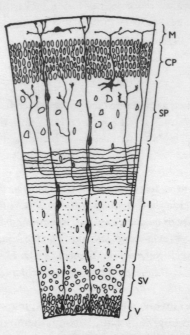

Figure 5. A cross-section through the developing cortex illustrating the six embryonic layers from the ventricular surface (bottom) to the pial surface (top). Spindle-shaped neurons migrate along radial glial fibres which span the entire thickness of the cortex. V, ventricular zone; SV, subventricular zone; I, intermediate zone; SP, subplate; CP, cortical plate; M, marginal zone. (Drawing by Dr P. Rakic, Yale University.)

protein called reelin which sticks to the molecular matrix surrounding them, and the suggestion is that reelin acts as a stop signal for each wave of arriving cortical neurons, telling them to get off the radial glial fibre and develop into a layer of mature neurons.

There are several human genetic mutations that seem to derail neurons on their journey to the proper location in the highly organized cortex. Most people with such mutations not only have epilepsy, but are also mentally retarded. The most severe of such human conditions is lissencephaly, a term meaning 'smooth brain' and is so named because the cerebral cortex lacks the ridges and valleys characteristic of a normal brain. Such brains also show abnormal cortical layering.

Cell fate determination

Cells in the ventricular zone face many choices in early development. At what point does a cell decide to become a neuron rather than a glial cell? If it decides to become a neuron, at what point does it decide to become a pyramidal or a non-pyramidal cell? Will it continue to proliferate after this decision is made? Is a particular cell programmed to reside in a certain layer before it makes its migratory journey? And at what point does the cell decide to form a particular set of connections and to produce a certain neurotransmitter? Knowing the stage at which a cell becomes committed to adopting a certain final form enables one to begin to narrow down the factors that might be involved in this developmental process. However, pinning down the times and understanding the mechanisms whereby a neuron becomes thus committed has proved hard going, both because of the brain's intricate structure and its inaccessibility during embryonic development. Even so, considerable progress has been made in addressing these questions in the developing cortex, and it is now clear that cortical neurons acquire their final form through a developmental interaction between their genotype and their immediate environment.

Genetic factors

Knowledge of the genealogical (lineage) relationships of cells in the cortex will help in understanding the mechanisms that underlie their developmental choices. This field of study was transformed in the mid-1980s by the advent of recombinant DNA technology. A method, the technicalities of which need not concern us here, was developed for introducing foreign genes into the genome of dividing progenitor cells, genes which would then be passed on to all the daughter cells in a particular lineage. If the gene codes for a protein which can be easily identified – for instance, by being capable of engaging in an enzyme reaction which can result in a coloured product being formed – all the cells which carry this specific gene (that is, a clone) can be recognized, using either light or electron microscopy, at any later time chosen. By choosing the time of insertion of the foreign marker gene in relation to particular phases of development and cell proliferation, the progeny arising from cells at that particular phase can be identified. This method gives valuable insights into how a cell's identity is determined, even though it cannot reveal the exact mechanisms involved. A complete understanding of how cells acquire their identity awaits more precise delineation of the genes involved and the factors that regulate their expression. Nevertheless, lineage analysis in the developing cortex has led to the notion that lineage or genetic factors do play a major role in dictating the identity of the different cell types.

Using this method in the developing rat cerebral cortex, my own, along with other laboratories, first addressed the question of whether there exist separate progenitor cells in the ventricular zone for neurons and the two classes of glia, astrocytes and oligodendrocytes; and if so, when do they arise? It turned out that clusters of related cells in the cortex are composed almost exclusively of one cell type, suggesting that as early as the onset of cortical neurogenesis there exist in the ventricular zone of the developing cortex progenitor cells dedicated to producing either neurons or glia. We then asked whether the two broad classes of neurons, the pyramidal and non-pyramidal cells, originate from a common progenitor. We examined clones of neurons in adult rats derived from cells which had the marker gene inserted into them at one of each successive day of cortical neuro-genesis (the last week of a 21-day gestation period in rats). The clones were composed almost exclusively of either all pyramidal or all non-pyramidal neurons, indicating that the ventricular zone contains sep-arate progenitor cells for these two classes of neurons. Such results mean that the proliferative zone of the developing cortex may be viewed as a mosaic of different progenitor cell types, and that lineage contributes significantly to the final form of cortical neurons and glia.

Using similar methods we have found that clones of neurons throughout the cortex homogeneously express the same neurotransmitter, pointing to an important role of lineage in determining the neurotransmitter expressed by cortical neurons. On the other hand, other proteins essential for neuronal functioning are not distributed in this clonally based manner, suggesting that their presence or absence depends on environmental rather than genetically driven developmental factors.

Examination of a large number of clonally related neurons from brains injected at different ages showed remarkable differences in the size and distribution of pyramidal and non-pyramidal neuronal clones. Non-pyramidal cells typically appeared as single cells or as clones of two neurons, and resided in the cortical layers that were just being generated at the time of injection. On the other hand clones of pyramidal neurons were larger and were dispersed in several layers following earlier injections, and the later the time of injection the smaller their size and more limited their distribution. This difference may explain the preponderance of pyramidal neurons in the mature cerebral cortex. It also suggests the existence of different mechanisms that generate the two main neuronal subtypes of the cerebral cortex.

Pyramidal neurons may be generated through two different patterns of cell division, either through asymmetrical (radially arranged clones) or symmetrical divisions (horizontal clones) as shown in Fig. 6; their distribution in discrete clusters suggests that their migration is radial. In contrast, non-pyramidal cells lose their spatial relationship with their clonal relatives and are dispersed in the cortex through horizontal migration. This means that non-pyramidal neurons must often represent the end branches of a family tree whose earlier branches may be pyramidal neurons. These findings suggest that clonally related cells, instructed to develop a particular pheno-—type, either have the ability to use a specific migratory pathway, or that cues encountered during radial and horizontal migration are responsible for the development of the pyramidal and non-pyramidal cell types.

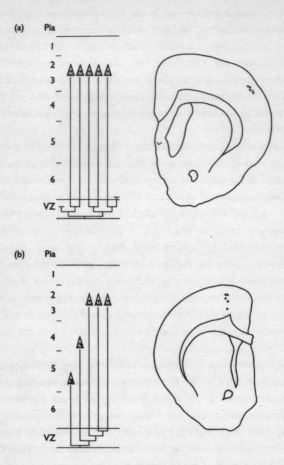

Environmental factors

Evidence for the production of cell diversity in the cortex points to the action of signals from the microenvironment of cells in or near the proliferative zones. Such signals include a multitude of chemicals: neurotrophic factors, neurotransmitters, neuropeptides and extracellular matrix molecules derived from many sources, including previously generated cells, the extracellular matrix, axons from

Figure 6. Pyramidal neurons in the cortex may be generated through two different patterns of cell division: symmetrical (horizontal clones, a) or asymmetrical divisions (radially arranged clones, b). In a, to obtain a clone of five neurons, progenitor cells must have divided symmetrically at least three times, corresponding to a clonal size of eight cells. The fact that only five cells were found in this clone suggests that at least one postmitotic (line ending above the ventricular zone) and one progenitor cell (line ending within the ventricular zone) were lost through death or migration from this cluster. In b, to obtain the five neurons the progenitors must have undergone three asymmetrical divisions and one symmetrical division after the incorporation of a marker gene to give rise to postmitotic daughters during the first three divisions and two terminal postmitotic cells from the last symmetrical division.

elsewhere in the developing brain, or the cerebrospinal fluid, to name but a few possibilities. The immature cells have receptors on their surface capable of recognizing and responding to such factors. The search for such signals and their precise role in the development of the cortex has intensified in recent years. For instance, the monoamines noradrenalin, dopamine and serotonin, discussed in more detail in the next chapter, are present in the developing brain long before they can be expected to function as neurotransmitters, and one at least, serotonin, has been found to promote the survival and differentiation of cortical pyramidal neurons.

As mentioned above, the expression in neurons of certain specific proteins is not genetically programmed but is likely to be induced by external factors. A variety of secreted growth factors play important roles in the proliferation and differentiation of cortical progenitor cells to a particular lineage. Depending on the presence or absence of such specific factors, the proteins will or will not be produced in particular neuronal subpopulations in the developing cerebral cortex. One such factor (called bFGF) helps keep cortical progenitor cells in a proliferative mode, but it has no effect on the rate at which the cells divide. In addition, the differentiation of neuronal, but not glial, progenitors is delayed by the presence of bFGF, thus confirming that proliferation and neuronal differentiation occur sequentially during development. Interestingly, bFGF also stimulates the expression of receptors for a particular neurotransmitter (GABA – see the next chapter) in progenitor cells in the ventricular zone of the developing cortex. In turn this neurotransmitter, produced in already differentiated cells, regulates cell production by providing a feedback signal that terminates cell division and promotes cell differentiation. How this is achieved is not yet known in detail, but the effect of the neurotransmitter may be to stimulate the expression of particular genes, which in turn induce neuronal differentiation. Discovery of how such growth factors as bFGF work thus forms a fruitful beginning to the task of identifying the factors that control proliferation and differentiation of different classes of neurons.

All in all, much recent evidence points to the fact that local environmental factors play important roles in the generation, survival, migration and differentiation of cortical neurons. Understanding the roles of both genetic and environmental influences, and their relative importance in determining the final forms and connections of neurons in the brain, is essential if we are to understand how the brain and its pathways develop.

Further reading

Ciba Foundation Symposium 193 (1995). *Development of the Cerebral Cortex*. Wiley.

Jacobson, M. (1991). *Developmental Neurobiology*. Plenum.

Kandel, E. R., Schwartz, J. H., and Jessel, T. M. (1991). *Principles of Neural Science*, 3rd edn. Elsevier.

McConnell, S. K. (1988). Development and decision-making in the mammalian cerebral cortex. *Brain Research Reviews* 13, 1–23.

Sanes, J. R. (1989). Analysing cell lineage with a recombinant retrovirus. *Trends in Neuroscience* 12, 21–28.

3

The Pharmacology of Thought and Emotion

TREVOR ROBBINS

The role of neurotransmitters

When a neuron is activated (or fired) it propagates electrical impulses or action potentials along its axons, which, as discussed in the previous chapter, interact with the next nerve cell across a gap, or synapse (see Fig. 1). Interaction occurs when, as a result of the arrival of the electrical signal at the synapse, a chemical neurotransmitter is released into the gap – the synaptic cleft – which rapidly diffuses across the cleft to the adjacent, postsynaptic cell where it binds to specialized receptor molecules embedded in the synaptic membrane. This binding changes the properties of the receptor molecules in a variety of ways, triggering the processes of electrical and biochemical activation in the postsynaptic neuron. Surplus neurotransmitter is swiftly destroyed by enzymes in the postsynaptic cell or sucked back up into the presynaptic cell by specific reuptake mechanisms.

The possibility that the brain uses a chemical code to enable communication among its billions of neurons was strengthened by discoveries about the principles of chemical neurotransmission in the early part of this century. These discoveries followed from the classification of the peripheral, involuntary or 'autonomic' nervous system and its two major functional divisions, each of which came to be associated with a different chemical neurotransmitter substance. Thomas Elliott, a physiology student at Cambridge University, provided the first good evidence that one of these divisions, the so-called 'sympathetic' nervous system, which was active in arousing potentially dangerous situations, released a substance closely related to the

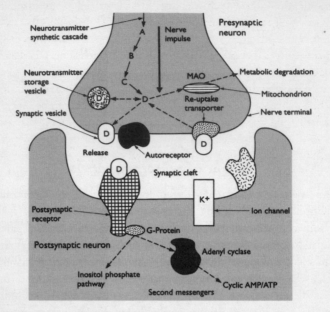

Figure 1. Schematic diagram of a synapse, the gap between two nerve cells or neurons. One type of neurotransmitter (possibly together with others) is released into the synaptic cleft consequent upon an action potential or nerve impulse. The neurotransmitter is synthesized from precursor substances such as amino acids via a biosynthetic sequence before its storage in the cytoplasm of the terminal (or swelling) of the presynaptic cell, or else in storage vesicles. Its levels are regulated by, for example, the enzyme monoamine oxidase (MAO), associated with the cell mitochondrion. It is also taken back into the cell by an active uptake process via a specific transporter molecule. Upon release it binds to specific receptors, some of which are associated with voltage-gated ion channels, and some with the induction of secondary and tertiary chemical messengers in the postsynaptic cell. The latter have a variety of functions including the regulation of calcium levels and direct effects on the gene expression of the postsynaptic cell.

hormone adrenalin, which was later characterized as noradrenalin. Over the next twenty years or so, Sir Henry Dale and Otto Loewi, among other physiologists and pharmacologists, were responsible for discovering a second neurotransmitter, acetylcholine, which helps to mediate the more mundane (but no less vital) functions of the other, 'parasympathetic' division of the autonomic nervous system.

While neuroscientists were content for many years to believe that the brain used this small number of neurotransmitters, it is now clear that a conservative estimate of the number of transmitters is over fifty. These include both a number of amine substances such as noradrenalin and acetylcholine, and also amino acids such as glutamate and gamma-amino-butyric acid, or GABA, and neuropeptides such as enkephalin and substance P (Table 1). We are still trying to guess why the brain uses such a diversity of substances. The probable answer is that diversity provides a rich grammar of interactions between neurons which optimizes the range and tuning of responses available in different situations.

Neurotransmitters have to be synthesized from their precursor

Table 1. Taxonomy of neurotransmitters and speculation on their roles

....

Excitatory or inhibitory amino acids: rapid information transmission and neural computation?
e.g. glutamate, aspartate, gamma-amino-butyric acid (GABA)

Biogenic amines: coarse representation of brain states and neuromodulation of signal/noise ratios?
e.g. noradrenalin, dopamine, acetylcholine, serotonin (or 5-hydroxy-tryptamine, 5-HT), histamine

Neuropeptides: specific coding and 'fine-tuning' by cotransmission?
e.g. enkephalin, beta-endorphin, substance P, cholecystokinin, corticotrophin releasing factor, neuropeptide Y (cholecystokinin is often released from dopamine-containing neurons and neuropeptide Y from noradrenalin-containing ones)

....

substances (often originating in the diet) by the neurons, stored in them, released when appropriate for binding to receptors on the postsynaptic cell, and either taken up again by the neurons after release or else degraded (Fig. 1). One way in which neurotransmitters work when they bind to their receptors is by causing the receptor molecules to change their conformation, opening up channels through which ions like potassium, sodium and calcium may pass. This will affect the voltage across the neuronal cell membrane and thus its ability to transmit action potentials. Depending partly on the ions they cause to enter the cell, some neurotransmitters increase the likelihood of action potentials being transmitted, and are hence excitatory. Others reduce the chance and are thus inhibitory. Alternatively the neurotransmitter may act via receptors that affect secondary and even tertiary chemical messengers in the postsynaptic cell. Triggering these chemical cascades may activate processes that regulate the levels of calcium ions within the cell, which also regulate its excitability. Other important actions that presumably can permanently alter the way in which a cell expresses its function include effects on its genetic material in the cell nucleus, for example by 'turning on' genes. Modern neuropharmacology or, sometimes, simple serendipity has provided us with means of interfering with these regulatory processes at every stage through the discovery of drugs with specific modes of action. The drugs include those used commonly in the treatment of depression, schizophrenia and anxiety, i.e. antidepressants, antipsychotics and anxiolytic drugs respectively. But they also include drugs used for 'self-medication', recreational drugs such as alcohol, caffeine and nicotine, as well as other drugs that may induce dependence such as cocaine, amphetamine and heroin. Apart from their everyday applications, we can infer much about the neurochemical basis of cognition and emotion from a knowledge of how such drugs act in the brain.

To gain some idea of how neurotransmitters may function, it is convenient to consider the brain in terms of sets of information-processing modules consisting of arrays of interconnected neurons. Such modules provide brain structures such as the neocortex, hippocampus, limbic system and striatum with colossal computing power, which cognitive scientists often try to simulate as connectionist networks. The fast computational functions of these networks are known to be mediated by excitatory neurotransmitters such as glutamate, whereas selectivity is conferred in part by the actions of the inhibitory transmitter GABA. Superimposed on these fast processing capabilities are the modulatory actions of neurotrans-mitters with slower modes of action, which may 'set the tone' of the network – that is, enable it to function in many different ways according to the general state or conditions under which it operates. These neuromodulatory transmitters include acetylcholine and nor-adrenalin and other amines such as dopamine and serotonin, as well as many neuropeptides (see Table 1). Many of these neuromodulators can also function as hormones in other parts of the body, perhaps helping to match the demands of different brain states to the most appropriate patterns of activity of the peripheral nervous system by a form of chemical coding (and incidentally suggesting a common evolutionary origin for nervous and hormonal systems in animals).

Sir Henry Dale espoused a coding principle that each nerve cell, when activated, released just one neurotransmitter substance, but 'Dale's law' has been undermined by the discovery that the same cell is capable of releasing at least two neurotransmitters, one of them often being a neuropeptide. Thus, the refinement of neurochemical signals does not simply stem from the capacities of a nerve cell to integrate the different signals emanating from the many presynaptic neurons with which it interacts, but also from the signal provided by a single presynaptic cell.

Chemical emotions: the psychopharmacology of drug addiction

In this chapter, I will first consider how neurochemicals can produce emotions so strong that they may lead to dependence or addiction. Drugs such as cocaine or amphetamine can induce subjective feelings such as euphoria and a sense of well-being which lead to further drug-seeking and drug-taking behaviour. This rewarding or reinforcing action probably depends on a host of factors including the genetic make-up of individuals, their previous experience and, most importantly, their present environmental circumstances.

Although it is impossible to know animals' subjective experience, much can be inferred about their emotional state from their behaviour. For example, they will readily choose to self-administer drugs such as amphetamine and cocaine, given the opportunity, this persistence being generally interpreted as indicating positive emotional experience. Based on animal studies, we now know that the capacity of drugs such as amphetamine and cocaine to induce such purposeful behaviour arises from their capacity to increase the activity of the dopaminergic neurotransmitter system – that is, the system of neurons which employs the amine dopamine as its major transmitter – in a forebrain structure called the nucleus accumbens. This region lies at the cross-roads in the brain between structures of the so-called limbic system which are involved in the memory of emotional events and structures that govern our behavioural responses (Fig. 2).

One interpretation of cocaine reward is that it amplifies the normal level of activity in the nucleus accumbens to enhance the significance or salience of the environment. Drugs which block dopamine receptors alter drug-taking behaviour for cocaine or amphetamine. Drugs which deplete dopamine from the nucleus accumbens actually prevent such drug-taking behaviour. It has even been shown that rats will self-administer amphetamine directly into the nucleus accumbens. It seems likely that this structure in the rat is involved in mechanisms analogous to those producing drug-induced euphoria in humans, and this clue is currently motivating studies using positron emission tomography (or PET) neuroimaging techniques to determine the neural systems activated by drugs such as amphetamine and cocaine in human volunteers.

It is unlikely that drug addiction by itself depends merely on the initial molecular site of drug action (e.g. cocaine binds to the proteins in the presynaptic cell responsible for dopamine reuptake, as shown in Fig. 1). Rather, one has to take into account the compensatory processes, including learning, that are engaged by the rest of the

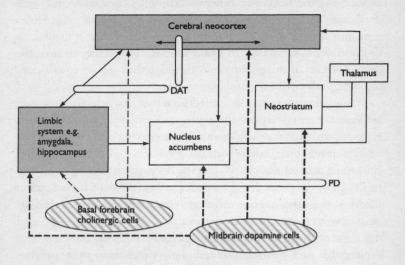

Figure 2. Schematic diagram to indicate the anatomical inter-relationships between some of the main forebrain structures and their innervation by the subcortical dopaminergic and cholinergic neurotransmitter systems (dashed lines). The arrows associated with solid lines indicate likely glutamatergic connections. The white bands indicate the predominant forms of neurochemical pathology associated with dementia of the Alzheimer type (DAT) and Parkinson's disease (PD). DAT leads to damage to cortical and limbic glutamatergic neurons, as well as to the basal forebrain cholinergic cells, while sparing much of the cortical dopaminergic projection. Note the contrasting pattern of pathology for PD.

brain in response to this potent drug-induced stimulus, operating over a considerable period of time. Perhaps unsurprisingly, these processes almost certainly involve structures of the limbic system known to be concerned with the emotions, including the amygdala and hippocampus, which have strong neuronal connections with the nucleus accumbens (Fig. 2). For example, rats will continue to seek the opportunity to self-administer a drug such as cocaine, even though it is not immediately available. They will continue to work as long as their behaviour generates stimulus cues associated with the drug by learning processes including classical conditioning. However, this drug-seeking behaviour is abolished if their amygdala is dysfunctional, as a result of brain lesions. The ability to take the drug, however, is still unimpaired, although the capacity to associate the drug with environmental cues is lost.

In human terms it may be conjectured that this neural interaction between the amygdala and the nucleus accumbens is normally what is responsible for the well-known 'drug craving' that results when addicts (even after rehabilitation) experience situations or cues (including people) associated with the drug, often leading to relapse to drug-taking. (This doesn't mean that a treatment for addiction might be the surgical removal of the amygdala, of course, even for willing volunteers! Quite apart from needing to know a good deal more about the precise nature of this limbic–striatal interaction, it is clear that such treatment would likely affect many other psychological processes, including vital ones associated with adaptive responding to cues associated with natural rewards or anxiogenic stimuli as described below.) Although the interaction between the amygdala and the nucleus accumbens almost certainly depends on the release of glutamate onto receptors in the nucleus accumbens, events which interact with the modulation provided by cocaine's action on the dopamine projection from the midbrain, again, it is exceedingly unlikely that a drug could be targeted to those particular glutamate receptors in order to prevent craving.

A dramatic demonstration of the importance of the rest of the brain in determining the subjective response to a drug is provided by studies of the role of expectancy. A recent experiment with amphetamine has confirmed what has been suspected for many years, on the basis of a famous study on the effects of adrenalin on human volunteers. This old research showed that adrenalin only produced measurable subjective emotional responses in volunteers when the subjects were uninformed or misinformed about which drug they were receiving, even though the peripheral, cardiovascular effects of the hormone were equivalent to those of informed subjects. Furthermore, the type of emotional response (anger or euphoria) appeared to depend simply on the social context at the time of receiving the adrenalin.

In the recent study by Harriet de Wit and colleagues at the University of Chicago, volunteers were administered either placebo or amphetamine on different occasions, sometimes receiving the treatment they were expecting and sometimes not. The powerful finding was that the subjective nature of the drug effect was different when it was expected and when it was not. Thus, the expected drug led to 'liking' and 'feeling' the drug, whereas the unexpected drug elevated subjective arousal and anxiety (Fig. 3). The effect of amphetamine clearly depended not simply on its initial molecular site of action, but also upon the cognitive context in which it was experienced. At a neural level this presumably reflects an interaction between the effect of amphetamine on brain dopamine function and the pattern of neural activity representing the learned expectancy of the drug's effects. Perhaps the drug effect can even be interpreted as mildly aversive (e.g. anxiety-inducing) if the subject is unprepared for it. Such findings emphasize that drug reward is a relative rather than absolute quantity. A further intriguing aspect of this study is that these contrasting subjective effects of amphetamine did not apparently diminish the subject's subsequent expressed preference to receive the drug. This implies that we must not necessarily equate the subjective effects of a drug with its reinforcing action, i.e. its capacity to engender self-administration behaviour. This consideration emphasizes the multifaceted nature of the emotions and the difficulty of equating a subjective experience such as euphoria or pleasure with the functioning of a single neurotransmitter system, especially without reference to the brain state or context within which it normally functions.

What is perhaps even more surprising is that several other drugs of abuse, often with quite different modes of action on different neurotransmitter systems, may all be acting ultimately on the same dopaminergic system to produce their reinforcing effects. For example, heroin, nicotine and alcohol may all work in part by indirectly increasing dopamine activity in the nucleus accumbens, even though they work at opiate, cholinergic and probably

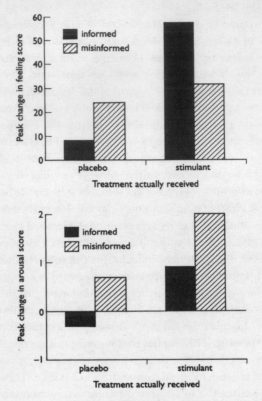

Figure 3. The influence of prior expectation on the subjective experience ('feeling drug effect' and 'arousal') of effects of amphetamine in human volunteers. The black columns indicate the responses when the volunteers were accurately informed about whether they were to receive the stimulant or placebo. The hatched columns indicate responses when the subjects were misinformed about which treatment they had actually received. Note that subjects expecting placebo and receiving amphetamine exhibited much higher levels of arousal (as well as anxiety, data not shown) than when they were expecting the stimulant. (Data redrawn from Mitchell et al., 1996, Psychopharmacology 125, 371–378, with permission from the authors and publisher.)

GABA-ergic receptors, respectively. A current mystery is the neuro-chemical basis of the withdrawal syndromes that often motivate further drug-taking behaviour. One theory points out that most drugs will act at different parts of the brain and so will potentially have many more effects than merely providing a form of chemical reward. Thus, drugs such as morphine and its chemical relative heroin may act in brain centres controlling the peripheral nervous system, as well as the central noradrenergic systems, with the result that, on withdrawal, control over these peripheral systems becomes dysregulated, leading to the characteristic unpleasant flu-like symptoms.

Another possibility is that the activation of the dopaminergic system is so intense that it takes some time to recover, and this produces a literal 'dopaminergic hangover', associated with depression and dysphoria. In this case, the emotional helter-skelter of drug addiction can be attributed in part to the fluctuations of the same neurotransmitter system. It is probably no accident that the dopaminergic system is one of the several monoamine transmitters whose functions are thought to be disturbed in clinical depression and that antidepressant drugs, as well as other treatments for depression such as electroconvulsive shock, mainly work by inter-acting with monoamine neurotransmitters.

A role for dopamine in cognitive function?

The midbrain dopamine system not only modulates emotional pro-cessing in the nucleus accumbens, but also plays an important part in the activation of movement itself. This has been known from the discovery that the motor symptoms of Parkinson's disease are caused by the degeneration of dopamine-containing cells of the midbrain which innervate an adjacent brain structure called the neostriatum. The symptoms of rigidity and difficulty in initiating movement that characterize Parkinson's disease are well known: what is less well realized is that this disorder is also associated with disorders of thinking and emotion. It is thought that some of these symptoms may also arise from a loss of dopamine cells, perhaps from the neostriatum, or the nucleus accumbens in the case of Parkinsonian depression, but quite possibly from the prefrontal cortex, which is associated with the highest levels of executive functioning in the brain and communicates with the striatum via several neural feedback loops (see Fig. 2).

Although Parkinson's disease is often categorized as a motor disorder, some of those who suffer from the condition exhibit subtle forms of cognitive dysfunction. For example, they may be slow to think and quite rigid in their thinking. There may also be mild forms of memory disturbance in so-called 'working memory', the ability to process information on-line while performing cognitive tasks. Some of these deficits appear directly to parallel the motor deficits. Thus, bradykinesia (slowed movement) is paralleled by 'bradyphrenia' – slowed thinking – in a task requiring the formation of a mental plan to solve a puzzle. Moreover, the motor rigidity of the syndrome may be accompanied by a lack of cognitive flexibility in tasks designed to assess this capacity. Many of these cognitive abilities are impaired in patients with frontal lobe damage, and this is consistent with the hypothesis that Parkinson's disease results in a disturbance of the functioning of 'cortico-striatal loops', perhaps because of dopamine depletion in the striatum or the frontal cortex itself.

Experiments with animals have suggested that the prefrontal dopamine systems may have specific roles in certain forms of cognition, notably working memory. However, recent evidence has suggested that, for some Parkinson's disease patients, dopamine may be almost as important for forms of cognition controlled by the prefrontal cortex, as it is for the retarded initiation of movement. The latter is often optimally treated by replacement therapy in which dopamine levels are increased by giving L-Dopa, from which the brain can synthesize dopamine. When Parkinson's disease patients had their L-Dopa medication temporarily removed for clinical reasons in a hospital setting, it was thus possible to test their cognitive functions both on and off the drug. The results showed that for all of the cognitive deficits associated with frontal lobe dysfunction, that is, of planning, attentional shifting and working memory, L-Dopa withdrawal produced a significant deficit (Fig. 4). This did not result simply because the Parkinson's disease patients were less capable of performing *any* functions, because their scores on certain tests of visual learning and memory were equally deficient both on and off the drug. The implications are that dopamine can modulate cognitive, as well as affective and motor functions. Perhaps the famous functional neuroanatomist Walle Nauta was correct when he suggested that certain forms of thought can be conceived as 'internalized action'.

Dementia and the cholinergic system

Some twenty years ago discoveries were made suggesting that the dementia caused by Alzheimer's disease might be associated with neurodegeneration of the basal forebrain cholinergic system (see Fig. 2). David Bowen and his colleagues in London and Elaine Perry's group in Newcastle found that the activity of the enzyme-synthesizing acetylcholine, choline acetyltransferase, was drastically reduced in patients who had died with Alzheimer's disease, and, furthermore, this reduction could be correlated with the deteriorating intellectual status of the patients when alive. A scenario was imagined in which Alzheimer patients, like those suffering with Parkinson's disease, could be treated with an appropriate neurotransmitter 'repletion therapy'. This cholinergic theory of geriatric memory dysfunction has long been shown to be too naïve, although there is little doubt that the cholinergic system plays at least some role in the complex cognitive symptomatology of Alzheimer's disease. Today it is generally believed that Alzheimer's disease results from neurodegeneration afflicting some of the neural networks of the posterior neocortex, such as the temporal and parietal lobes. The neuronal loss is the culmination of a neurogenerative process that includes the over-production, or incorrect synthesis, of specific proteins, in particular those known respectively as beta-amyloid and tau. Particularly at risk are the glutamate-containing pyramidal cells of the cortex that participate in informational transactions between different parts of the cerebral cortex and between the cortex and its subcortical targets. Thus, no amount of boosting of neuromodulation by the cholinergic

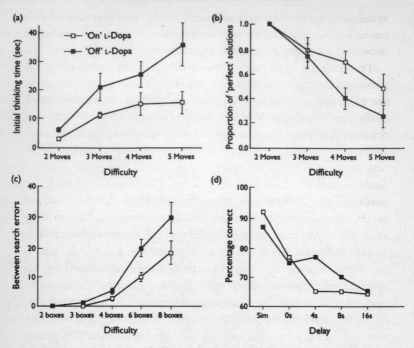

Figure 4. Summary of effects of L-Dopa withdrawal on a variety of cognitive functions in patients with Parkinson's disease (PD). The graphs plot mean scores of 10 patients with PD tested both on and off L-Dopa therapy. The vertical bars around the points in panels (a), (b) and (c) indicate the standard errors of the mean scores, a conventional index of variability. The top two panels indicate beneficial effects of the drug on (a) the time taken to think about problems on the Tower of London puzzle and (b) the accuracy of solutions. The problems require solutions of increasing difficulty based on the number of moves needed for one arrangement of coloured balls to match another. Also shown (c) is the beneficial effect of the drug on a task requiring 'self-ordered' working memory, but the lack of effect (at all levels of difficulty) on visual recognition memory (d), using the same task that is so sensitive to cholinergic receptor blockade by the drug scopolamine. (Data redrawn from Lange et al., 1992, Psychopharmacology 107, 394–404, with permission.)

system that innervates the neocortex from its subcortical origins could be expected to be effective, because the very informational network that it usually modulates has grossly degenerated.

The evidence favouring a role for the cholinergic system in cognition did not derive solely from biochemical evidence obtained from the post-mortem examination of brains from patients dying with Alzheimer's disease. When administered to young adult volunteers, drugs antagonizing the cholinergic receptors in the brain (such as scopolamine) could be shown to produce significant, though temporary, deficits, superficially resembling those of Alzheimer patients. Some of this evidence is based on the effects of scopolamine on performance in a test of visual recognition memory known to depend on the integrity of the temporal neocortex in young subjects. The subject is shown a complex, coloured visual pattern for a short while (about 4 seconds) only, and a few seconds later is asked to pick it out from an array of similar patterns. The resultant deficits are specific impairments of short-term visual memory, rather than some perceptual aberration or general confusion, and can be shown to mimic those seen in the earliest stages of Alzheimer's disease. Mere analogy does not of course demonstrate a direct relationship between these different phenomena, but the results clearly indicate some role for acetylcholine in short-term memory, perhaps because its release in defined conditions helps to amplify signals processed by the cortex above levels of background neural 'noise'.

The frustrating failure in most cases of cholinergic therapy (for example, via drugs acting to simulate the action of acetylcholine at cortical receptors or to delay the breakdown of whatever acetylcholine can be released at intracortical synapses) to produce a long-lasting boosting of memory function in Alzheimer patients can probably be put down to the more general disruption of this processing produced by degeneration of cortical circuits themselves. While this loss of the basic cortical circuitry is obviously not a problem for young volunteers, we should not infer that cholinergic therapy would necessarily produce cognitive-enhancing effects. The possible use of cholinergic drugs as 'mental steroids' would be counteracted by the fact that subjects are probably already performing at optimal levels. For example, it has been shown that treatment of chess players with physostigmine, an anticholinesterase which boosts synaptic levels of acetylcholine, improves the ability of poor players to solve chess problems, but only impairs the perform- ance of good players.

Another problem for the cholinergic model described above is that the full breadth of cognitive deficits observed in Alzheimer's disease is not always seen following anticholinergic drugs. For example, as shown in Fig. 5, volunteers treated with scopolamine can still learn a number of visual associations (the locations of up

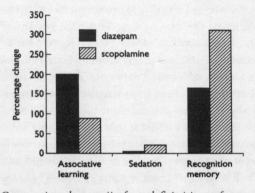

Figure 5. Contrasting changes (in fact, deficits) in performance on two tests of visual memory or learning in human volunteers receiving either diazepam (Valium) or scopolamine. Scopolamine significantly impaired visual recognition memory on the delayed matching to sample test, producing three times as many errors as under placebo, at the highest dose used (as shown here), while non-significantly increasing the number of errors in a learning task in which subjects had to associate abstract visual patterns with particular locations on a computer monitor screen. Diazepam (Valium), again at the highest or most effective dose, impaired the learning task rather than that of visual recognition memory. Both drugs had mild sedative effects at these doses, but this could not account for the pattern of effects observed. (Data taken from results of James Semple and colleagues and from a Cambridge University undergraduate research project.)

to eight computer graphic 'junk' stimuli on a computer screen), even though this task is a devastating one for demented individuals. It appears likely that different forms of learning and memory may depend on different brain systems (see Chapter 4) with different forms of chemical neuromodulation.

Amnesia and the benzodiazepines

The learning of new associations can be profoundly impaired by drugs such as the benzodiazepines that have been much used clinically as anxiolytic agents. It has been known for several years that these drugs, including Librium (chlordiazepoxide) and Valium (diazepam), in addition to their 'anxiolytic' properties, may also produce reversible anterograde amnesias – that is, deficits in new learning. These synthetic compounds can bind to receptors in several relevant regions of the brain, including not only some portions of the limbic system, where the anxiolytic effects may occur, but also those areas of the cerebral cortex and limbic system where new memories may be laid down. When the benzodiazepines bind to their receptors it has been shown that a ion channel in the inhibitory GABA receptor is opened. Therefore, these drugs effectively increase inhibitory neurotransmission via GABA neurons in many areas of the brain. The hippocampus, as will become apparent from Chapters 4 and 5, is a region specialized for the learning of new associations between environmental events. It is plausible that the learning deficits produced by the benzodiazepines may result from a disruption of GABA-ergic transmission in regions such as the hippocampus. What is interesting is that the more 'passive', less associative form of recognition memory that is so specifically affected by the anticholinergic drug scopolamine is much less impaired by Valium than is new learning (see Fig. 5). These results indicate the probable importance of the fast inhibitory transmission via GABA mechanisms for the optimal functioning of learning networks.

These results may also indicate that treatment with benzodiazepine drugs may provide a more suitable model of the cognitive deficits of Alzheimer's disease. This view is strengthened by evidence that drugs such as Valium can also produce impairments on the tests of 'executive' functioning described above that are determined by structures such as the prefrontal cortex. Thus diazepam can impair performance on cognitive tests of planning, working memory and flexibility of thinking in a way qualitatively similar to frontal lobe lesions, but unrelated to general sedative actions. This would be accounted for by the disruptive effects of potentiated GABA-ergic function on the functioning of structures such as the prefrontal cortex. This action differs from that produced by neuromodulatory systems such as the dopaminergic system; for example, Valium does not result in a slowing of thinking time on the planning task, as occurs in Parkinson's disease.

The theoretical excitement about drugs such as L-Dopa and benzo-diazepines which affect both emotional and cognitive functions is that there may be genuine links between these two psychological domains. While the anxiolytic actions of the benzodiazepines may be distinct from their cognitive effects, and may arise simply because of common molecular actions in very different types of brain processing modules, it remains distinctly possible that the two psychological effects are related. The very existence of the benzodiazepine ligand itself presumably suggests that there is a hitherto undiscovered naturally occurring neurotransmitter system that normally acts via these receptors.

The discovery of 'inverse agonists', which also act at benzodiazepine receptors, opens up the prospect of 'cognitive-enhancing drugs' that may facilitate the functioning of relevant neural networks, subject to the constraints mentioned above. These drugs have been shown to have some beneficial effects on memory in laboratory studies. However, just as they have opposite effects to those of benzodiazepines on memory, they have convulsant and anxiety-generating actions that also mirror those of these compounds. Thus, the search is on for inverse agonists that would have memory facilitatory actions without these potentially dangerous side-effects.

There is another potential theoretical problem in the use of this class of cognitive-enhancing drugs. These would have to be taken peripherally into the body and so would affect many different sets of GABA-ergic systems in different parts of the brain. Thus, the capacity to target the system that is affected would be much restricted, and the possibility of unwanted effects arising from actions on brain systems controlling other functions, many of them not cognitive, would remain high. Perhaps this is why it is so hard to detect cognitive enhancing effects in normal individuals, especially if they are already functioning at close to their optimal level. One possible hope for the future is that it will be possible to target particular brain systems in a more selective way because of subtle differences in the ways in which the receptors are composed from their protein subunits across different brain regions.

Are our conscious thoughts and emotions no more than chemical events?

This brief description of the actions of certain drugs on cognitive and emotional processes may lead some to despair that we are *en route* to 'chemical emotions', in which psychological constructs such as fear and learning essentially become redundant as we improve our understanding of these processes at the molecular level. There are several arguments against such an agenda, some of which have already been raised above. The first is the argument of the appropriate and useful level of description of psychological events. Understanding such processes in terms of neurotransmitter systems is, of course, only a beginning for scientists with a reductionist orientation. Further explanations can be framed in terms of the cascade of neurochemical and ionic events that follow the binding of a neurotransmitter substance to its receptor. However, just as chemistry has survived the advent of explanations of atomic and subatomic events at the quantum mechanical level, so will psychology survive the assault from biochemistry. The real issue is the level of description which makes sense, that is, that level at which phenomena can be explained and predicted at both the theoretical and practical levels – for example, that treatment with L-Dopa will improve aspects of cognitive function via its action on the forebrain dopamine systems.

Moreover, it is clear that the functioning of chemical neurotransmitter systems cannot be understood in a vacuum. Identical chemical events in one brain region may have completely different functional, as well as subjective, outcomes, depending on the interactions of the system in question with others. Thus, the effects of a drug may depend on such factors as environmental context, previous experience, time of day, baseline level of performance and so on, all of which may bear on the overall mode of functioning of the neural network with which the neurotransmitter system interacts. While the effects of drugs on emotions and cognition may continue to provide amazing opportunities for understanding the chemical architecture of the mind, and new options for the treatment of patients suffering from pathology of cognition or affect, they are unlikely radically to alter our understanding of these processes at the subjective or psychological levels of discourse.

Further reading

Altman, J., Everitt, B. J., Glautier, S., Markou, A., Nutt, D., Orietti, R., Phillips, G. D., and Robbins, T. W. (1996). The biological, social and clinical bases of addiction: commentary and debate. *Psychopharmacology* 125, 283–345. A recent survey of work on drug addiction.

Cooper, J. R., Bloom, F. E., and Roth, R. (1996). *The Biochemical Basis of Neuropharmacology*, 7th edn. Oxford University Press. For further information on neurotransmitter systems and biochemical mechanisms of drug action.

Feldman, R. S., Meyer, J. S., and Quenzer, L. F. (1997). *Principles of Neuropharmacology*. Sinclair Associates. A recent up-to-date textbook.

Robbins, T. W., and Everitt, B. J. (1995). Arousal systems and attention. In: *The Cognitive Neurosciences* (ed. M. Gazzaniga *et al.*), pp. 703–725. MIT Press. For further information on the monoamine and cholinergic neurotransmitter systems at the functional level.

Scientific American. Special issue: Mind and Brain, September 1992. See especially the articles 'Major disorders of mind and brain', by E. Gershon and R. O. Reider, and 'Aging brain, aging mind', by D. J. Selkoe.

4

Memory and Brain Systems*

LARRY R. SQUIRE

Neuroscience concerns itself with two great problems, the brain's 'hard-wiring' and its capacity for plasticity. The former refers to the issue of how connections develop between cells, how cells function and communicate with each other, and how the functions we are born with are organized, such as sleep–wake cycles, hunger and thirst, and the ability to perceive the world through our five senses. Thus, nervous systems have inherited through millions of years of evolution many capabilities important for survival, adaptations that are too important to be left to the uncertainties of individual experience. The capacity for plasticity refers to the fact that nervous systems also inherit the ability to adapt or change as the result of experiences that occur during an individual lifetime. The experiences we have can modify the nervous system, and we can later behave differently as a result. This capacity gives us the ability to learn and to remember.

All the animals, all the brains, illustrated in Fig. 1 have the capacity for plasticity. There is a gradual increase in the size of the brain, with the vertebrates closest, in evolutionary terms, to humans. Monkey brains, for instance, are only one-tenth the size of the human brain. Yet all contain the same basic cell types, with very similar cellular and molecular properties, arranged within regions which correspond across species; and as a first approximation, these brains have the same pattern of connections between these regions. Someone examining

* An earlier version of this chapter appeared previously in *Neuroscience, Memory and Language, Decade of the Brain*, Vol. 1. Richard Broadwell (ed.). US Government Printing Office.

and comparing these brains in anatomical detail might be more impressed with the similarities than the differences. Thus, neuroscientists suppose that differences between species, differences for example in cognitive ability and in memory, are due to the number of neurons and to the details of how they are connected with each other. Hence we can learn a great deal about the properties and

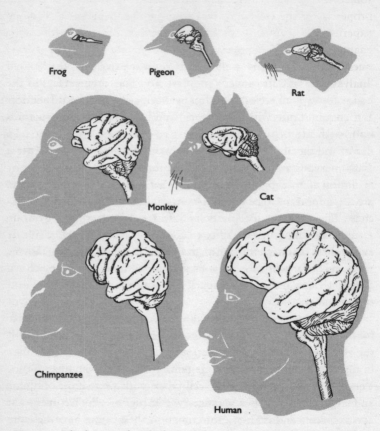

Figure 1. The brains of several vertebrate species, ranging from the frog through the monkey to the human. (From M. R. Rosenzweig and A. L. Leiman, 1982, Physiological Psychology, D. C. Heath & Co.)

mechanisms of the human brain from studying those of other animals, and in particular the brains of monkeys, so close to us in evolutionary terms. As a result, for many years the monkey has been a precious and valuable experimental animal for the study of the nervous system.

From a biological point of view, the problem of memory is sometimes defined as a problem of neural plasticity – how the cellular properties of the cells and their connections change as a result of experience. This is the issue addressed by Tim Bliss in the following chapter. But many important aspects of memory are systems-level questions that can only be answered at a relatively global level of analysis. Even if one understood how synapses change to alter the connectivity between neurons, many other questions would remain. Is there one kind of memory or many? What are the brain structures and pathways involved in memory and what jobs do they do? To provide a sketch of our current understanding, I consider here three issues, illustrating each with some examples.

First, the brain is organized such that memory is a distinct and separate cognitive function, which can fruitfully be studied in isolation from perception and other intellectual abilities. Particular brain structures, including the hippocampus, are essential for the ability to lay down in memory an enduring record of experience. Damage to these structures causes an amnesic syndrome, a circumscribed impairment in the ability to learn and remember. While significant information has come from the study of human amnesic patients, the bulk of our understanding about the anatomy of memory continues to come from the kind of systematic and cumulative work that is possible only in experimental animals.

Second, memory is not a single faculty of the mind but is composed of multiple separate systems. That is, there is more than one kind of memory, not just in a semantic or philosophical sense but in the specific biological sense that different kinds of memory have different brain organizations and depend on different brain systems. The major distinction is between conscious knowledge of facts and events, which is impaired in amnesia, and other non-conscious knowledge systems that provide for the capacity of skill learning, habit formation, the phenomenon of priming, and certain other ways of interacting with the world.

Third, new technology, including positron emission tomography (PET) and functional magnetic imaging (fMRI), is providing direct anatomical and functional information about memory in living human subjects.

Amnesia and the anatomy of memory

The modern era of this problem began in 1953 when a patient, who was to become known as HM, sustained a neurosurgical procedure intended to relieve severe epilepsy. The surgery involved the removal in both hemispheres of a section of the brain about 5 cm long – the medial temporal region shown in Fig. 2. The surgery was successful in relieving the epilepsy to a point where it could be controlled by medication. However, it also resulted in an unexpected and severe memory impairment for day-to-day events. HM, who was 27 years old at the time of surgery, retained an above-average intellectual ability, intact immediate (digit span) memory, intact knowledge from early life, and a personality that according to his family was unchanged by surgery. Currently, in the late 1990s, HM is in his early seventies and remains an active participant in research. He is profoundly forgetful, such that he does not recognize his examiners with whom he has frequent contact. It is also reported that he does not now recognize a photograph of himself. Apparently, he has been unable to learn about his appearance as it has changed during the 40+ years since his surgery. This case has taught two important principles about how the brain accomplishes learning and memory. First, the medial temporal lobe is important for memory function. Second, the brain has to some extent separated perceptual processing and other intellectual processing functions from the capacity to lay down an enduring record of the memories that ordinarily result from such processing.

This case is often cited as providing evidence that the hippocampus is important for memory. However, as Fig. 2 indicates, HM's lesion,

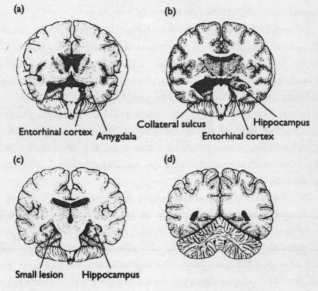

Figure 2. *This diagram of the human brain indicates the extent of surgical removal in the well-known amnesic patient HM, as revealed by magnetic resonance imaging. The inset at the top is a ventral view of the human brain showing the rostrocaudal extent of the ablation. A to d are drawings of coronal sections, arranged from rostral (a) to caudal (d), showing the extent of the lesion. Note that although the lesion was made bilaterally, the right side is shown intact to illustrate structures that were removed. (From S. Corkin, 1997,* Journal of Neuroscience 17, *3964–3979.)*

while including the hippocampus, also involved a number of adjacent areas of the medial temporal lobe: the amygdala, parahippocampal cortex, entorhinal cortex and perirhinal cortex. Emphasis was initially placed on the posterior half of the lesion, because other patients who underwent temporal lobe surgery appeared to develop memory impairment only when the removal extended far enough posteriorly to include the hippocampus and the underlying cortex. Nevertheless, many years passed before investigators could determine which brain structures within HM's large lesion were the crucial ones important for memory function.

Two major developments contributed to progress on this problem. First, anatomical information became available from other carefully studied single cases of memory impairment. These cases, which became available in the 1980s and 1990s, provided strong and direct evidence for the importance of the hippocampus itself in human memory. The second development was the establishment in the early 1980s of an animal model of human memory impairment in the monkey. The animal model set the stage for identifying the major structures and connections in the medial temporal lobe important for memory.

The first of these human cases was patient RB. This patient developed memory impairment in 1978 at the age of 52 following complications of open-heart surgery which resulted in his brain temporarily losing its blood supply (ischaemia). He recovered and survived for five years, during which time the only cognitive deficit that could be detected was a moderately severe memory impairment – an example of the problems he faced is shown in Fig. 3. Studies of his brain after his death showed that an entire section of the hippocampus (known as CA1) was destroyed. Studies of experimental animals have indicated that the CA1 field is particularly vulnerable to ischaemic damage. Moreover, the anatomical facts of hippocampal circuitry are such that damage restricted to the CA1 region of the hippocampus would disrupt the flow of information into and out of the hippocampus. These findings, and those from other patients subsequently, suggested that the hippocampus is a critical component of the medial temporal lobe memory system.

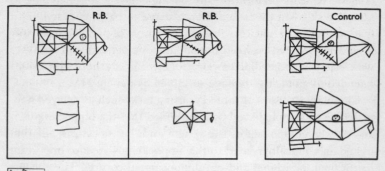

Figure 3. Amnesic patient RB was asked to copy the figure illustrated in the small box to the lower left. Then, without forewarning, he was asked to reproduce the figure from memory 10 to 20 minutes later. The left panel shows RB's copy (top) and his reproduction (bottom) 6 months after the onset of his amnesia. The middle panel shows RB's copy and reproduction 23 months after the onset of his amnesia. The right panel shows the copy and a reproduction of a healthy normal subject matched to RB for age and education. This normal subject's data were selected as average from a group of six normal subjects. (From S. Zola-Morgan et al., 1986, Journal of Neuroscience *6, 2950–2967.)*

From humans to monkeys

In the early 1980s investigators began to pursue these same problems systematically in the monkey. Monkeys could be prepared with bilateral surgical lesions of particular brain structures, and their memory then evaluated quantitatively using specially designed tasks. Although many tasks have been used to assess memory in monkeys, the one most widely used has been delayed non-matching to sample. In this test, a single object is presented to the monkey and then after a short delay two objects are presented, the original object and a novel one. To obtain a food reward, the monkey must select the novel object. New pairs of objects are used on each trial. Human amnesic patients perform poorly on the delayed non-matching to sample task when the task is administered to patients exactly as it is administered to monkeys. Indeed, a number of parallels have now been demonstrated between human amnesic patients and monkeys with lesions of the medial temporal lobe, including those with lesions intended to mimic the damage sustained by patient HM.

Cumulative studies of monkeys using tasks such as delayed non-matching to sample have both confirmed that the hippocampus is an essential component of the system and that structures adjacent to and anatomically related to the hippocampus are also important (entorhinal, perirhinal and parahippocampal cortex). These structures together with the hippocampus comprise the full medial temporal lobe memory system (Fig. 4). Such lesion studies have also indicated that other major related brain regions such as the amygdala are not directly involved in the same kind of memory, although they are important in other functions, including attributing salience to emotional components of events, which may be relevant to whether they are subsequently stored in memory. The medial temporal lobe is not the only area of the brain where damage can cause severe memory impairment. Bilateral damage in deep brain structures such as the thalamus can also result in amnesia which resembles medial temporal lobe amnesia in many ways. Each brain region can be considered as a crucial part of a memory system involving both limbic and diencephalic brain regions.

Multiple forms of memory

One of the profound insights to emerge in the past decade is that memory is not a single entity but is composed of several different abilities. Prior to this development, memory was understood to vary in strength and accessibility and could be expressed in various tasks, but it could still be regarded as a single biological and psychological phenomenon. Memory could be seen as a special case of neural plasticity, dependent on synaptic change, whereby experience leads to a change in behaviour. This unitary view has now been replaced by the view that there are multiple memory systems in the brain.

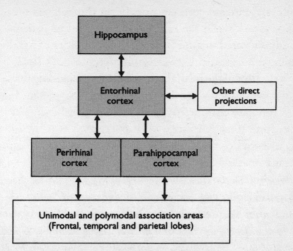

Figure 4. The components of the medial temporal lobe memory system are shown as tinted boxes. The entorhinal cortex is the major source of projections to the hippocampal region (hippocampus proper, dentate gyrus and subicular complex). Nearly two-thirds of the cortical input to the entorhinal cortex originates in the adjacent perirhinal and parahippocampal cortices, which in turn receive input from unimodal and polymodal areas in the frontal, temporal and parietal lobes. The entorhinal cortex also receives other direct projections from orbital frontal cortex, cingulate cortex, insular cortex and superior temporal gyrus. All these projections are reciprocal. (From L. R. Squire and S. Zola-Morgan, 1991, Science 253, 1380–1386.)

Some of the most compelling evidence for the modern view has come from findings that amnesic patients, who are severely impaired on conventional memory tests that assess recall and recognition of previously encountered material, are nevertheless fully intact at many kinds of learning and memory. They are impaired at remembering facts and events (declarative memory), but they are intact at non-declarative memory, which includes skill learning and habit learning and certain kinds of conditioning. They are intact as well at the phenomenon of priming, that is, they show enhanced perception or

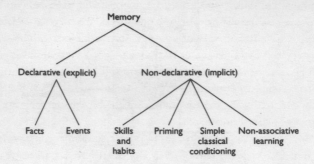

Figure 5. Declarative memory refers to conscious recollection of facts and events and depends on the integrity of limbic/diencephalic structures. Non-declarative memory refers to a heterogeneous collection of abilities. In the case of non-declarative memory, experience alters behaviour non-consciously without providing access to any memory content. (From L. R. Squire and S. Zola-Morgan, 1991, Science 253, 1380–1386.)

detection of items that have not previously been experienced (Fig. 5). This distinction is not based on a simple recounting of what amnesic patients can and cannot do. Several independent lines of evidence suggest that studies of amnesia reveal a biologically natural division in how the nervous system has organized its capacity for acquiring, storing and retrieving information. An important implication of this idea is that the limbic/diencephalic structures, which when damaged produce severe and disabling amnesia, are needed for a specific kind of memory. These structures are involved in the acquisition of declarative knowledge (fact and event memory), which is then available as conscious recollection. Declarative memory is what we normally mean when we speak of human memory.

Non-declarative memory is a heterogeneous collection of abilities, all of which are independent of the limbic/diencephalic brain structures damaged in amnesia. Non-declarative memory is non-conscious. Information is acquired as changes within specific perceptual or response systems, or as changes encapsulated within specific knowledge systems, without affording access to any prior memory content. Nondeclarative memory is independent of conscious memory for the prior encounters that led to behavioural change. The rich variety of non-declarative memory abilities can be appreciated by considering the sorts of tasks that amnesic patients can acquire normally, such as motor-skill learning, perceptual-skill learning (such as learning to read mirror-reversed text) and cognitive-skill learning (such as the ability to improve performance on certain computer-based problems).

Very specific information about prior encounters can be supported by non-declarative memory. For example, amnesic patients exhibit intact acquisition and retention of a text-specific reading skill. The reading aloud of several lines of text increases the speed with which the same text is subsequently read, but no such facilitation occurs for a novel text.

Amnesic patients also exhibit intact and specific long-lasting priming effects for the names of objects. For instance, subjects were first shown pictures of simple objects, one at a time, and asked to name each picture as quickly as possible. Then, either 2 or 7 days later, subjects were shown more pictures and were asked again to name them as quickly as possible. The results indicated that both amnesic patients and normal subjects named the old pictures substantially faster than the new pictures. The familiar pictures were named some 10 per cent faster than the unfamiliar ones. Moreover, when a different version of the original picture was used, but one that had the same name (e.g. a picture of a beagle instead of a retriever, both of which would be identified as dog), the facilitatory effect was significantly reduced. Thus, priming was greatest when the exact physical characteristics of the stimuli were maintained across their two presentations. This suggests that a substantial component of the priming effect is based on specific visual information. This priming effect, therefore, is likely to be based on changes at relatively early stages of visual information processing. They are presemantic in the sense that the effect is highly perceptual and does not require an appreciation of the name of the stimulus or what it means. In contrast to the findings for priming, amnesic patients were greatly disadvantaged when they were asked simply to identify which pictures they had seen before (79 per cent correct for normal subjects, 59 per cent correct for amnesic patients; chance performance would be 50 per cent).

Functional anatomy of human memory

Most of the available information about the anatomical structures and connections involved in memory functions has come from analysis of the effects of lesions in memory-impaired patients and experimental animals. The development of brain imaging methods, based on positron emission tomography (PET) and functional magnetic resonance imaging (fMRI), has provided the opportunity to study the anatomy of declarative and non-declarative memory directly in normal subjects. In collaborative research with Marcus Raichle and his colleagues at Washington University, we have used PET to monitor local blood flow while subjects performed one of several similar tasks. The strategy is to use a rapidly decaying radioisotope to monitor regional cerebral blood flow. To do this, water labelled with an isotope of oxygen that decays with a half-life of about 2 minutes is injected into the artery leading to the brain. The distribution of the radioactivity, and hence the blood, can then be detected while subjects are performing particular tasks. Local changes in cerebral blood flow are thought to reflect local changes in neural activity. In the typical experiment, the brain image produced during a 40-second period in one cognitive state is subtracted from the image produced during a second related state in order to isolate changes in regional blood flow associated with specific cognitive operations.

In the first study of declarative and non-declarative memory using PET, eighteen normal volunteers participated in four task conditions and four separate PET scans during a single 2-hour session. Prior to each scan, subjects studied common English words four to eight letters in length, which were presented one at a time (e.g. MOTEL, INCOME). About 3 minutes after the words were presented, subjects saw word stems (three-letter word beginnings) one at a time. Each word stem (e.g. MOT, INC) could form at least ten common

English words. During presentation of these stems, and while local blood flow was being monitored in the PET scanner, subjects performed one of four physically identical tasks. (1) No response: subjects viewed the word stems but made no verbal response, and none of the stems could form words that had been studied. (2) Baseline: subjects completed the word stems to form the first word to come to mind and spoke that word aloud. Again, none of the stems could form study words. (3) Priming: the same as the baseline condition, except that now half of the stems could form study words. (4) Memory (cued recall): subjects attempted to complete the word stems to form study words, and they spoke these words aloud. Half of the stems could potentially be completed to form study words.

There were three major findings in the PET study. Figure 6 shows one of the two largest blood-flow changes in the brain that was observed when the memory condition was subtracted from the baseline condition. The locus of change was in the right posterior medial temporal lobe in the area occupied by the hippocampus and the parahippocampal gyrus. The priming task also engaged the hippocampal region to some extent, probably because during the priming condition recollection could potentially occur for words that had been presented at study. Indeed, many of the subjects became aware of the link between the word stems and the target words. Because of this complication, it was important that the memory task activated the hippocampal region to an even greater extent than the priming task.

It might seem surprising to hear that activation occurred in the right hippocampal region in a verbal memory task like the one used here. Ordinarily, one thinks of the left side of the brain as the side more involved in verbal processing and the left hippocampal region as the region more involved in verbal memory. This generalization is accurate as a first approximation but it is simplistic and potentially misleading. In fact, the right hemisphere appears to be more important for words than the left hemisphere when performance is based on the visual form of words rather than their sound or meaning. This principle was established many years ago. The importance of

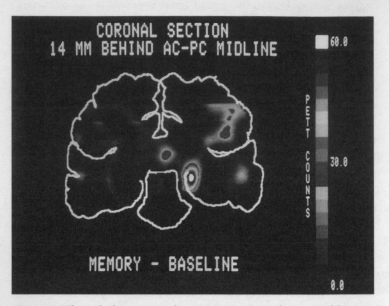

*Figure 6. The right hippocampal region was activated in normal human
subjects who were engaged in a memory task. The image is a 2 mm thick
coronal section, 14 mm posterior to the midpoint of the line joining the
anterior and posterior commissures (AC–PC midline). The section
shows the major findings produced by a memory task in comparison to a
baseline condition. The circular area in the right ventromedial lobe
shows the area that was activated. (From L. R. Squire* et al., 1992,
Proceedings of the National Academy of Sciences **89**, 1837–1841.)*

the right hemisphere for certain kinds of verbal tasks was also
demonstrated in recent divided-visual-field studies of normal subjects
that were designed specifically to illuminate the findings from PET.
When word stems are presented to the left or right visual fields (that
is, to the left or right of a central fixation point), the anatomy of
visual processing in the brain dictates that the material presented to
the left of fixation arrives first to the right cerebral hemisphere
(and then reaches the left side indirectly by crossing the cerebral
commissures). Correspondingly, material presented to the right of

fixation arrives first to the left cerebral hemisphere. In our study with normal subjects, it was observed that cued recall (and also priming, see below) was better when word stems were presented to the left of fixation than when they were presented to the right of fixation. That is, in the study with normal subjects, in agreement with the PET findings, cued recall (and priming, see below) depended more on the right hemisphere than on the left.

The second finding was that the right prefrontal cortex was activated in the memory condition in comparison to the baseline condition. This region exhibited little activity in any of the other task conditions. Activation of right prefrontal cortex has been reported previously in PET studies in tasks requiring response selection. In addition, damage to prefrontal cortex impairs performance on tasks that require search strategies and sustained attention.

The third finding was observed when brain activity in the baseline condition was subtracted from brain activity in the priming condition. This subtraction revealed a reduction of activity in right occipital cortex corresponding to parts of its visual areas. These PET findings provide direct support for the idea that priming can involve rather early-stage perceptual processing stations, and also suggest an interesting explanation for the phenomenon of repetition priming. For a time after the presentation of a word or other perceptual object, it seems that less neural activity is required to process the same stimulus.

The findings from PET illuminate two ways in which experience can modify the nervous system and influence subsequent behaviour. Enhanced performance due to repetition priming depends on changes in relatively early-stage visual-processing centres. Which brain regions support priming can be expected to vary depending on the precise nature of the stimulus material and on the similarity between the material presented for study and for test.

Implications of multiple memory systems

Conscious and non-conscious memory systems ordinarily cooperate with each other in learning, in the sense that many learning tasks are amenable to multiple strategies and to both declarative and non-declarative kinds of learning. Thus, one's behaviour towards a familiar face or stimulus object can be expected to be a combination of declaratively guided conscious recollections about the stimulus and its significance, as well as non-declarative, non-conscious dispositions shaped by previous encounters.

The existence of multiple memory systems has implications for traditional notions about the construct of the unconscious mind. In considering the effects of past experience on subsequent behaviour, it matters how one understands the nature of memory. By the traditional view, material that is unconscious is below some threshold of accessibility and could potentially be made available to consciousness. Yet, experimental inquiry has led to a distinction between a kind of memory that is conscious (declarative memory), which by its nature can potentially be brought to mind as either a proposition or a visual image, and other kinds of memory that are non-conscious in the sense that the acquired knowledge is expressed through performance without affording any awareness of memory content. For example, in the case of non-conscious memory, an experience very early in life can affect subsequent behaviour by causing a phobia, which creates a particular behavioural disposition towards a set of objects. But the persistence of the phobia does not imply that a record of the event itself has also persisted. Behaviour has simply changed.

Thus, an experience can result in altered dispositions, preferences, conditioned responses, habits or skills. Often, of course, individuals will also establish independently and in parallel a declarative conscious record of what it was that happened. However, the point is that the creation of behavioural dispositions, preferences, habits and skills in non-declarative memory does not necessarily afford the potential for an awareness that behaviour is being influenced by past experience. Nor need there be any declarative record of the event itself. For example, if an unpleasant experience with a dog occurred during the first two years of life, prior to the time that long-term declarative memory can be established, the experience could result in a persistent phobia but there would be no declarative record of what actually happened. In this circumstance, the presence of a non-declarative memory does not imply the possibility of uncovering any conscious recollections about the first two years of life; the unconscious cannot become conscious. Behaviour can change by acquiring new habits that supersede old ones, or one can become sufficiently aware of the existence of a habit such that one can to some extent alter it through practice or limit the stimuli that elicit it. However, one does not become aware of the memory content of a habit in the same sense that one knows the content of a declarative memory. Declarative memory is independent of, and parallel to, non-declarative memory.

Conclusions

Memory is localized in the sense that different parts of the brain store different aspects of information, but memory is distributed in the sense that multiple areas of neocortex participate in representing even simple pieces of information (Fig. 7). If distributed activity in the cortex, which subserves perception and short-term memory, is to persist as stable and enduring long-term declarative memory, then at the time of learning information must converge into the medial temporal lobe memory system. Through associative mechanisms in the medial temporal lobe, conjunctions are formed and stored that are able to bind together the distributed record of a whole event. For a time after learning, these conjunctions, these sites of plasticity, retain the capacity to revivify, even from a partial cue, the separate components in neocortex that together constitute a whole memory.

Diencephalic structures, particularly medial thalamic structures, also participate in this process, perhaps as a way of accessing the frontal lobes so that conscious recollections can be translated into action. In any case, the limbic/diencephalic system that supports declarative memory provides for the possibility of conscious

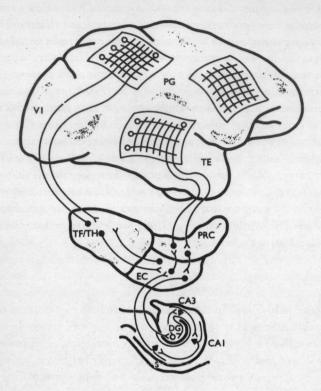

recollection. Declarative memory is fallible, in the sense that forgetting can occur as well as failures of retrieval. Declarative memory is also precious, giving rise to our capacity for personal autobiography and the possibility of cultural evolution.

Other kinds of memory also exist, such as skills, habits, priming or conditioning. These memories are acquired, stored and retrieved without the participation of the limbic/diencephalic system. Nondeclarative memory is fundamental, phylogenetically early and essential for survival. For example, through conditioning, it provides a relatively automatic way to learn about the causal structure of the world. In contrast to declarative memory, non-declarative forms of memory are reliable and consistent, adapted for slow and incremental

*Figure 7. The components of the medial temporal lobe memory system
are illustrated in this schematic drawing of the primate cortex. The
networks in the neocortex show putative representations of visual object
quality in the inferotemporal cortex (area TE) and of object location in
the posterior parietal cortex (area PG). At the time of learning,
information from the neocortex arrives initially at the parahippocampal
cortex (area TF/TH) and the perirhinal cortex (PR, areas 35 and 36),
and then at the entorhinal cortex (EC, area 28), the gateway to the
hippocampus. Further processing occurs in the stages of the
hippocampus, the dentate gyrus (DG) and the CA3 and CA1 regions,
and information ultimately exits this circuit by way of the subiculum (S)
and EC, where widespread afferents return to the neocortex. Not shown
here are the several projections connecting the medial temporal lobe
system to medial diencephalic structures and the projections from the
medial temporal lobe and diencephalic structures to the frontal lobe,
which may be important for making conscious recollections available as
the basis for action. (From L. R. Squire, 1990, in:* The Biology of
Memory, *ed. L. Squire and E. Lindenlaub, p. 648, Schattauer Verlag.)*

change. These forms of memory are the basis of much of our
personality and provide for myriad, non-conscious ways of
responding to the world. And in no small part, by virtue of the
non-conscious status of these kinds of memory, the nature of non-
declarative memory creates some of the mystery of human experience. Here emerge the dispositions, habits and preferences that are
inaccessible to conscious recollection, but that nevertheless arise
from experience, influence us and are a part of who we are.

Further reading

Schacter, D. L. (1996). *Searching for Memory*. Basic Books.
Schacter, D. L., and Tulving, E. (eds.) (1994). *Memory Systems 1994*. MIT
Press.
Squire, L. R. (1987). *Memory and Brain*. Oxford University Press.
Squire, L. R., and Knowlton, B. (1994). Memory, hippocampus and brain
systems. In: *The Cognitive Neurosciences* (ed. M. Gazzaniga). MIT Press.

Squire, L. R., and Zola, S. (1996). Memory, memory impairment, and the medial temporal lobe. In: *Cold Spring Harbor Symposia on Quantitative Biology*, Vol. LXI. Cold Spring Harbor Press.

Squire, L. R., and Zola-Morgan, S. (1991). The medial temporal lobe memory system. *Science* 253, 1380–1386.

Squire, L. R., Ojemann, J. G., Miezin, F. M., Petersen, S. E., Videen, T. O., *et al.* (1992). Activation of the hippocampus in normal humans: a functional anatomical study of memory. *Proceedings of the National Academy of Sciences* 89, 1837–1841.

5

The Physiological Basis
of Memory

TIM BLISS

For the neurophysiologist the problem of memory is the problem of how a particular pattern of nervous activity in the brain, a pattern which is the neural representation of the event to be remembered and which is all that the brain can know about that event, is able to produce physical changes in the brain which allow the representation of the event to be stored and subsequently recalled. It is neural activity itself which is the agent driving these changes, and the changes which occur must in some way represent the event itself. The easiest way to envisage how this might happen is to suppose that activity strengthens the connections between just those nerve cells which were active during the event, and that subsequently a relevant cue triggers a recapitulation of the original pattern of activity. Activity in neural nets spreads by the electrical conduction of nerve impulses along nerve fibres, and then by the chemical process of synaptic transmission at the synapses between neurons. Because nerve impulses are invariant in amplitude (nerve cells either fire an impulse of constant amplitude or no impulse at all, the so-called all-or-none property of neurons), the only plausible candidate for the site of activity-induced changes is at the synapses themselves. In order for information to be stored, therefore, there must be a mechanism which allows activity-dependent changes in synaptic efficacy to occur. In the late 1960s a phenomenon called long-term potentiation was discovered in the hippocampus; as we shall see, long-term potentiation has most of the properties which one would like to see in a neural memory device.

Memory in a dish?

Much of what I shall be discussing in this chapter is based on experiments performed on thin slices of brain tissue, maintained in a small bath and perfused with an oxygenated saline solution containing glucose. Thus nourished, nerve cells in the slice remain healthy and responsive for several hours. They will, if stimulated, fire impulses, release transmitter, and respond appropriately to excitatory and inhibitory inputs from other neurons in the slice. But what can such a reduced preparation, cut off from all sensory information, lying passive and inert in its dish, possibly tell us about memory, that most precious of cognitive functions, the faculty of mind which above all others endows us with the sense of our own identity? About the psychology of memory, of course, very little; but about the physiology of memory, the neural mechanisms which are likely to encode information at the level of synaptic interconnections between neurons, we have learnt a great deal from such experiments in the last two decades. Unlike other, less tractable, problems discussed in this book, such as the relationship between brain processes and consciousness, perception or free will, there is a widespread feeling among neuroscientists that the nature of the link between synaptic plasticity and memory is a problem which we now have the experimental tools to answer.

The region of the brain which is most widely investigated in studies of the physiological basis of memory is the hippocampus, shown in Fig. 6 of Chapter 4 (see p. 66). Two factors have been responsible for the popularity of the hippocampus among neuroscientists interested in memory. First, as argued by Larry Squire in the previous chapter, the hippocampus is intimately involved in memory processing: in humans it is essential for the formation of new memories and for the consolidation of older memories into a permanent memory store. This became strikingly and tragically clear in the case of HM, whose hippocampus was removed by surgery in a last-ditch attempt to control his incapacitating epilepsy. The operation resulted in his losing all ability to form memories of the day to day events of his life. HM retains memories for events before his operation, although he shows a 'gradient of forgetting' – he is better at remembering events which occurred many years before his operation than more recent events. The study of HM and other amnesic patients has shown that the hippocampus is necessary for the formation of new declarative memories, but that the permanent long-term store for such memories must lie elsewhere in the brain. The gradient of forgetting implies that it can take several years to complete the transfer from hippocampal to non-hippocampal stores, a process known as consolidation.

The second reason for studying the hippocampus is more practical, but it has nevertheless played an important role in the story I have to tell: its structural organization is relatively simple, and this makes it possible to carry out the kind of long-lasting physiological experiments which are necessary when studying neural processes underlying memory. When Terje Lømo and I set out nearly 30 years ago to see whether we could identify neurons in the brain which possessed the kind of properties which would enable them to act as memory elements, we chose to work on the hippocampus – not just because we knew that the hippocampus was involved in some way in laying down new memories, but because it was only in the hippocampus that we could design the appropriate experiments. Science, as Peter Medawar observed, is the art of the soluble, and we pick our questions and preparations accordingly.

In humans, the hippocampus lies tucked within the medial wall of the temporal cortex (see Fig. 1a), while in rats, the animal most commonly used for experiments on the mechanisms of long-term potentiation and its relationship to learning and memory, it lies immediately beneath the dorsal surface of the cortex. The neural organization of the hippocampus is very similar in all mammals, from rats to monkeys to humans (Fig. 1b). We can be reasonably confident that just as the patterns of nerve connections to, from and within the hippocampus are similar in different mammals, so there will be similarities and homologies in the functional properties of hippocampal neurons.

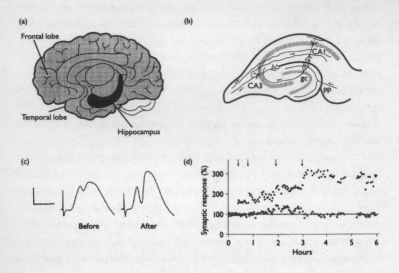

Long-term potentiation

The hypothesis discussed above – that neural activity produces enduring changes in synaptic efficacy, and that it is these changes which constitute the physical memory trace – was popularized over a hundred years ago by the great Spanish anatomist Raman y Cajal, who first established the existence of synaptic junctions between neurons. Neurophysiologists did not doubt that he was right, if only because there was no obvious alternative. The problem was to find synapses which displayed the appropriate property. Most synapses, when activated by a tetanus (a high-frequency train of electrical pulses delivered through a fine stimulating electrode which induces in the presynaptic nerve fibre a corresponding train of nerve impulses), demonstrate a short-term increase in efficacy known as post-tetanic potentiation. But this effect lasts only a minute or two. Are hippocampal synapses any different? To find out, Lømo and I stimulated the main pathway into the hippocampus, the perforant path, and recorded the responses generated by the target neurons, the type known as 'granule cells' in the dentate gyrus (see Fig. 1c). The

Figure 1. The hippocampus and long-term potentiation of synaptic transmission. (a) Midline view of the right hemisphere of the human brain, showing the position of the hippocampus in the temporal lobe. (b) Diagram of the neuronal organization of the mammalian hippocampus. Processed sensory information enters via the fibres of the perforant path (pp), projecting to the granule cells (gc) of the dentate gyrus, which project to the pyramidal cells of area CA3; these in turn project to the pyramidal cells of area CA1, completing the 'trisynaptic loop' through the hippocampal formation. (c) Synaptically evoked responses recorded from granule cells of the dentate gyrus, before and after the induction of long-term potentiation. The first spike is an electrical artefact marking the moment of stimulation. The subsequent upward-going slope is the synaptic response generated in the granule cell population by the synchronous volley of impulses in perforant path axons initiated by the electrical stimulus; superimposed on this is a downward-going spike which reflects the synchronous firing of granule cells; note that after the induction of LTP (see (d)) the synaptic response is steeper, and more cells fire impulses. The calibration bars represent 5 ms and 3 mV. (d) Experiment in which synaptic responses are evoked by single electrical pulses delivered through stimulating electrodes placed in the perforant path on both the left (open circles) and the right dentate gyrus (solid circles). Arrows mark the times at which high-frequency trains of stimuli were delivered on the right half of the brain, producing immediate and persistent enhancement of the response to single stimuli. This is the phenomenon of long-term potentiation, or LTP.

perforant path carries highly processed visual, auditory and olfactory information from the entorhinal cortex to the dentate gyrus. We found that when a brief tetanus was given to this path there was, in addition to the expected post-tetanic potentiation of the responses of the granule cells, a much longer increase in synaptic efficacy. We called this enduring change long-term potentiation, or LTP.

Our first experiments were carried out on anaesthetized rabbits and showed that LTP can persist for several hours (Fig. 1d); further experiments on awake rabbits, in which electrodes were implanted into the hippocampus under anaesthesia some days earlier, demonstrated that LTP could last at least for several days, but that the potentiated responses do eventually decay back to base line. (Whether this is true of LTP in other pathways in the hippocampus is not known; presumably there are synapses in the cortical circuits which support long-term memory, in which LTP, or something like it, can last a lifetime.) At the end of the paper in which we described these results, Lømo and I wrote: 'Our experiments show that there exists at least one group of synapses in the hippocampus whose efficiency is influenced by activity which may have occurred several hours previously – a time scale long enough to be potentially useful for information storage.' Since then, LTP has been found at other

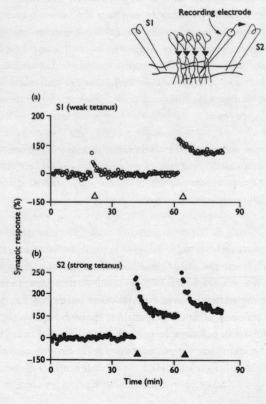

excitatory pathways in the hippocampus, as well as at synapses in several other cortical regions. Unlike post-tetanic potentiation, however, LTP is not exhibited by every cortical synapse.

It soon turned out that LTP had other characteristics which greatly enhanced its potential as a neural memory device, the two most important of which are input specificity and associativity. These two properties can be most easily demonstrated in the hippo-campal slice, as illustrated in Fig. 2. In this experiment, responses of pyramidal cells in a different region of the hippocampus, area CA1, were recorded. A pair of stimulating electrodes was placed on either side of the recording electrode to activate the axons of CA3 cells, a class of large neurons in the CA3 region of the hippocampus, called from their shape pyramidal cells. These axons make excitatory synapses with CA1 cells. The two stimulating electrodes were posi-tioned so as to activate separate sets of fibres converging on the same population of CA1 cells. With this 'two pathway' arrangement, it is easy to show that a tetanus which induces LTP in one pathway has no effect on synaptic efficacy on the other pathway, providing the second pathway is not active at the time of the tetanus. The

Figure 2. Long-term potentiation is input-specific and associative. The diagram at the top shows how electrodes can be placed so as to excite different sets of fibres projecting to the same population of CA1 cells. The strength of stimulation is set so that one electrode (S1) excites too few fibres to produce LTP, while the other is above threshold for LTP. Single stimuli are given alternately to S1 and S2 and the synaptic responses plotted in (a) and (b) respectively. High-frequency stimulation to S1 (open arrow head in (a)) produces only a brief potentiation; high-frequency stimulation to S2 (solid arrowhead in (b)) produces LTP in the pathway activated by S2, but no potentiation in the S1 pathway. This is the property of input specificity. If the high-frequency train to S1 (which when given alone does not produce LTP) is given at the same time as the train to S2 (aligned open and solid arrowheads in (a) and (b)), then the weak pathway is also potentiated; this is the property of associativity.

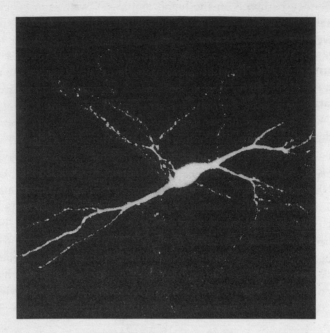

Figure 3. Spine City. A living pyramidal cell in area CA1 of the rat hippocampus, filled with a fluorescent dye. Note that the cell is encrusted with dendritic spines, each of which is the site of an excitatory synapse. Pyramidal cells can have as many as 20,000 spines.

property of input specificity shows that, in principle, each synapse can act as an independent computing device. Since there can be more than 20,000 synapses on a typical pyramidal cell, this enormously increases the potential amount of information the neuron can store.

If the stimulus to the second pathway is sufficiently weak, a tetanus to this pathway becomes incapable of inducing LTP. Remarkably, however, if the weak tetanus is given at the same time as the stronger tetanus to the first pathway, then the second pathway is also potentiated. This is the property of *associativity*, which provides a neural model for the ubiquitous form of learning known as classical conditioning. (Remember Pavlov's dogs: after repeated trials during which a bell was rung immediately before the delivery of food, the dogs began to salivate to the sound of the bell alone. They had learned the association between bell and food, as, by analogy, the second set of synapses, stimulated only at low frequency, had 'learned' the association with the high-frequency train.)

What can we learn about the mechanisms responsible for the induction of LTP from the properties of input specificity and associativity? The fact that LTP is produced by high-frequency but not by low-frequency stimulation suggests that the target cells need to be strongly activated, a conclusion strengthened by the observation that weak high-frequency trains, activating fewer fibres, are also relatively ineffective at inducing potentiation. We can formulate an induction rule for LTP which takes account of the requirement for strong activation, and also predicts the properties of associativity and input specificity. As described in Chapter 3, when a nerve impulse travels down an axon and reaches a presynaptic terminal, a transmitter substance – either excitatory or inhibitory – is released from the nerve terminal, traverses the narrow synaptic cleft, and binds to receptor molecules embedded in the neuronal cell membrane on the postsynaptic side of the synapse. If the transmitter is excitatory, this process results in an influx of positive ions (principally sodium) through channels in the receptor molecules, and into the postsynaptic neuron, resulting in a reduction in the electrical potential (*depolarization*) of the dendritic membrane; if membrane depolarization is sufficiently intense, the postsynaptic cell itself will discharge an impulse. Inhibitory transmitters oppose this process, and usually produce an increase in the potential across the membrane (*hyperpolarization*). With these definitions in mind, we can now state the induction rule for LTP:

An excitatory synapse in the hippocampus will be potentiated if it is active at a time when the dendrite on which it is located is strongly depolarized.

This rule accounts for the fact that a weak tetanus does not induce LTP (it causes insufficient depolarization), and also explains input specificity (synapses must be active) and associativity (a weak input, provided it is active at a time when a strong input has led to sufficient dendritic depolarization, will satisfy the two conditions set by the induction rule). Note that the rule says nothing about strong high-frequency stimulation. If sufficient depolarization can be produced in some other way, then the induction rule predicts that active synapses will be potentiated. A direct test of this prediction was made by Holger Wigström and his colleagues in Sweden in 1986. They impaled a single pyramidal cell with a fine glass electrode, and passed electrical current across the cell membrane, mimicking the depolarization produced by a strong tetanus. They used a two-pathway protocol in which single stimuli were given alternately to each of two pathways, with the stimulus to one pathway coinciding with an artificially induced depolarizing pulse, and the stimulus to the other pathway out of phase with the depolarizing pulse. The result was exactly as predicted by the induction rule: after several pairings, LTP was induced in the in-phase pathway, but not in the out-of-phase pathway.

Receptor mechanisms

During the 1980s, in what is probably the major success story of research in this field to date, the molecular mechanisms responsible for the induction of LTP were worked out. It is now possible to give an explanation for the induction rule in terms of the properties of a single protein. The story hinges on the nature of the excitatory transmitter and the receptor proteins to which that transmitter binds. The major excitatory transmitter in the brain is the amino acid glutamic acid (usually referred to simply as glutamate). The particular effect that a transmitter exerts depends on the receptor to which it binds, and it is now known that for each transmitter a family, or even several families, of receptors exists. We will concentrate on two glutamate receptor families – AMPA receptors and NMDA receptors. The names are the acronyms of synthetic glutamate analogues, the use of which produced the first evidence for the existence of different types of glutamate receptor: both types, by definition, respond to glutamate; but AMPA receptors respond to AMPA and not to NMDA, and NMDA receptors respond to NMDA and not AMPA. Further progress came with the development of specific antagonists to glutamate receptors; these are compounds which mimic the native transmitter in binding to glutamate receptors but do so in such a way that does not allow channels to open and ion fluxes to flow. Transmission at all known fast excitatory synapses in the mammalian brain is completely blocked by broad-spectrum glutamate antagonists which bind to all glutamate receptor subtypes. In the hippocampus, it became clear in the 1980s that specific antagonists of the AMPA receptor were almost as effective as broad-spectrum antagonists at blocking transmission at perforant path synapses and the synapses on CA1 pyramidal cells. It seemed as if transmission at these synapses was mediated by AMPA receptors alone. Consistent with this interpretation, a compound called APV, a specific NMDA receptor antagonist, had very little effect on transmission at these synapses.

Then came a breakthrough. Graham Collingridge, now at the University of Bristol but working at that time in Vancouver, discovered, with colleagues, that although APV did not affect synaptic transmission in area CA1 in the hippocampal slice, it completely blocked the induction of LTP. But if LTP was first induced by tetanic stimulation in the absence of APV, then the subsequent application of APV had no effect. Evidently, activation of the NMDA receptor was the trigger for the induction of LTP, but, once triggered, the receptor played no further part in the expression of the enhanced response. The next piece in the jigsaw came from researchers in Paris and the USA, who found that the NMDA receptor, and the ion channel associated with it, displays some highly unusual properties. For a start, its behaviour is voltage-dependent; this means that it is not enough, as for other receptors, for transmitter to bind to the receptor in order for the ion channel to open; this only happens when the cell – or the dendrite on which the NMDA receptor is located – is strongly depolarized; at membrane potentials near to the resting level, the channel of the NMDA receptor is blocked by magnesium ions, which bar the passage of other ions

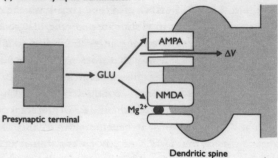

(a) Normal synaptic transmission

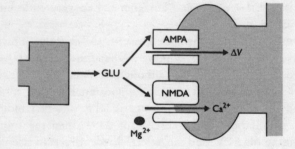

(b) Induction of LTP

even when transmitter is bound to the appropriate part of the receptor. Only strong depolarization will drive the magnesium ions out of the channel and allow the free passage of other ions. Thus two conditions have to be met for the NMDA receptor-associated channel to open: transmitter must bind to the receptor, and the dendrite on which it is located must be sufficiently depolarized.

Hebb's postulate

Put this in the context of the synapse, and it will be seen that the conditions for the opening of the NMDA channel are formally

*Figure 4. The role of the NMDA receptor in the induction of LTP. (a)
In normal transmission at excitatory hippocampal synapses, the
transmitter glutamate (GLU) is released from the presynaptic terminal
and binds to receptors located on the apposing dendritic spine on the
target neuron. The receptors are of two kinds, labelled AMPA and
NMDA. The synaptic response is mediated largely by AMPA receptors
which on binding glutamate undergo a conformational change, allowing
sodium ions to enter the interior of the cell, leading to a reduction in
voltage (ΔV) across the cell membrane. The NMDA receptor also binds
transmitter, but the channel in the protein through which the ions pass is
blocked by magnesium ions (Mg^{2+}), so that in normal circumstances the
NMDA receptor contributes little to the evoked response. (b) During
intense synaptic activation, as during a high-frequency train, more
transmitter is released, leading to a greater ion flux through the AMPA
channel and consequently to a greater reduction in membrane voltage.
The block of the NMDA receptor by magnesium ions is
voltage-dependent; when the reduction in membrane voltage is more
than about 30 mV, magnesium ions are expelled from the channel,
allowing other ions to pass. Calcium ions (Ca^{2+}) pass easily through the
NMDA receptor channel, and it is the entry of calcium into the spine
which is believed to be the trigger for the induction of LTP.*

identical to the induction rule for LTP; the induction rule is simply
a reflection of the properties of the NMDA receptor. Because two
conditions need to be met for the NMDA receptor to become
functional – binding of transmitter and strong depolarization – it has
been called a 'molecular AND gate'; another common description
is 'molecular coincidence detector'. Both these terms reflect the
associative property of the receptor – its operation depends not only
on transmitter release at its own synapse, but also on simultaneous
excitatory events occurring in neighbouring synapses, which can
cooperate to produce the necessary depolarization. The NMDA
receptor also embodies the molecular machinery for what is often
known as the Hebb synapse, after the Canadian psychologist Donald
Hebb, whose book *The Organization of Behavior*, published in 1949,

first made explicit a possible rule for learning based on changes in synaptic efficacy. Hebb's famous postulate states:

When an axon of cell A is near enough to excite a cell B and repeatedly or persistently takes part in firing it, some growth process or metabolic change takes place in one or both cells such that A's efficiency, as one of the cells firing B, is increased.

What matters is the coincident activity of the population of cells (A cells) which project to the target cell B; only those synapses belonging to A cells which are active at the same time will be strengthened, since only in those circumstances will conditions be satisfied for the opening of the NMDA channel. In effect, the NMDA receptor detects conditions in which there is coincident firing of A cells, leading to strengthening of synapses which are active together. Coincidence detection may also be an important process in the developing brain where, for example, it has been suggested that it helps bring about the organization of the neurons of the visual cortex so as to separate, on the basis of their activity, the inputs from the two eyes.

Another unusual feature of the NMDA receptor is the high permeability of its channel to calcium ions. A number of lines of evidence strongly suggest that it is the entry of calcium through the NMDA channels in the postsynaptic membrane which is the trigger for LTP. For instance, the capacity for LTP is abolished if the cell is injected with calcium chelators – agents which trap free calcium ions. There are many enzymes and biochemical cascades which are stimulated or initiated by a rise in intracellular free calcium (that is, calcium existing unbound or unsequestered, in free ionic form). A number of such cascades have been implicated in LTP, including the activation of a class of enzymes, protein kinases, which can chemically alter the receptor proteins by linking phosphate to certain amino acids within the protein chain, thereby altering their function. Activation of protein kinases can also lead to gene transcription and the synthesis of new proteins, the function of which may be to construct larger synapses. While the details of these biochemical cascades remain to be worked out, LTP, like memory itself, can be divided into two components: an early component, lasting up to a few hours, which does not require new protein synthesis, and a later, more-persistent phase which is dependent on protein synthesis.

Presynaptic v. postsynaptic mechanisms

The discussion so far might lead one to suppose that while presynaptic activity is required for the induction of LTP (transmitter must be released), the persistent increase in the strength of synaptic transmission that ensues is maintained by postsynaptic mechanisms – for instance, by phosphorylation of glutamate receptors or by insertion of new receptors into the postsynaptic membrane. This is an active area of current research, and, though the evidence is not yet conclusive, it seems very likely that postsynaptic mechanisms of this sort are involved in the expression of LTP. This may not be the whole story however. Presynaptic mechanisms, leading to a persistent increase in the amount of transmitter released, are also thought to play a role in the expression of LTP. One line of evidence pointing to a presynaptic component is an increase in the release of glutamate from synapses following the induction of LTP, an increase which is abolished if induction is blocked with the NMDA receptor antagonist, APV.

Another line of evidence comes from what is known as quantal analysis. Transmitter is released at individual synapses in packages known as quanta (these are physiologists' quanta, by the way, and have nothing to do with the way that physicists use the term); release is a probabilistic event, and usually one quantum at most is released at hippocampal synapses. Analysis of the variation of synaptic responses at individual synapses before and after the induction of LTP can, in principle, give insights into whether LTP is governed by pre- or postsynaptic mechanisms; an increase in the probability of release without any change in quantal amplitude, for instance, would suggest a presynaptic mechanism. However, this is a contentious area; while the majority of such experiments indicate that expression is at least in part presynaptic, there are wide disagreements both about the nature of the changes and the interpretation that should be placed upon them. At the moment there is little sign that consensus is about to break out among the disputants. Nevertheless, the evidence as a whole points to the conclusion that LTP is maintained at least in part by presynaptic mechanisms.

Presynaptic changes pose an intriguing theoretical problem: if the trigger for induction is entry of calcium through the postsynaptic NMDA receptor channel, how does the presynaptic side of the synapse get to know about this critical event? As we have seen, LTP is not induced by weak tetani: so release of transmitter is not enough by itself to produce LTP. Perhaps there is communication between axons, so that in an associative protocol, the weak input is aware that a strong input is simultaneously active? The conjunction experiment of Holger Wigström disposes of that idea – LTP can be produced by weak inputs, providing that the postsynaptic cell is strongly depolarized. It seems that there must be a signal emanating from the postsynaptic site of induction, and traversing the synapse to act at the presynaptic terminal, setting in motion the biochemical events leading to a persistent increase in transmitter release. That, in brief, is the argument for a retrograde messenger, the search for which has preoccupied several laboratories in the last three or four years. There are two main candidates. One is a gas, nitric oxide, now known to play an important part in many physiological processes, including a powerful effect in dilating blood vessels. The other is a lipid, arachidonic acid, which is a normal component of cell membranes. At this point, the evidence is not conclusive for either of these candidates. Most intriguingly, there is experimental support for the existence of an unidentified diffusible substance which acts to modulate synaptic strength at all synapses in the immediate vicinity of a potentiated synapse. These experiments suggest that the diffusible messenger can modulate transmission in a non-Hebbian manner – the affected synapses can be on a different cell from the one in which LTP was induced, and may not even have been active at the time of induction. These are heretical ideas in terms of the orthodoxy of the last two decades, and their progress will be watched with more than usual interest.

LTP is the brain's way of boosting synaptic strength, but there must surely be a limit to the process. If repeated episodes of tetanic stimulation are given to hippocampal pathways, potentiation eventually becomes saturated. (Technical difficulties have so far prevented a detailed analysis of LTP at single synapses and it is not known if at this level LTP is all-or-none. When many synapses are activated, as in Fig. 1(d), the graded increase in the level of LTP can be explained either by a gradual increase in the level of potentiation at individual synapses, or by an increase in the proportion of potentiated synapses, where individual synapses can be in one of two states, not potentiated or maximally potentiated.) If all synapses became saturated, there would be no scope for further activity-induced plasticity, and, according to our central hypothesis, further learning would become impossible. Learning is a life-long process, so where is the flaw? We can save our hypothesis in various ways. First, we do not know how many memories the hippocampus stores, nor how many synapses are assigned to each memory. It may be that the representation of each memory requires relatively few synapses and that a temporary memory store like the hippocampus is in no danger of filling up even if LTP does saturate. In any case, LTP is not permanent, at least in the dentate gyrus of the hippocampus. These two possibilities have not satisfied theorists, who have urged the experimentalists to look for procedures which will produce long-term depression rather than long-term potentiation, and, in particular, for procedures to switch off LTP once it has been induced (depotentiation). Evidence for both long-term depression and depotentiation has now been found as a consequence of particular patterns of repetitive low-frequency stimulation, although such depression is more difficult to produce experimentally than LTP.

LTP and learning

Soon after the discovery of LTP, physiological psychologists set out to establish whether they could establish a link between LTP and learning and memory in their favourite experimental animal, the rat. It had previously been established that rats with hippocampal lesions could no longer learn to find their way around spatial mazes;

this and other evidence, including the discovery of 'place' cells in the hippocampus (cells which increase their firing rates when the rat is in a particular place in the room) led John O'Keefe and Lynn Nadel in London to suggest that the hippocampus established a 'cognitive map' of the rat's world. Carol Barnes, in Canada, compared LTP and learning ability in rats of various ages, and showed that in general there was a good correlation between the duration of LTP and performance in a navigational task – the kind of task which requires an intact hippocampus. This was consistent with the hypothesis that LTP provides the neural underpinning for spatial learning.

But the most influential such experiment had to wait until after the crucial role of the NMDA receptor in the induction of LTP had been uncovered. Richard Morris, then at St Andrew's University in Scotland, infused the NMDA receptor antagonist APV into the hippocampus of rats. He then compared the performance of APV-treated rats with a control group in a task which he had earlier devised to study the role of the hippocampus in spatial learning. In this task, called the water maze, the rat is placed in a circular pool filled with warm, opaque water, from which it can only escape by climbing on to a small platform located just below the surface and invisible to the rat. Initially, the animal swims at random until by chance it bumps into the platform. The time between placing the rat in the water and its climbing onto the platform is logged. With successive trials the time in the water steadily diminishes, eventually levelling out as the rat learns, on the basis of visual cues in the surrounding environment, to swim directly to the platform when released from any position at the periphery of the pool. Rats with lesions of the hippocampus cannot learn this task. What Morris now showed was that when treated with APV, a drug whose only known effect was to block the induction of LTP and which did not otherwise interfere with synaptic transmission in the hippocampus, performance was reduced to a level comparable to that of animals with hippocampal lesions. This experiment provided powerful evidence for the hypothesis that LTP is required for the acquisition of the neural representation of spatially oriented learning. Morris himself was at pains to stress, however, that his results did not force this conclusion. He could not be certain that the drug had not spread outside the hippocampus and was producing its effect by blocking NMDA receptor-mediated transmission elsewhere, or that the drug had other and unknown effects which were responsible for the impairment in learning.

In the decade since Morris's pioneering experiment, the waters of this particular pool have if anything become more rather than less opaque. Morris himself, with colleagues, has found that once a rat has been trained to find the submerged platform in one pool, it can learn the position of another platform, in another pool in a different room, even when treated with APV, a result which implies that it is learning *about* spatial tasks – learning to learn – which is sensitive to APV. The simple link between LTP and spatial learning is thus called into question.

Genetic confusions

Other approaches have also produced equivocal results. The new techniques of genetic engineering have made it possible to produce mice in which a given gene can effectively be eliminated from the genome and hence the protein for which it codes cannot be made. Some such proteins are essential for survival and the mutation is therefore lethal – as is the case for the NMDA receptor gene, for instance. On the other hand, many different genes can apparently be knocked out without major effects on the animal's survival capacity, allowing the effects of such knockouts on LTP and behaviour to be studied. The first animals to be examined in this way were those which lacked genes for particular protein kinases. Initial results were encouraging. The knockout animals were impaired in spatial learning and showed significantly less LTP than their normal siblings. So far, so good. But between 1993 and 1996 twenty or more different types of knockout mice, each with deletion of a different gene, were examined in this way, and it has become clear that in some cases normal spatial learning can proceed despite severely impaired LTP in one or more hippocampal pathways.

However, there is as yet no case in which a knockout has shown no LTP in any hippocampal pathway, and yet has displayed normal spatial learning. This is the minimal result required to disprove the hypothesis that LTP is necessary for learning. Even if such an animal is found it does not disprove the slightly weaker hypothesis that hippocampal LTP is used by the normal animal for spatial learning.

The limitations of this technique are that it does not allow for the developmental plasticity that all living organisms show. There may after all be many routes by which the brain can achieve a particular outcome, and compensatory mechanisms may well come into play during development which allow neural encoding of spatial learning to proceed elsewhere. Recently developed genetic technology promises to answer some of these problems – the production of region-specific, inducible knockouts. The goal is an animal in which the gene of interest can be knocked out in a specific region at a time of the experimenter's choosing. Two recent reports show that this goal is close to being achieved. Experimenters at Susuma Tonegawa's laboratory at MIT have studied LTP and spatial learning in a mouse in which the NMDA receptor was deleted only from cells in area CA1, and nowhere else in the brain. This restricted deletion of the NMDA receptor is not lethal, and so the experimenters were able to study both spatial learning and LTP in these animals. Both were impaired. In another study from Eric Kandel's laboratory at Columbia University, mice were generated which expressed a mutant form of a protein kinase restricted to the hippocampus. Spatial learning was severely impaired in this mutant and LTP was modified; tetanic stimulation at 10 Hz, which in the normal mouse produces LTP, now produced depression instead. Their dazzling new trick was this: expression of the mutant kinase could be suppressed by injecting the animal with a bacterial antibiotic. When this was done, LTP was obtained in the hippocampus and normal performance in the spatial learning task was restored. These exciting new experiments provide the strongest evidence so far that LTP is exploited by the brain for at least one form of memory – that required for rats to find their way about in the world.

One thing emerges clearly from this discussion of the relationship between LTP and memory: an unequivocal proof of a causal relationship is not going to be easy to establish. On the other hand – if not LTP, what? Surely it is the activation of synapses made stronger by LTP that brings irresistibly to my mind Mark Twain's remark about the author of the *Iliad*: if it wasn't Homer, then it must have been another old blind Greek poet of the same name.

Further reading

Bliss, T. V. P., and Collingridge, G. L. (1993). A synaptic model of memory: long-term potentiation in the hippocampus. *Nature* 361, 31–39.

Kandel, E. R., and Hawkins, R. D. (1992). The biological basis of learning and individuality. *Scientific American* 267, 78–87.

Morris, R. G. M. (1996). Learning, memory and synaptic plasticity: cellular mechanisms, network architecture and the recording of attended experience. In: *The Lifespan Development of Individuals: Behavioural, Neurobiological and Psychosocial Perspectives*, pp. 139–160. Cambridge University Press.

Rose, S. P. R. (1992). *The Making of Memory*. Bantam.

6

Ageing of the Brain:
Is Mental Decline Inevitable?

A. DAVID SMITH

Omnia fert aetas, animum quoque; saepe ego longas
cantando puerum memini me condere soles:
nunc oblita mihi tot carmina . . .

Time wastes all things, the mind too: often I remember how
in boyhood I outwore long sunlit days in singing:
now I have forgotten so many a song . . .

Virgil, *Eclogue IX* (trans. Mackail)

Was Virgil right? Is it really true that a decline in our mental
and cognitive functions is an inevitable part of ageing? It is well
established that the proportion of people with dementia, the most
extreme form of cognitive deficit, is greater in the elderly and it is a
popular view that we get more forgetful as we age, but what do the
experts say? Some of them take the extreme view not only that
cognitive decline with ageing is inevitable but also that it is due to
a disease process, most commonly Alzheimer's disease. Thus, we
find the Nobel prizewinner Carleton Gajdusek saying in 1994: 'Alzheimer's disease is an accelerated form of brain amyloidosis [the
accumulation of the amyloid protein] of normal ageing. We shall
all get Alzheimer's disease if we live long enough.' On the other
hand, most of us know people in their ninth and tenth decades of
life who have remarkable memories. So, are there some people who
will escape Alzheimer's disease? In this chapter we will discuss the
idea that cognitive decline may not be an inevitable part of ageing
but rather that it reflects a disease process which is more likely to
affect us as we get older. If cognitive decline is a consequence of

disease, then it should be possible to discover ways of preventing it from happening by identifying the nature of the disease. It will not be necessary to understand the whole process of ageing in order to extend the useful life and mental well-being of the elderly.

The scale of the problem facing society

In a very short period of time in relation to the time humans have lived on this planet, the average life-expectancy has increased from around 25 years to more than 70 years. The main factors that have led to an increased life-expectancy are improvements in family income, in nutrition and in medical care, notably the introduction of drugs that combat infections. We only have to recall that the composer Gustav Mahler (born 1860) was one of fourteen children in his family and that six of his brothers and sisters died in childhood from infectious diseases. Mahler himself died at the age of 51 of streptococcal septicaemia, something that today could have been cured by antibiotics. Indeed, if we were to nominate one single biological discovery of the twentieth century as having given the greatest benefit to humanity, it would probably be the discovery of the ability of penicillin to treat bacterial infections, made in Oxford in 1941 by Howard Florey and his colleagues, following the original discovery of the bacteriocidal action of penicillin by Alexander Fleming.

Along with the extension of a productive and healthy life for the majority, these improvements in life-expectancy have also increased the number of sufferers of age-related diseases. Dementia is one such disease, whose prevalence approximately doubles for each successive 5-year period over the age of 60. For countries in the European Union and North America dementia already places a major burden on healthcare since about one in sixty of the populations of these countries suffers from dementia: some 6 million in the EU and about 5 million in North America. The costs per year have been estimated to be around $100 billion for the USA and about £3 billion for the UK. Dementia has been called the 'silent epidemic' because so little attention has been given to the scale of the problem by national governments. For example, in 1992 the Medical Research Council of the UK was only spending approximately 1 per cent of its budget on research into Alzheimer's disease, which is responsible for most cases of dementia, while ten times as much was spent on AIDS research. It is similar in the USA: more than 10 per cent of the entire budget of the National Institutes of Health is spent on AIDS research, while less than 3 per cent is spent on research into dementia in the elderly.

The future demographic predictions are alarming. Between 1990 and 2030 the proportion of people over 60 will grow by about 75 per cent in OECD countries, with a dramatic rise of almost 100 per cent in Japan. So we can expect the proportion with dementia to increase by a similar amount. Since the population of the EU is predicted to remain at around 370 million, we can expect more than 10 million with dementia by the year 2030.

The situation in Japan is so serious that the government there has developed a plan (New Gold Plan) to prepare for the rise in the costs of care of the elderly. In 1950 only 5 per cent of the Japanese population was over 65 years old, while in 2020 they will comprise more than 25 per cent. Special taxes have already been introduced to provide for the increase in the cost of pensions, but little can be done about the anticipated rise in the number of people with dementia except to hope that increased support for basic research in neuro-science, in the form of a new institute to be headed by Professor Masao Ito, will lead eventually to new drug treatments. The answer to a crucial question will determine the strategy of such basic research: *is dementia an inevitable part of natural ageing?* If it is, then it will be necessary to understand the process of ageing in order to develop rational new drug therapies.

Can neuropsychologists tell us whether cognitive decline is part of normal ageing?

There have been many studies of cognitive performance in the elderly in comparison with that in younger people and the overall view has emerged that there are certain aspects of higher cognitive function

Table 1. Mental functions and ageing as described by neuropsychologists

Well preserved	Decline with age
Sensory memory	Explicit secondary memory
Explicit primary memory	Executive functions
Implicit memory – priming	Implicit memory – classical
Implicit memory – visual	conditioning
Language – phonology, lexicon,	Visuospatial functions
syntax	Language – semantic
	Intelligence-test performance

in which the elderly are deficient. Table 1 summarizes these findings. It is important to realize that the great majority of such studies are 'cross-sectional' in design: in other words they compare a group of elderly people with a group of younger people. From this kind of comparison it is not correct to conclude that there is a 'decline' in cognitive function with age; all that can be said is that the two groups differ in their performance, i.e. the elderly show a 'deficit' in comparison with the young. There could be many reasons why the two groups differ in their performance in cognitive tests apart from their age. How do we know that the elderly group did not have a lower cognitive performance than the young group at the time when they were the same age as the young group? After all, they were born much earlier, when environmental factors, such as nutrition, may have been very different. So they might have started from a lower baseline and in fact have shown no decline with age at all. This situation is known as the 'cohort effect' and it is a major problem in research of this type. It would be much better, but it is also much more difficult, to study the same group of subjects longitudinally over a period of many years. Only then would it be possible to identify a decline in cognitive abilities by looking at changes in performance over time in individual subjects. But even the longitudinal design has its problems. If cognitive decline is indeed found in some of the subjects over time, how do we know that this decline is not due to the onset of a disease process? In order to avoid this problem, most of those carrying out cross-sectional and longitudinal studies take great care to exclude from their subject groups those who show any signs of disease. For example, they use standard screening procedures to exclude people with dementia. But these tests are designed to detect frank dementia and so are not at all sensitive to the very early stages of a dementing disease. In a longitudinal study it is important to detect those who might be in the earliest, presymptomatic, stages of dementia, but we do not yet know how to do that.

Is Alzheimer's disease an inevitable part of ageing?

Alzheimer's disease is the commonest cause of cognitive deficit in the elderly and there is a widely held view that it is an inevitable part of ageing and that we will all develop it if we live long enough. It is supposed that some people's brains age more rapidly than others and so they succumb to Alzheimer's disease earlier. This view arose out of the pioneering research carried out in Newcastle in the 1960s by Garyl Blessed, Bernard Tomlinson and Martin Roth. They found that the characteristic microscopic changes (the deposition of plaques of amyloid protein which become scattered through the brain and the 'tangled' appearance of the small fibres within individual neurons) of Alzheimer's disease were in fact also present, although to a lesser degree, in the brains of people who appeared to have been cognitively normal during their life. Roth and his colleagues suggested that there was a continuum from normal ageing to Alzheimer's disease and that the difference was merely a quantitative one. This view appears to be supported by the finding that the prevalence of amyloid plaques in the brain increases with age, most dramatically after the age of 60. However, we must be careful not to equate 'prevalence' with 'density'. There is no doubt that the number of people having amyloid plaques in their brains increases with age, but recent work has shown that the density of these plaques in any individual who displays them is constant at all ages. Thus, it may not be correct to assume, as does Gajdusek, that the density of amyloid plaques continually increases in our brains as we age, eventually crossing a threshold that leads to Alzheimer's disease.

What is needed is a biological 'state' marker for Alzheimer's disease that lets us follow the course of the disease in life. We could then compare the changes in this marker with those happening in normal ageing. So far, no way has been devised of following the deposition of amyloid plaques or of neurofibrillary tangles in the brain in life: these remain markers for the pathologist to assess after death. However, work by the Oxford Project to Investigate Memory and Ageing (OPTIMA) has shown that structural brain imaging using X-ray computed tomography (CT) can provide such a 'state' marker. We chose to examine the part of the brain that, after death, shows the greatest density of neurofibrillary tangles: the medial temporal lobe. This tiny part of the cerebral cortex comprises only 2 percent of the volume of the whole cerebral cortex but includes the hippocampus, a structure known to be crucial for memory (see the previous two chapters). Furthermore, the neurons of the medial temporal lobe are connected with almost all other parts of the cerebral cortex. Thus, any damage to this part of the brain is likely to have consequences for the functioning of much of the rest of the cerebral cortex. X-ray CT images of the medial temporal lobe show that this region is markedly smaller in demented subjects who eventually die of Alzheimer's disease than in age-matched control subjects without cognitive deficit (Fig. 1). The smaller medial temporal lobe is thus likely to become a useful aid to the diagnosis of Alzheimer's disease in life.

Why is the medial temporal lobe smaller in Alzheimer's disease? We showed that the degree of atrophy correlated well with the density of neurofibrillary tangles found in the hippocampus after death. It is likely that the presence of tangles inside neurons leads them eventually to die and so their processes die back, the number of synaptic contacts is reduced and the volume of tissue is less. Thus, measurement of the size of the medial temporal lobe is an indirect way of revealing the development of pathological change. This led us to distinguish three potential explanations to account for the

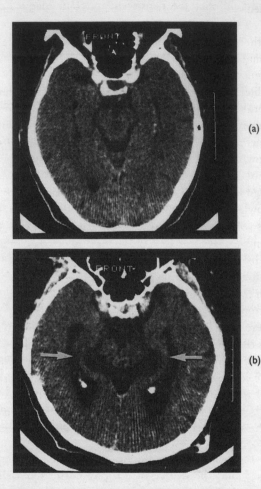

Figure 1. X-ray computed tomograms oriented along the long axis of the temporal lobe. (a) Cognitively screened normal control male subject aged 80 years old when scanned. Histopathological examination of the brain after death revealed no obvious pathology. (b) Female patient who was clinically diagnosed as demented and scanned at age 62 years. Histopathologically confirmed Alzheimer's disease. Note marked atrophy of the medial temporal lobes (arrows).

smaller medial temporal lobes in subjects with Alzheimer's disease (Fig. 2):

(i) does the development of pathological change occur steadily over many years, but at an accelerated rate in subjects with Alzheimer's disease, or

(ii) are subjects with Alzheimer's disease born with a thinner medial temporal lobe that shrinks at the same rate as in controls, or

(iii) does atrophy of the medial temporal lobe occur very rapidly, as if triggered by an event in the brain?

By following the changes in the medial temporal lobe by serial CT scans over periods of several years, we have been able to show that in cognitively screened control subjects this part of the brain shrinks slowly as we age, at about 1 to 1.5 per cent per year. However, in subjects with Alzheimer's disease the medial temporal lobe atrophied at an alarming rate, some 15 per cent per year, so supporting the third hypothesis. An independent study from Denmark also supports this view. In normal ageing, there is a loss of some of the neurons in the hippocampus, but the part of the hippocampus that loses neurons in Alzheimer's disease is quite distinct; in the latter region, there is no detectable loss of neurons in normal ageing. The symptoms of Alzheimer's disease correlate best with the density of neurofibrillary tangles in the medial temporal lobe and with the loss of synaptic connections in the cerebral cortex. Since neurons in the medial temporal lobe send processes to many parts of the cerebral cortex, it is the loss of these processes following the death of the neurons from which they originate that is partly responsible for the loss of synaptic connections.

We can conclude that Alzheimer's disease is distinct from normal ageing and that it cannot simply be an acceleration of normal ageing. The pathological changes in the medial temporal lobe seem to follow some event in the brain, an event which is increasingly likely as we age, but which is not inevitable. This finding provides new hope for understanding and for treating Alzheimer's disease, since we no longer have to understand the process of ageing but instead we can look for the biochemical changes that accompany the atrophy and the factors that trigger the start of the pathological process. If we

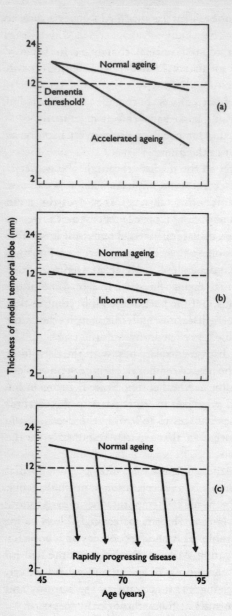

Figure 2. Different hypothetical ways that could lead to atrophy of the medial temporal lobe in subjects with Alzheimer's disease. (a) The normal age-related atrophy of the medial temporal lobe is accelerated. (b) Subjects with Alzheimer's disease are born with a thinner medial temporal lobe that atrophies at the normal rate. (c) An event takes place in the brain in subjects with Alzheimer's disease that leads to rapid atrophy of the medial temporal lobe.

could find out what the mechanisms are that lead the nerve cells to die, then we could identify chemically sensitive sites at which drugs could be designed to act to stop the neurons from dying. In this way, we could devise therapies for patients who show the early signs of Alzheimer's disease in the hope that the progression of the disease could be slowed down or halted.

Even more important would be to discover the trigger factors that initiate the process. Just like other common diseases, such as cancer and heart disease, it is likely that Alzheimer's disease is a multifactorial disease and that several trigger factors must come together in order to initiate the 'catastrophic event' in the medial temporal lobe. Some of these trigger factors will be genetic. That does not mean that having certain genes will determine whether or not a person will get Alzheimer's disease, as in familial Alzheimer's disease. This kind of cause is very rare, perhaps accounting for only 5 per cent of all cases worldwide. In the common non-familial form of the disease, having certain genes will increase the risk of developing Alzheimer's disease, but these genes on their own will not cause the disease. There have to be other risk factors present, possibly other genes but also factors intrinsic to the body and environmental factors. In 1993 a research group at Duke University, North Carolina, under Allen Roses, discovered a powerful genetic risk factor for Alzheimer's disease: a common variant of the protein apolipoprotein E. Subjects that carry the variant called E4, which occurs in about 15 per cent of the Caucasian population, have about a five-fold increased risk of developing Alzheimer's disease. It was then found that a much rarer variant, E2, seemed to protect carriers from developing Alzheimer's disease. These two variants of the most common form, E3, each differ from it by only a single amino acid in the protein chain. The search is now on for the molecular basis of these effects, since the hope is that discovery of the way in which these proteins act could lead to the development of new drugs to treat Alzheimer's disease. However, it should not cause anyone alarm to discover that they carry the gene for apolipoprotein E4, since studies have shown that many cognitively normal elderly people have this gene and, furthermore, about 35 per cent of all people with Alzheimer's disease do not carry this gene.

The search for non-genetic risk factors for Alzheimer's disease is made difficult by the problem of obtaining an accurate diagnosis in life. The epidemiological studies that have been done should thus be interpreted cautiously. One thing is absolutely certain: increased age is a major risk factor. What it is in the ageing process that increases the risk is not known. Other risk factors that have been suggested are listed in Table 2, but they all need validation in other

Table 2. Risk factors for Alzheimer's
disease as described by epidemiologists

....

Age
Head injury with concussion
Myocardial infarct (women)
Atherosclerosis
Oestrogen deficiency (women)
Low education
Dietary/absorption deficiency

....

studies, preferably with subjects who have died and so have a confirmed histopathological diagnosis. Such studies are very important because the identification of a non-genetic risk factor could make it possible to devise measures that would reduce the risk of Alzheimer's disease developing in a population (see below).

A distinction between successful ageing and pathological ageing

In 1987 Rowe and Kahn suggested that it was helpful to distinguish between 'usual' and 'successful' ageing. They defined 'usual' ageing as that which occurs in the population as a whole but postulated that it is heterogeneous, comprising a subgroup who are ageing successfully, i.e. without cognitive decline, and a subgroup who are suffering from pathological changes that are associated with cognitive decline. Thus, if we take the population as a whole it would appear that cognitive decline does increase with age, but if we rigorously exclude those with pathological changes, such as early Alzheimer's disease, it is possible that a majority will not show any significant decline.

This hypothesis is consistent with the work of OPTIMA described above. Since Alzheimer's disease is the consequence of some event in the brain, an event determined in part by genetic risk factors and in part by the environment, we can re-examine the evidence of cognitive decline in the elderly that has been described by the neuropsychologists (see Table 1). In fact, almost all the areas of 'decline' shown on the right of the table are characteristic features of the early stages of Alzheimer's disease. Alzheimer's disease is not the only disease process that can affect cognitive performance: the second most common cause of dementia is due to cerebrovascular disease. Perhaps the areas of cognitive deficit detected by the neuropsychologists in the elderly are in large part due to the early stages of these two disease processes. These early stages would not have been detected by the methods normally used to screen for dementia.

The problem in practice is how do we distinguish those who are beginning to age pathologically? We have found that the medial temporal lobes in about 12 per cent of normal elderly subjects (aged over 70) show rapid atrophy even though there is no detectable change in cognitive status using standard screening tests for dementia. This finding suggests that annual CT scans to measure changes in the size of the medial temporal lobe in normal elderly people might be a way of detecting those who are destined to develop the clinical signs of Alzheimer's disease. If more sensitive cognitive tests are used, then it is possible that a decline in performance would be detectable and that is now being investigated. If such brain imaging and neuropsychological tests can indeed detect early disease, then they could be used to screen subjects at risk and so allow the administration of drug therapies at a very early stage, when they are more likely to be effective.

What can we do to achieve successful ageing?

Is there anything society as a whole, or we as individuals, can do to improve our chances of achieving successful ageing? It should be clear from the arguments above that society should adopt policies that favour the prevention of diseases such as cerebrovascular disease and Alzheimer's disease in order to reduce the proportion of those who will become demented due to these diseases.

It is noteworthy that several of the risk factors for Alzheimer's disease listed in Table 2 are similar to risk factors for vascular disease, raising the question whether measures that prevent vascular disease will also help to prevent Alzheimer's disease. It is of special importance to clarify whether or not environmental risk factors are involved, since these could be controlled. The idea that exposure to aluminium is a risk factor for Alzheimer's disease is one of the oldest (based on the fact that the abnormal brain structures found in the disease contain accumulations of aluminium), but has no sound basis; the concentration of aluminium appears to be a consequence and not a cause of the condition. An environmental risk factor is, however, suggested by the finding that dementia and clinically diagnosed Alzheimer's disease is much more common in Japanese people living in Hawaii than those living in Japan. The gene pool from which these two populations originate is virtually identical, so pointing the finger at some aspect of the environment.

It has been suggested from epidemiological studies that there is an association between a low intake of vitamin C and the subsequent development of cognitive deficit. OPTIMA's recent work has shown that there is a strong association between low blood levels of the vitamins folic acid and B_{12} and confirmed Alzheimer's disease. It will be very important to see whether these associations are in fact causal, i.e. does a relative vitamin deficiency actually contribute to the causation of Alzheimer's disease? In order to answer this question, large-scale trials will have to be carried out in which subjects at risk of developing Alzheimer's disease are given dietary supplements of these vitamins for many years.

If it is indeed found that a deficiency in a vitamin is a definite risk factor, then supplementation of the diet of elderly people could reduce the incidence of Alzheimer's disease. Such a policy of prevention could have a huge impact on millions of people and is far preferable to waiting for people to develop the disease and then treating them. However, since Alzheimer's disease is multifactorial, it is likely that correction of a single risk factor would only prevent a proportion of those at risk from progressing to the disease. Women taking HRT postmenopausally have also been shown to be less at risk of the disease than matched controls not on HRT; levels of oestrogen may well turn out to be protective against the disease. It may thus be necessary to prescribe hormone replacement therapy as well as a dietary supplement. We are a long way from such an optimistic scenario: first of all, environmental risk factors will have to be firmly established; second, large-scale intervention studies will be needed to see if such interventions do indeed reduce the incidence of the disease.

The most puzzling of the risk factors that have been proposed is the level of education. In studies from several parts of the world, an association has been found between low levels of education and an increased risk of developing dementia. None of these studies has been validated by histopathological diagnoses, and so we cannot be sure that they are not due to an artefact of the procedure used to detect dementia. Nevertheless, it has been suggested that education builds up a 'reserve' in the brain, so that it takes longer for cognitive decline to be revealed. There is some experimental evidence consistent with this hypothesis, since the density of synaptic connections in the cerebral cortex can be influenced in animals by the richness of the environment when they are young. Does that mean that we have some control over our own destiny? In his famous treatise on old age, Cicero made some suggestions about what individuals can do to improve their chances of ageing successfully. He particularly promoted the idea of using one's brain to the full and, as an example, he learnt Greek in the last years of his life. He wrote that it is important to give one's brain exercise:

To keep my memory in training, every evening I run over in my mind all that I have heard during the day. That is my intellectual exercise, my running track for the brain.

It is striking that modern studies are beginning to confirm Cicero's vision. Elderly people who are regularly given simple cognitive tasks to perform, such as completing crosswords and jigsaw puzzles, show an improvement in cognitive performance that persists for several months. Successful ageing is also enhanced by regular physical activity, by maintaining social activities and by autonomous living. A study from the south of France has even suggested that those who participate in travelling, social activities and odd jobs, like knitting or gardening, have, three years later, a reduced likelihood of becoming demented. If such studies can be confirmed, then clearly we as individuals and society as a whole can adopt policies that favour successful living and so enhance the quality of later life for the increasing numbers of elderly in the population. We must abandon the fatalistic view that mental decline is an inevitable accompaniment of ageing.

Further reading

Olshansky, S. J., Carnes, B. A., and Cassel, C. K. (1993). The aging of the human species. *Scientific American* **268**, 46–52.

Rowe, J. W., and Kahn, R. L. (1987). Human aging: usual and successful. *Science* **237**, 143–149.

Schaie, K. W. (1994). The course of adult intellectual development. *American Psychologist* **49**, 304–313.

Schneider, E., and Rowe, J. (eds.) (1995). *Handbook of the Biology of Aging*, 4th edn. Academic Press.

Smith, A. D., and Jobst, K. A. (1996). Use of structural imaging to study the progression of Alzheimer's disease. *British Medical Bulletin* **52**, 575–586.

7

Why There Will Never Be a Convincing Theory of Schizophrenia

RICHARD BENTALL

> My theory on schizophrenia is the best one around,
> which isn't saying much.   Paul Meehl, 1996

Over the last century or so, it has become so commonplace to regard insanity simply as a medical condition that it has become difficult to think of it in any other way. It is true that some critics have challenged this approach (most notably the American psychiatrist Thomas Szasz, who argued that mental disorders should not be considered illnesses unless some kind of biological pathology could be demonstrated), but they have not been influential in the long term. Indeed, what started as a project by nineteenth-century alienists to assimilate insanity into the field of general medicine has now become a part of ordinary language. We speak unreflectively about 'mental illness', about psychiatric 'patients' and about their 'treatment' by doctors and nurses.

Not surprisingly, scientists and clinicians who have advocated biological theories have increasingly dominated research into the causes of insanity. These investigators have assumed that the bewildering forms of behaviour which are observed in the psychiatric clinic can be broken down into a small number of diseases, and that these diseases can in turn be explained in terms of different pathologies of the central nervous system. Enthusiasm for this approach has been maintained by periodic rallying cries by prominent psychiatrists, designed to sustain the faithful and to downplay the value of alternative approaches which have emphasized psychological or social factors. An editorial published in the *Journal of Mental*

Science (now the *British Journal of Psychiatry*) in 1858 proclaimed: 'Insanity is purely a disease of the brain. The physician is now the responsible guardian of the lunatic and must ever remain so.' Exactly the same prejudice about the explanation of psychiatric disorder was expressed in an 1989 editorial in the journal *Psychological Medicine* written by the American psychiatrist Samuel Guze, who argued: 'There can be no such thing as a psychiatry that is too biological.' Of course, dramatic developments in the basic neurosciences have also played a role in stimulating biological research into psychiatric disorders, for example the discovery of the neurotransmitters and the invention of new methods of imaging the brain. However, the application of these discoveries in the field of psychiatry has always followed the assumption that psychiatric disorders are fundamentally biological in origin and are similar, in many ways, to the kinds of illnesses treated in physical medicine – after all, neurotransmitters and brain-imaging technologies were undreamt of in 1858.

In this chapter, I will challenge some of the assumptions of biological psychiatry by considering research into 'schizophrenia', the psychiatric disorder that has attracted more biological research than any other and that has been the focus of my own research career. I will not attempt to deny the importance of biological studies of behaviour in general and abnormal behaviour in particular. However, I will try to show that such research can only contribute to the understanding of behaviour – normal or disordered – if placed in the context of a proper psychological understanding of the behaviour in question. Outside of that context, biological research is conceptually little more advanced than phrenology (the nineteenth-century pseudoscience that hypothesized correlations between personality and bumps on the skull on the assumption that skull shape reflects the shape of the brain).

When I first began to study schizophrenia in the mid-1980s, it was somewhat unusual for a psychologist to be interested in the more severe forms of psychiatric disorder. It was then widely assumed that the symptoms experienced by schizophrenia patients were incapable of psychological analysis, that the disorder was genetically determined, and that the underlying disease of the central nervous system was almost certainly biochemical (abnormal functioning of those parts of the brain containing the neurotransmitter dopamine was thought to be the most likely candidate). It was also assumed that breakthroughs in the understanding of schizophrenia could only follow from the application of new methods of studying the brain and from attempts to determine the structure of the human genome. (Indeed, I once returned home to watch a television news report in which it was claimed that 'scientists' had discovered the gene for schizophrenia, and briefly wondered whether, as a psychologist, I should consider researching into something else!) In the decade since, these approaches have provided fascinating insights into the workings of the brain, yet the promises they seemed to hold for the understanding of schizophrenia have yet to be fulfilled. I will argue that this failure should have been expected. Indeed, I will suggest that there never will be a convincing theory of schizophrenia, because the very concept of schizophrenia is incoherent.

Kraepelin, Bleuler, Jaspers and Schneider: how we came to think about schizophrenia

Walking on to a psychiatric ward can be a confusing experience, even for a visitor who does not suffer from a psychiatric problem. Patients sit around, waiting to receive their medication, while over-stretched nurses wrestle with paperwork in the nursing office, or struggle to manage the numerous personal crises that make up the day-to-day life of the ward. The uninitiated are likely to be baffled by the range of distressing experiences reported by the patients. Many suffer from extremes of emotion – usually depression, anxiety, panic or irritation, but sometimes extreme elation. Others report hearing voices (auditory hallucinations) or bizarre beliefs (delusions), for example that they are being persecuted by secret organizations (paranoid or persecutory delusions), or that they have impossible powers (grandiose delusions). Some patients appear to be 'burnt out' both emotionally and behaviourally – they may sit silently and unexpressively for hours on end, unable or unwilling to respond to those around them. Usually, nothing much of a therapeutic nature seems to be happening.

The task of the psychopathologist – the scientist who is interested in those phenomena which (for want of a better word) are sometimes grouped together under the label of 'insanity' – is to explain these behaviours and experiences. Traditional approaches to explaining insanity are based on two assumptions: first, that insanity can be divided into a small number of disease entities (of which schizophrenia is one) and, second, that the manifestations or 'symptoms' of insanity cannot be understood in terms of the psychology of the individual. These assumptions were spelt out explicitly by the early psychiatrists whose writings have most influenced modern psychiatric thinking.

Psychiatrists of the mid and late nineteenth century quite reasonably supposed that progress would not be made in the understanding of insanity in the absence of an adequate method of classifying the disorders they were observing in their patients. Various taxonomies of mental disorders were proposed, but it was the one suggested by the German psychiatrist Emil Kraepelin that became most influential and that has been embraced by most researchers even to this day.

Photographs of Kraepelin reveal a bearded, stern-faced man. In later life he became a fervent German nationalist and wrote sentimental poetry about his fatherland. His approach to classifying disorders was influenced partly by his brother, a botanist who worked on the classification of plant species, and partly by a period of study with the psychologist Wilhelm Wunt, who emphasized the need for precise descriptions of mental states. Putting these ideas together, Kraepelin assumed that a detailed examination of the way that symptoms of mental disorder co-occurred would lead to a workable system of diagnostic classification, and thence to an understanding of the biological abnormalities assumed to be responsible for insanity:

Judging from our experience in internal medicine it is a fair assumption that similar disease processes will produce identical symptom pictures, identical pathological anatomy and an identical aetiology. If, therefore, we possessed a comprehensive knowledge of any of these three fields – pathological anatomy, symptomatology, or aetiology – we would at once have a uniform and standard classification of mental diseases. A similar comprehensive knowledge of either of the other two fields would give us not just as uniform and standard classifications, but all of these classifications would exactly coincide. (Kraepelin, 1907)

Kraepelin therefore kept detailed records of the symptoms reported by his patients, and also of what happened to them over the course of time, assuming that different disease processes would be revealed as clusters of symptoms that occurred together and which led to different outcomes. In 1896, on the basis of these kinds of observations, he proposed that there were only two major types of mental disorder: *dementia praecox* and *manic depressive illness*.

Dementia praecox was so-named because it was seen as a form of degenerative brain disease (or dementia) that appeared to have a very poor outcome, and that almost always occurred in late adolescence or early adulthood (*praecox* = young). Sufferers experienced severe intellectual deterioration, from which they inevitably failed to recover, and also from disorders of thinking, bizarre or delusional beliefs, and hallucinations. In contrast, manic depression (of which simple or unipolar depression was seen as a special variant) was characterized by extremes of mood (either depression or elation) and usually had a fairly good long-term outcome.

It was the Swiss psychiatrist Eugen Bleuler who, in 1911, suggested that the term dementia praecox should be replaced by the term *schizophrenia*. Bleuler took this view partly because he felt that Kraepelin's description of the disorder was flawed: schizophrenia sufferers were not invariably young when first ill (although they often were) and the outcome was often not as bleak as Kraepelin had supposed (although Bleuler remarked that he had never seen a patient who had completely recovered from the disorder). To the confusion of Hollywood scriptwriters ever since, he proposed the new term schizophrenia, not because patients experienced a splitting of the personality, but because the different facets of mental life –

perception, thought, emotion – appeared to become split off from each other as the disorder advanced.

Whereas Kraepelin had emphasized intellectual deterioration as the main feature of dementia praecox, Bleuler argued that four rather subtle symptoms, since known as 'Bleuler's four As', should be seen as fundamental: disordered *affect* (or emotion), *ambivalence*, *autism* and loosening of the *associations*. Although he assumed that schizophrenia was biological in origin, he attempted to understand these symptoms by combining some simple insights into human cognitive processes (which he thought were associative in nature) with concepts borrowed from psychoanalysis.

It is notable that neither Kraepelin nor Bleuler regarded the most obvious manifestations of insanity – hallucinations and delusions – as core characteristics of schizophrenia. Indeed, it was two later German psychiatrists, Karl Jaspers and Kurt Schneider, who first emphasized the importance of these symptoms. Jaspers, a distinguished philosopher as well as a psychiatrist, was concerned to draw a dividing line between everyday attitudes and experiences and the apparently bizarre beliefs and attitudes of schizophrenia patients. He suggested that a fundamental difference could be drawn between beliefs and experiences that were *ununderstandable*, or incomprehensible in terms of an individual's personality and background, and the understandable beliefs and experiences of ordinary people. Whereas understandable beliefs and experiences were comprehensible in psychological terms, ununderstandable beliefs and experiences such as delusions and hallucinations were not, and could therefore only be explained in terms of a disorder of the brain. This account is somewhat similar to the distinction made by some modern philosophers, for example Dan Dennett, between the 'intentional stance' (when we take the view that a person's behaviour or experiences can be explained by prior mental states) and the 'design stance' (when we take the view that behaviour or experiences are best understood in terms of the machinery of the brain). As Dennett has observed, it is natural to fall back on the design stance when behaviour is unintelligible from the point of view of the intentional stance: we assume that behaviour must be a product of some kind of breakdown in the machinery of the brain precisely because we cannot understand it.

Schneider was concerned with positive symptoms for less philosophical reasons. In an attempt to define schizophrenia more precisely, he described eleven *first-rank symptoms*, each a form of hallucination (for example, hearing thoughts spoken out aloud; hearing voices speaking about the individual in the third person), delusion (for example, a delusional perception in which the individual suddenly draws some bizarre conclusion about something seen or heard), or passivity experience (for example, believing that feelings are being caused or controlled by others), any one of which was, in his view, sufficient to justify a diagnosis of the disorder. This approach proved popular partly because these symptoms were much more easy to identify than Bleuler's four As.

Modern diagnostic manuals employed by psychiatrists, for example the fourth edition of the American Psychiatric Association's *Diagnostic and Statistical Manual* (known as DSM-IV and published in 1994) and the tenth edition of the World Health Organization's *International Classification of Diseases* (ICD-10, published in 1992), embrace Kraepelin's distinction between schizophrenia and manic depressive illness but, following Schneider, place most emphasis on hallucinations and delusions (sometimes called positive symptoms) rather than the negative or deficit symptoms emphasized by Kraepelin.

Will the real cause of schizophrenia please stand up!

The philosopher Ian Hacking has noted how the idea of *the* cause can be so mesmeric that it often paralyses critical thinking about diagnostic categories. As soon as we are presented with a causal explanation (no matter how implausible) of some diagnostic entity or other, it becomes natural to assume that the entity has some basis in reality. Of course, mental life is very complex, so it would be foolish to expect that even precisely defined diseases are the product of a single causal process. As another philosopher, Ted Honderich, has pointed out, even simple physical processes such as the ignition of a match are the product of complex causal circumstances: not only must the match rub against a rough surface with a certain force but the match head has to be of a certain chemical composition and it must have been kept in a place that is dry for a period prior to ignition. We can anticipate that, by comparison, psychiatric disorders will be much more complex, and will involve interactions between biological, psychological and social processes.

Research into the causes of schizophrenia has been pursued vigorously in the century since Kraepelin first described the disorder. Despite the widely held assumption that schizophrenia must be determined by some relatively fixed aspect of a person's biological development rather than by some part of their life experience, some authors have disagreed. For example, research since the 1930s has shown that an unexpectedly large number of people suffering from schizophrenia live in inner city areas. Other clinical studies, conducted in the 1960s, seemed to indicate that schizophrenia patients come from families in which the other members are somehow odd or disordered in their communications with each other. However, accounts of schizophrenia that have exclusively implicated stressful environments or family dynamics have not survived the test of time particularly well. It is now known that people with severe psychiatric problems, who are usually unemployed and poor, often move to inner city areas where accommodation is cheap. Although there is good evidence that family atmosphere can influence the course of most psychiatric disorders (patients tend to do better if close relatives are accepting and relaxed and worse if their relatives are highly critical or overprotective), there is no evidence that family difficulties alone are sufficient to explain the very disabling symptoms that lead to a diagnosis of schizophrenia.

Although this apparent failure of psychological research might at first sight give encouragement to biological researchers, biological theories of schizophrenia have not fared much better. Since the 1930s, genetic studies have seemed to support the idea that schizophrenia is inherited. For example, identical twins are more likely to be concordant for schizophrenia (that is, if one twin is diagnosed as suffering from schizophrenia there is a good chance that the other twin will receive the same diagnosis) than non-identical twins. As identical twins share exactly the same genes whereas non-identical twins do not, this observation appears consistent with genetic determination. Unfortunately, early studies were poorly designed, so that, for example, very loose diagnostic criteria were employed and the clinicians making the diagnoses were not blind to the status of the twins being studied. Later, more methodologically rigorous studies have produced much lower estimates of the contribution that heredity makes to schizophrenic breakdowns. Moreover, the inconsistent way in which schizophrenia runs in families suggests that there is no single schizophrenia gene, and that the disorder may be heterogeneous for genetic determination (that is, that genes may play a more important role in some patients than in others). Nonetheless, some researchers remain enthusiastic about a genetic approach, most notably Tim Crow, who argues in the following chapter that the genetic contribution to schizophrenia is linked to the evolution of language and the way in which the left and right hemispheres of the brain specialize for different functions. However, the basis for this claim, the curious observation made in a World Health Organization study that the incidence (number of new cases per given period of time) of schizophrenia is constant the world over, has been disputed by some epidemiologists, who have suggested that the WHO study was poorly designed to detect cultural differences in the incidence of psychiatric disorders.

Similar disputes exist about theories of schizophrenia that implicate disorders of the brain. In the 1950s it was accidentally discovered that the antihistamine drug chlorpromazine (known also as Largactil) appeared to quell the symptoms of severely disturbed schizophrenia patients. Subsequent studies showed that other similar drugs, now known by the collective name of neuroleptics, also had antipsychotic properties, precipitating a search for the mechanisms by which this therapeutic effect was achieved. Animal experiments revealed that all the effective antipsychotic drugs available at the time blocked receptors in the brain that employed the neurotransmitter dopamine. The simultaneous observation that chemicals that mimic dopamine's action (agonists), used to treat Parkinson's disease, sometimes also caused delusions and hallucinations led to the compelling theory that schizophrenia was caused by some kind of overactivity of the dopamine system.

Unfortunately, the dopamine theory, although undoubtedly elegant, has withstood the test of time no better than the environmental and genetic theories of schizophrenia. Although dopamine-blocking drugs help a considerable number of patients who suffer from severe psychiatric problems, a considerable proportion of patients fail to respond to them. Even when these drugs are effective, this may not be the consequence of any specific effect on the dopamine system. The search for evidence of abnormal dopaminergic functioning in the brains of schizophrenia patients (for example, by measuring the amount of dopamine in the brain or counting the number of dopamine receptors) has yielded contradictory findings. Experiments using the new brain imaging technologies have failed to find a correlation between the extent to which antipsychotic drugs block receptors in particular patients and the benefits experienced by them. Finally, new antipsychotic drugs such as clozapine have recently become available and these seem to be very non-specific in their action on the brain, and do not vigorously block dopamine receptors.

There are, of course, other ways of studying the brain. Brain imaging studies have revealed abnormalities in the structure of the brains of some schizophrenia patients. Although these abnormalities have varied across different studies, the most common observation has been enlargement of the fluid-filled cerebral ventricles. However, enlarged ventricles have also been observed in a proportion of patients diagnosed as suffering from manic depression, so this abnormality is probably not specific to schizophrenia nor necessary for it to occur. Performance on neuropsychological tests, which are known to be sensitive to brain damage, has also been observed to be poor in many schizophrenia patients, but the precise deficits observed seem to vary widely from patient to patient.

Not surprisingly, given the difficulties experienced by genetic, biochemical and neurological researchers, theories of schizophrenia have become progressively more exotic. Diet theories were briefly fashionable in the 1970s – the Nobel-prizewinning biochemist Linus Pauling advocated treating schizophrenia patients with massive doses of vitamins. Renal dialysis was also briefly studied as a treatment for schizophrenia, on the assumption that toxins accumulating in the blood might be responsible for the disorder. The most recent biological theories, perhaps inspired by research into infectious diseases such as AIDS, have implicated viruses. People born in the spring appear to have a slightly greater chance of developing schizophrenia than those born at other times of the year. This has provoked the suggestion that a viral infection suffered by a pregnant mother in winter might cause subtle neurological deficits in the foetus that become manifest as schizophrenia in adulthood. Perhaps the strangest theory of this sort has been proposed by two American epidemiologists, E. Fuller Torrey and Robert Yolken, who dispute the World Health Organization's claim that schizophrenia occurs with equal frequency in all parts of the world, and who have suggested that the schizophrenia virus might be transmitted to expectant mothers from the domestic cat. (According to their data, the incidence of schizophrenia is highest in those countries where cats are kept as pets.)

The sceptical observer might be forgiven for feeling baffled by this wide range of apparently contradictory theories, and for questioning whether there really has been much progress in understanding the aetiology of schizophrenia in the century that has passed since Kraepelin first described the disorder. After all, just about every variable known to influence human behaviour has been singled out as *the* cause of schizophrenia at one time or another. Of course, it is possible that schizophrenia is simply a much harder disease to understand than other diseases – for example, Parkinson's disease and various types of cancer – for which substantial scientific progress has been made. However, given the numerous contradictory findings of schizophrenia research, it seems much more likely that patients diagnosed as schizophrenic suffer from many different kinds of problems, and that the problem lies not in the methods used to study schizophrenia but in the very concept itself.

Is there really such a thing as 'schizophrenia'?

To determine whether the concept of schizophrenia is useful for either clinical purposes or research we must submit it to two tests: *reliability* and *validity*. The former test refers to the extent to which clinicians can agree with each other about who merits the diagnosis, whereas the latter refers to the extent to which the diagnosis is coherent as assessed by other means (for example, whether symptoms cluster together in the way supposed, whether they have a particular outcome, and whether they respond to a particular treatment). Reliability is a necessary but insufficient criterion for validity. A diagnosis cannot be valid unless it is first reliable, whereas it can be reliable without being valid. (Consider the highly reliable diagnosis of Bentall's disease, which consists of the following 'symptoms': naturally red hair, more than three times as many summer colds as winter colds over the past three years, and more than three Pink Floyd CDs in the patient's music collection. Although we could all agree about who suffers from Bentall's disease and who does not, no-one would seriously consider committing even the smallest fraction of the nation's research resources towards elucidation of its origins.)

In the 1960s and 1970s many researchers became concerned about the reliability of the schizophrenia diagnosis for two reasons. First, studies showed that clinicians often disagreed about who was schizophrenic and who was not. Second, it became apparent that the diagnosis was used much more widely in North America than in Western Europe. It was these concerns that led to the development of diagnostic manuals (for example, DSM-IV and ICD-10) that specify precisely what symptoms are required before a diagnosis of schizophrenia can be made. There is no doubt that clinicians using the same diagnostic manual usually agree about who suffers from schizophrenia and who does not. However, it is important to realize that the criteria outlined in the diagnostic manuals have not been written on the basis of empirical research but are, in effect, psychiatric folklore institutionalized by committees of distinguished psychiatrists. Agreement between the different diagnostic manuals is often very poor, leading the British psychiatrist Ian Brockington to observe that the babble of disagreement between clinicians about who has schizophrenia has been replaced by 'a babble of precise but different formulations of the same concept'.

Evidence on the validity of schizophrenia is no more comforting to the traditional viewpoint. As already indicated, one way of addressing this problem is by considering whether the symptoms of schizophrenia cluster together in the way that Kraepelin and Bleuler supposed. Complex statistical analyses of symptom data collected from large numbers of patients have consistently shown that they do not. Recent studies have suggested that there are at least three and perhaps more relatively independent clusters of schizophrenia symptoms. Hallucinations and delusions do tend to occur together (although even this is not invariably the case). Similarly, the negative or deficit symptoms of apathy, loss of emotion and social withdrawal also tend to occur together. There also seems to be a cluster of symptoms that include attentional difficulties, bizarre thinking and disordered speech. So many patients experience a combination of symptoms normally attributed to schizophrenia and symptoms normally attributed to manic depression that the term *schizoaffective* disorder is now commonly used to describe those who fail to fall cleanly into one of Kraepelin's two major diagnostic categories.

The diagnosis of schizophrenia also fails to meet acceptable standards of predictive validity. Whereas Kraepelin, and to a lesser extent Bleuler, held pessimistic views about the outcome of the disorder, modern studies show that the outcome is enormously variable. In Western countries, about one-third of patients completely recover, about one-third remain permanently or almost permanently ill, and about one-third have an intermediate outcome characterized by alternating periods of illness and normal or near-normal functioning. Although antipsychotic drugs undoubtedly make symptoms more tolerable for many patients, there is no evidence that modern patients do better in the long term than patients in Kraepelin's day. Curiously, there is strong evidence that patients in third-world countries do better over time than those in the developed world, a difference that is usually attributed to the more relaxed way in which third-world families cope with a psychiatric crisis.

The final test of the value of a diagnosis, and the test which should matter most to clinicians, is the extent to which it can predict response to treatment. A diagnosis should tell a clinician what kind of treatment will work and what kind of treatment will not. Since the discovery of chlorpromazine it has been widely believed that neuroleptics are the treatment of choice for schizophrenia, whereas other drugs, for example lithium carbonate, are the treatment of choice for manic depression. In fact, some schizophrenia patients respond to lithium carbonate and some patients with manic depression respond to neuroleptics. In a trial conducted at Northwick Park Hospital in the UK in the 1980s, psychotic patients were randomly assigned a neuroleptic, lithium carbonate, both or neither, regardless of their diagnosis. Response to these medications was found to be symptom-specific but not diagnosis-specific: hallucinations and delusions tended to respond to neuroleptic medication, regardless of the patient's primary diagnosis, whereas those experiencing extremes of mood tended to respond to lithium carbonate, again regardless of their primary diagnosis.

It would seem that schizophrenia is an illness that consists of no particular symptoms, that has no particular outcome, and that responds to no particular treatment. No wonder research has revealed that it has no particular cause.

Can we live without the diagnosis of schizophrenia?

If the concept of schizophrenia is as unhelpful in our quest to understand insanity as these findings suggest, why does the diagnosis continue to be used? One reason is that clinicians and researchers are reluctant to accept that a concept in which so much effort has been invested could be meaningless. As one young psychiatrist once protested to me, 'The diagnosis of schizophrenia must be useful . . . because we continue to use it.' Of course, much the same kind of argument could be used to defend astrology. In fact, there is a remarkable similarity between Kraepelinian psychiatry and astrological hypotheses. In each case, it is widely believed that diagnostic concepts ('schizophrenic', 'Libran') reveal something important about the individual and predict what will happen in the future. In each case, evidence in favour of such explanatory and predictive power is strikingly absent.

A second reason why clinicians and researchers have been reluctant to abandon the concept of schizophrenia has been the lack of an alternative way of thinking about insanity. The biomedical view of psychiatric disorder has become so pervasive that researchers find it difficult to conceptualize the behaviour and experiences of psychiatric patients except in terms of diagnostic categories of one sort or another. For this reason, it is widely assumed that researchers have no choice but to stick with the Kraepelinian system until some better method of psychiatric classification has been discovered.

However, there is a logical alternative to the Kraepelinian approach which does not require the discovery of a new diagnostic system. We could abandon diagnosis altogether! Instead of studying psychiatric patients grouped according to broad diagnostic categories, we could study them according to the actual problems that they bring to the psychiatric clinic. After all, patients and their friends and relatives rarely if ever complain about *schizophrenia* – they complain about particular types of behaviour or experience that are troubling to them, for example hearing voices, feeling paranoid, or having difficulty in maintaining work or relationships with other people. These types of behaviours and experiences are what psychiatrists call *symptoms*, and they, rather than meaningless diagnostic categories, could and should be the focus of research.

In the last ten years or so, a number of investigators have begun to conduct studies of this sort. In what remains of this chapter I will describe some of this work, focusing on my own studies of delusions and hallucinations.

Understanding persecutory delusions

Recent research on the psychology of delusions has followed from the assumption that delusional beliefs (for example, 'There is a conspiracy to do me harm involving both the CIA and the Royal Family') are influenced by much the same processes that influence normal, non-delusional beliefs (for example, 'If I don't get this chapter completed for Steven Rose in the next few days, he'll never talk to me again, and that will be bad for my career'). Fig. 1 shows a simple model of the factors involved in the acquisition and maintenance of beliefs that I (quite literally) drew on the back of an envelope when I began my own research on this issue. The model is pretty crude and would no doubt be rejected as hopelessly inadequate by any self-respecting cognitive psychologist, but we can nonetheless use it to speculate about what might be going on when someone develops a belief that looks bizarre and obviously abnormal to everyone else.

The model suggests that we do not simply pick our beliefs out of some kind of metaphysical hat but that, on the contrary, they are usually based on things that happen in the world. Once relevant data in the world have been perceived and attended to, we might make certain inferences about their significance. If we are true

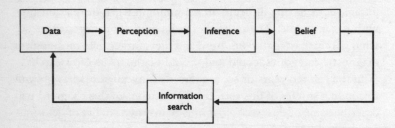

Figure 1. A 'bargain-basement' model of belief acquisition, not to be taken too seriously, which highlights processes that may be involved in the acquisition of both normal and delusional beliefs. (From R. P. Bentall, 1990, in: Reconstructing Schizophrenia, *ed. R. P. Bentall, pp. 23–60, Routledge.)*

rational scientists we might then search for more information relating to our beliefs, although most of the available evidence indicates that normal individuals go about this in a pretty irrational fashion. (Philosophers of science, following Popper, have observed that it is most logical to search for evidence that might potentially refute a theory. Because a theory can be definitively disproven but never definitively proven, negative evidence should be particularly persuasive. Research, however, shows that ordinary people, if they look for further evidence at all, search specifically for data that would confirm their theories.)

Unusual events at each of these stages may play a role in the generation of the kind of beliefs that lead directly to the psychiatric clinic. An old joke runs: 'Just because I'm paranoid doesn't mean that people are not out to get me.' Although the hypothesis that patients suffering from paranoid delusions might sometimes be genuine victims of persecutory experiences has not been taken all that seriously by researchers, there is at least anecdotal evidence that paranoid ideas usually arise in situations in which the individual feels powerless, or victimized by others. An example of this from our work at Liverpool concerns a lady who was examined by my research assistant Sue Kaney as part of a research project we were conducting. The lady complained that the local professor of gynaecology was turning her into a portfolio, a delusion that appeared incomprehensible until we discovered that she was suffering from an unusual gynaecological condition which was being studied by the professor.

Perceptual abnormalities can influence delusions by causing the individual to be exposed to a data set that apparently requires an unusual explanation. There are many examples of this in the psychiatric literature, but perhaps the clearest concern *delusional misidentifications*. The most common delusion of this sort involves the patient believing that one or more people have been replaced by alien imposters, *doppelgängers* or robots, and was first described by the French psychiatrist Capgras in 1923. Studies by neuropsychologists, particularly Andy Young in Cambridge and Haydn Ellis in Cardiff, have indicated that Capgras patients suffer from deficits in the neuropsychological mechanisms responsible for recognizing faces. These mechanisms are highly developed in primate species because recognizing faces is a skill that has considerable survival value. Because these mechanisms are not functioning properly, Capgras patients are left with the dreadful feeling that people they know well look as they should but don't seem familiar to them. The delusion can be seen to be, at least in part, a response to this experience.

Much of my own research has focused on the kinds of inferences made by patients suffering from paranoid delusions. A type of behaviour that we human beings persistently indulge in is *explaining things*. We explain what happens to us to other people and, if other people are not around, we explain the things that happen to us to ourselves. Martin Seligman and his colleagues in the USA have suggested that a statement (technically called an *attribution*) including the word *because* or implying the word *because* can be found for every few hundred words of ordinary speech. They have argued that such explanations vary across three fundamental dimensions known as *internality* (whether the cause is something about the self or something about other people or circumstances), *stability* (whether the cause will inevitably be present in the future), and *globalness* (whether the cause will influence all or only some areas of the individual's life). According to research carried out by Seligman and his colleagues, we are likely to become depressed if we attribute negative events (for example, having our latest research manuscript rejected for publication by a major journal) to causes that are internal, stable and global (for example, 'I am stupid') rather than causes that differ in one or more of these dimensions ('It was not my best effort'; 'The editor is a scurrilous rogue').

In research which my colleagues and I have conducted using a variety of measures, and since replicated by other investigators, we found that patients suffering from persecutory delusions, like depressed patients, tend to blame negative events on causes that are unusually stable and global. However, in contrast to depressed patients, they also attribute such events to causes that are excessively external (caused by other people or circumstances) rather than internal (self-blaming), as shown in Fig. 2. Although normal subjects also show this tendency to take credit for success and to attribute blame for failure elsewhere (known to social psychologists as *the self-serving bias*), it is present to a much lesser degree than is the case for paranoid patients.

The self-serving bias is widely believed to be a mechanism that ordinary people use to regulate self-esteem. If we attribute difficult

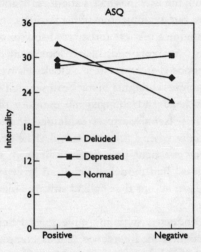

Figure 2. Internality scores for positive events (e.g. becoming rich) and negative events (e.g. failing to obtain a job) obtained from deluded, depressed and normal subjects, who completed the Attributional Style Questionnaire (ASQ). Subjects were asked to think of the most likely cause of these hypothetical events. High internality scores indicate that participants tended to blame themselves, whereas low scores indicate a relative tendency to blame other people or circumstances. Note that depressed patients tend to blame themselves more for negative than for positive events. Normal subjects show a 'self-serving bias'. Deluded patients show this bias to a significantly greater degree than the normal subjects – they are masters of the art of blaming others when things go wrong and themselves when things go right. (Data from S. Kaney and R. P. Bentall, 1989, British Journal of Medical Psychology 62, 191–198.)

experiences to external causes ('Steven Rose is a hard taskmaster'), we find it much easier to feel good about ourselves in embarrassing situations than would be the case if we blamed ourselves ('I should have completed the chapter earlier'). It is therefore natural to assume that the excessive self-serving bias exhibited by paranoid patients is a protective system that serves the function of protecting the patient from harbouring negative beliefs about the self.

In clinical practice with paranoid patients, this protective function is often evident from the way in which patients talk about particular failure experiences. For example, one of my patients recently turned up half an hour late for a session and offered the following excuse: 'The problem was,' he explained, 'that I looked in my diary and saw that I was supposed to come at 3 o'clock. However, the man down the road who puts thoughts in my head wanted me to be late, so he got into my head and changed my memory of the time to half past three.' It was only after I explained that I was a bad timekeeper, especially when I felt stressed, that he decided that he may have forgotten the right time because he, too, was suffering from stress. Because I had modelled being an 'acceptable failure', he too became able to accept that he had simply failed to arrive at the right time.

Recent work conducted with my colleagues Peter Kinderman and Sue Kaney has provided evidence that is consistent with the hypothesis that paranoid patients have fragile self-esteem. We have found that, on obvious and straightforward psychological measures, paranoid patients report little difference between how they see themselves and their ideals. However, on more subtle measures paranoid patients respond as if they have a much more negative view of the self. The measures employed in these studies are quite complex, so I will give only one example here, taken from a study conducted by Peter Kinderman. He asked paranoid subjects to tick a checklist of positive and negative adjectives according to how well they described the self, finding (as expected) that they endorsed many more positive than negative words. He then presented the same words printed in different ink colours and asked the patients to ignore the meaning of the words and instead report the colours. On a test of this sort, known as a Stroop test after its inventor, colour naming is much more difficult if the words are emotionally salient and hence grab the reader's attention. (Under these conditions, conflict occurs between naming the colour of the ink and the almost irresistible urge to read the word itself.) As predicted, the paranoid patients, like depressed controls but unlike ordinary people, showed slowed colour naming especially for the negative adjectives. Taken with the attributional findings already described, these results support the hypothesis that paranoid delusions are the product of (perhaps repeated) attempts to blame others for personal short-comings, which in turn are motivated by an extremely fragile sense of self-esteem.

Of course, this account, while illuminating the mental mechanisms by which delusions are generated, tells us very little about the role of more distant aetiological factors. To understand these, we need to understand the origins of the attributional abnormalities exhibited by the deluded patients. Although there are very few research data that address these questions, there is some evidence in favour of two possibilities.

First, there is evidence from depressed patients that particular styles in making attributions tend to run in families. This suggests that the attributional abnormalities exhibited by deluded patients may be learnt. Although there is no evidence from paranoid patients that directly addresses this issue, it is not difficult to imagine family circumstances that would tend to encourage the systematic allocation of blame to others.

A second, equally intriguing, possibility is that paranoid attributions are partially caused by more fundamental cognitive deficits. Suppose you encounter a friend who does not acknowledge you as you walk by. Most ordinary people in this kind of situation make some kind of excuse for the friend. For example, you might imagine that your friend is not feeling well, is preoccupied by worry, or is having a particularly bad day. In order for you to make this attri-bution you have to try and see the world from the friend's point of view. To use the rather misleading terminology of developmental psychologists who have studied this special kind of empathy, you must have a *theory of mind* about your friend. Absence of such an ability might conceivably leave paranoid patients with only two choices in this kind of situation: blaming themselves (which they are extremely reluctant to do) or attributing the friend's behaviour to some kind of dispositional feature of the friend ('He's a person who can't be trusted!'). Consistent with this possibility, data collected by Chris Frith and his colleagues at the Institute of Neurology in London suggest that paranoid patients in particular may find imagining the mental states of others quite difficult.

Understanding hallucinations

Similar progress to that achieved in understanding delusions has been made in the case of hallucinations. Most research has focused on auditory hallucinations (hearing voices) because these are the kind of hallucination most commonly reported by patients diagnosed as suffering from schizophrenia. However, two relatively recent observations have challenged the view that hallucinations, auditory or otherwise, should necessarily be seen as associated with mental illness.

First, it seems that the experience of hallucinations and the attitudes that people have towards them vary enormously from culture to culture. For example, in native Hawaiian culture, it is relatively common to see dead ancestors. Even in the WHO studies of the incidence of schizophrenia (which allegedly indicated that schizophrenia symptoms are invariant the world over), it was observed that visual hallucinations are much more commonly reported in developing countries than in the West.

More remarkably, perhaps, in recent years it has been discovered that many more people experience hallucinations than seek psychiatric help, even in developed countries. Surveys have consistently shown that the prevalence rate of hearing voices far exceeds even the most generous estimates of the prevalence rate of schizophrenia. A Maastricht-based psychiatrist, Marius Romme, has even formed a national organization for Dutch people who hear voices, many of whom manage to follow perfectly happy lives. (Romme once very gently chastised me for my efforts to develop psychological treatments for hallucinations on the grounds that people who hear voices are in some sense analogous to homosexuals in the 1950s – more in need of liberation than cure.)

The hallucinations experienced by psychiatric patients often have negative or unpleasant content, which is why they seek treatment. As in the case of delusions, the content usually concerns patients' relationships with others, or their discomfort with themselves. I will never forget one of my first patients who drew this vividly to my attention by telling me that his voice kept repeating the phrase, 'Give cancer to the crippled bastard!' He said he had no idea who the 'crippled bastard' could be, but the answer to this conundrum was obvious to me – my patient was seated in a wheelchair, his legs shattered by a suicidal fall from a high window. (It subsequently transpired that his mother had died of cancer, and that he felt quite guilty about his failure to support her in her final days.)

In recent years, research has led to something of a consensus about the psychological mechanisms involved in hearing voices. All ordinary people have an inner voice – called *inner speech* by psychologists – which we use when thinking and regulating our own behaviour. We use this internal dialogue to monitor our own actions, to make plans for the future, and to decide what to do. Usually we conduct the dialogue silently, although most people talk out loud to themselves when they are on their own or under stress. Even when thinking silently in words, however, small movements of the vocal cords can be detected by sensitive electromyography (EMG) equipment. This phenomenon is called *subvocalization* and reflects the fact that thinking in words is literally internalized self-talk.

Subvocalization as measured by EMG has been detected in psychiatric patients when they hear voices. Consistent with this observation, brain imaging studies conducted by Philip McGuire and colleagues at the Institute of Psychiatry in London using single-photon emission tomography (SPET) have shown that the left hemisphere centres responsible for language are active when patients hear voices. Moreoever, activities that tend to inhibit inner speech, such as reading aloud, tend to block auditory hallucinations. These observations are powerful evidence that people who hear voices are mistaking their own inner speech for voices that are alien or external to themselves.

The reasons why people who hear voices make this kind of mistake are not well understood. One possibility is that they suffer from some kind of fundamental deficit in those brain mechanisms responsible for discriminating between self-generated actions and perceptions. Plausible though this hypothesis may seem, the results of studies we have conducted to put it to the test have been somewhat equivocal. However, it is clear that individuals' judgements about the source of inner speech can be influenced by their beliefs about what kinds of events are likely to occur in the real world: people see ghosts because they believe in them. For example, experiments have shown that the judgements made by hallucinating patients about the source (internal or external) of perceived events can be heavily influenced by suggestions made to them. If ordinary people are asked to close their eyes and are told that they will hear a familiar tune (for example, 'White Christmas'), a small proportion will report hearing the tune, even if it is not in fact played. Several studies, including one conducted by myself and colleagues, have shown that psychiatric patients and ordinary people who report a history of hallucinations are especially susceptible to this effect.

This observation helps make sense of apparent cultural differences in the experience of hallucinations. After all, ideas about the kinds of events that are likely to be 'real' and the kinds of events that are likely to be 'imaginary' are heavily embedded in cultural values and practices; for example, Western people are more materialistic and much less likely to believe in the reality of ghostly ancestors than people from some other cultures. The role of beliefs and expectations in determining hallucinatory experiences also helps make sense of the apparent association between hallucinations and delusions. If beliefs help determine hallucinations, it is perhaps not surprising that deluded patients are especially vulnerable to hallucinatory experiences.

There is *meaning in madness, or why Jaspers was (mostly) wrong*

It will be recalled from the historical introduction to this chapter that modern accounts of insanity have been based on two assumptions: first, following Kraepelin, that insanity can be divided into a small number of disease entities and second, following Jaspers, that the 'symptoms' of insanity cannot be understood in terms of the psychology of the individual. I have, I hope, adequately dealt with the first of these assumptions. By way of a conclusion to this chapter, I would like to make some observations about the second.

Karl Jaspers held that psychotic experiences were not understandable as products of patients' experiences. This assertion amounts to the claim that psychotic experiences lack true intentionality, where the term *intentionality* refers to the *aboutness* that connects normal mental states to the world in which we live. On this view, when patients diagnosed as suffering from schizophrenia express a delusional belief or report a hallucination, they are not really referring to anything at all. In the words of the distinguished historian of psychiatry German Berrios, delusions are 'empty speech acts, whose informational content refers to neither world nor self. They are not the symbolic expression of anything.' Of course, if we accept this view, there is no alternative but to explore possible biological causes of these empty speech acts.

Because most psychologists who have studied psychotic symptoms have tacitly accepted Jaspers' analysis, the psychological tests they have employed have usually been designed to detect *cognitive deficits* – gross failures of attention and information processing of the sort that would be expected if the brain is suffering from some kind of global malfunction. Such tests involve emotionally neutral or even meaningless stimulus materials. For example, many studies have required patients to recall series of digits, with distracting stimuli either present or absent, in order to show that schizophrenia patients have difficulty when attending to events in their environment.

Although cognitive deficits undoubtedly play a role in psychotic symptoms, many of the measures described in the previous sections have been designed to detect *cognitive biases* or *content-specific information processing and reasoning*. Such measures compare the individual's response to some kinds of stimuli versus others, for example by asking them to attend to, recall or explain both positive (success) and negative (failure) events. Organisms which have intentionality must be able to deal with different kinds of information in different ways, according to its significance to the individual. Measures of cognitive bias therefore provide evidence about whether particular psychiatric symptoms have the property of intentionality.

It should be apparent from the account I have given of psychological research into delusions and hallucinations that intentionality is not compromised in at least the majority of psychotic patients. Consistent with this, the content of the delusions and hallucinations expressed by patients nearly always concerns the patient's position in the social universe or wider existential themes. Recognition of the intentionality of psychotic symptoms has at least two important implications.

First, there are therapeutic implications. Other psychiatric problems that are known to reflect content-specific information processing – for example, depression, which is characterized by preferential attention to and recall of negative information about the self, the world and the future – are also known to be susceptible to psychological treatments in which patients are encouraged to critically question the contents of their own thoughts. Despite the view, widely held among biological psychiatrists, that delusions and hallucinations are best treated with neuroleptic medication, recent studies conducted in the UK have indicated that psychological treatments may also be helpful. Such treatment requires great skill by the therapist as it can be very difficult to engage patients who, by their very nature, tend to be frightened and suspicious. Nonetheless, a number of small-scale trials have yielded promising results, and larger-scale trials are now under way.

Equally importantly, the results of psychological studies of psychotic symptoms suggest that any biological abnormalities observed in psychiatric patients must be understood in terms of the particular symptoms experienced by those patients and the psychological processes involved. As these symptoms, at least in part, reflect exaggerations of those cognitive idiosyncrasies that often lead to errors of thinking in everyday life, it will no longer be possible to draw a neat dividing line between the 'us' who are sane and the 'them' who are not.

Further reading

Bentall, R. P. (ed.) (1990). *Reconstructing Schizophrenia*. Routledge. This is an edited book which includes critical discussions of the history of the schizophrenia concept, the problems of psychiatric diagnosis, the genetics of schizophrenia and research into treatment. It is getting slightly dated, but I do not believe that any of the conclusions in it are in need of substantial revision.

Bentall, R. P. (1993). Deconstructing the concept of schizophrenia. *Journal of Mental Health* 2, 223–238. This article summarizes the arguments against the schizophrenia concept outlined in this chapter, and provides references to most of the studies I have discussed. It forms part of a special edition of the *Journal of Mental Health* devoted to controversies about schizophrenia, and the articles that accompany it, two by medical researchers and one by a psychologist who suffered a psychotic breakdown, give contrasting accounts of what the diagnosis means.

Boyle, M. (1990). *Schizophrenia: A Scientific Delusion*. Routledge. This book provides a critical history of the schizophrenia concept and raises many of the same issues discussed in my own work.

Reider, O. (1974). The origin of our confusion about schizophrenia. *Psychiatry* 37, 197–208. This is a classic critique of the schizophrenia concept.

For more detailed accounts of psychological research into hallucinations and delusions the reader might consult the following:

Bentall, R. P. (1990). The illusion of reality: a review and integration of psychological research on hallucinations. *Psychological Bulletin* 107, 82–95. Although beginning to look slightly dated, this article gives a reasonably comprehensive review of research into hallucinations.

Bentall, R. P. (1994). Cognitive biases and abnormal beliefs: towards a model of persecutory delusions. In: *The Neuropsychology of Schizophrenia* (ed. A. S. David and J. Cutting), pp. 337–360. Lawrence Erlbaum. This chapter reviews the research literature on delusions in some detail.

Other chapters in the same book present more conventional biological accounts of schizophrenia.

There are many general reviews of schizophrenia research, most of them edited volumes that are heavy, expensive and short on information about psychosocial approaches. A recent volume that meets all of these criteria, but which is otherwise well written and reasonably comprehensive, is: Hirsch, S. R., and Weinberger, D. R. (eds.) (1995). *Schizophrenia*. Blackwell.

8

Nuclear Schizophrenic Symptoms as the Key to the Evolution of Modern *Homo sapiens*

TIM J. CROW

In the course of a lifetime, approximately 1 per cent of the population will suffer from a 'schizophrenic' illness. These individuals may become withdrawn and socially isolated, experience hallucinations (most characteristically voices), develop delusions (beliefs held in the teeth of contrary evidence), and have difficulty in formulating their thoughts. In addition, the ability of sufferers to express or even experience emotion can be severely blunted. Such symptoms tend to persist and recur, are associated with an increased (at least twentyfold) risk of suicide, substantial loss of employment capacity, and disruption to social and family relationships.

What is the cause of these symptoms? In what sense is this a disease? In what field – sociology, psychology or genetics – should one seek answers to questions such as these? Is schizophrenia a single disease entity for which a single causal agent is responsible? Is such an agent to be expected in the environment or is it intrinsic to the individual? Is it something that we might hope to eliminate, for example by public health measures or a programme of eugenics?

Is schizophrenia an entity?

These questions require that the problem be formulated in such a way that a coherent answer can be expected. In fact there are serious doubts about the reality of 'schizophrenia' as a discrete category. As discussed in the previous chapter, the origin of the concept lies clearly in the distinction that Kraepelin drew between dementia praecox and manic-depressive insanity. On the one hand, Kraepelin argued, there are diseases in which mood change (depression or elation) is prominent, and psychotic symptoms (delusions and hallucinations) can be seen as congruent with and perhaps secondary to the mood change. These illnesses Kraepelin grouped together under the heading of manic-depressive insanity, from which a complete recovery can usually be expected. On the other hand, there are disease states in which the psychotic phenomena cannot be understood in this way. These illnesses he called dementia praecox (with a generally earlier age of onset) and paraphrenia (with a later age of onset), and the outcome is less good. Until recently the separation of dementia praecox and manic-depressive insanity (the 'schizophrenic' and 'affective' groups of psychoses) has gone largely unchallenged. Indeed it can be said to underpin most if not all modern psychiatric classifications, and exerts a profound influence on aetiological thinking. Schizophrenia, as dementia praecox, following Bleuler, has come to be called, and affective (manic-depressive) psychoses are generally regarded as distinct entities with separable patterns of symptoms, treatments and outcomes. By implication they have separate aetiologies.

But Kraepelin himself developed doubts. Thus he wrote of 'the difficulties which prevent us from distinguishing reliably between manic-depressive insanity and dementia praecox. No experienced psychiatrist will deny there is an alarmingly large number of cases in which it seems impossible, in spite of the most careful observation, to make a firm diagnosis . . . it is becoming increasingly clear that we cannot distinguish satisfactorily between these two illnesses and this brings home the suspicion that our formulation of the problem may be incorrect.'

Whereas it is undeniable that there are profound differences between different forms of psychotic illness, and that there is a relationship between form of illness and outcome – psychotic illnesses with affective features generally have a better outcome than those which lack such features, and this generalization is Kraepelin's legacy – it is far from established that any categorical distinction can be drawn. 'Schizoaffective' illnesses are common and, in the absence of principles by which they can be subclassified, undermine the Kraepelinian dichotomy.

A continuum of psychotic illness

Schizophrenia itself is an elusive entity as demonstrated by lack of agreement as to how it should be defined. In 1982 Jean Endicott and her colleagues applied different sets of diagnostic criteria to a series of forty-six patients, who met at least one of these definitions, admitted to the Psychiatric Institute in New York. By the most liberal criteria forty-four patients suffered from schizophrenia, but by the most restrictive there were only six. Such findings engender justifiable scepticism regarding the existence of any such 'disease entity'. But closer scrutiny reveals that the differences in this study between the sets of criteria are to a large extent accounted for by the extent to which different sets allocate patterns of illness to the categories of 'schizoaffective' and 'affective' psychosis. The more liberal criteria allocate more patients to the category of 'schizophrenia' and fewer to these diagnoses; the stricter criteria allocate the cases excluded from a diagnosis of 'schizophrenia' to the categories of 'schizoaffective' or even 'affective' psychosis. The category boundaries are arbitrary. The findings fit more readily with the notion that there exists a continuum of psychotic illness that stretches from more 'understandable' manic-depressive psychoses at one end to the less understandable schizophrenic psychoses at the other.

What does the existence of a psychotic continuum imply? While a categorical concept is readily compatible with an exogenous (environmental) causation, a continuum suggests rather that the disorder represents a component of variation that is intrinsic to the individual – that is, it is an extreme of variation in the normal population. A continuum concept might be thought difficult to investigate, but this problem can be overcome. There is a set of symptoms (those described as nuclear or of the first rank) that can be used to define the most characteristic core of the schizophrenic syndrome. While these symptoms fail to identify a category distinct from psychotic illnesses that lack these features, first-rank symptoms do define a threshold that yields crucial information on the population characteristics of psychosis.

Nuclear symptoms include:

(1) hearing voices that talk about oneself in the third person, or hearing one's thoughts spoken aloud;

(2) certain convictions concerning one's thoughts, for instance that thoughts that are not one's own are inserted into one's head, that thoughts are removed from one's head, or that one's thoughts are broadcast to others.

A feature is their incomprehensibility. For someone who has not experienced such a thing, it is difficult to conceive what it must be like to have thoughts 'inserted into one's head'. By definition, so to speak, one's thoughts are surely one's own. But this experience is described, and complained of, by sufferers of very different backgrounds and life histories.

What the symptoms seem to represent is some sort of loss of the boundary between the self and the outside world or, perhaps more specifically, other persons. Crucially, they reflect on the relationship between thought and language.

The World Health Organization ten-country study of incidence

One can ask how frequently do such phenomena occur and do they vary across environmental circumstance? As comprehensive an answer to these questions as we have comes from the 1992 WHO ten-country study of incidence. In each of ten centres dispersed across populations as different as those of Japan, India, Northern Europe and Hawaii, a relevant catchment area was defined and those facilities to which individuals experiencing psychotic symptoms for the first time might present were identified. The authors adopted standardized interviewing procedures and were able to demonstrate good reliabilities between centres in eliciting symptoms and reaching a diagnosis.

The findings are salutory. Whereas with a 'broad' definition of schizophrenia (that included diagnoses allocated by the hospital clinicians as well as those of the researchers adopting liberal criteria) there were significant differences between centres in incidence, when the criteria were defined more narrowly, specifically by the presence of the nuclear or first-rank features, the differences between centres became less and, in this comparison, were not significant.

If there were real differences in incidence between populations, as the criteria were drawn more restrictively one would expect the differences in incidence to become greater. But this is not what is seen. In fact they become less (and the variance is reduced). This finding is consistent really only with a second interpretation – that incidence is constant across populations, and that the differences with broad diagnostic criteria arise from differences in the levels at which the threshold is drawn.

Schizophrenia, it seems, is constant across populations that differ widely in geographic, climatic, industrial and social environment and the utility of first-rank symptoms has been to demonstrate this fact. These symptoms define a level of severity or non-understandability at which it is highly likely that an individual who experiences them for the first time will present to a psychiatric or related service, and thus be enumerated as in the WHO study.

The conclusion is challenging. If schizophrenia is independent of the environment, it differs from common physical diseases such as coronary artery disease, diabetes and arthritis. These represent an interaction between genetic and environmental aetiological factors in a way that schizophrenia does not. Schizophrenia it seems is a characteristic of human populations. It is a disease (perhaps *the* disease) of humanity.

How old is the schizophrenia mutation?

If the variation underlying these psychological phenomena is genetic, one can ask: how old is the schizophrenia mutation? Either the mutation (i.e. genetic variation) or the mechanism that gives rise to it must have preceded the separation of the populations in which it is now present. Given that the Japanese, Indian and North European populations have been separated for thousands (probably at least 10 thousand) years, the mutation is clearly old. When one considers in addition that schizophrenia with essentially the same features is present in the Australian aboriginal population that separated from the rest of modern *Homo sapiens* at least 50 thousand years ago, it is apparent that the genetic variation must be very old – in fact must have preceded, or been coincident with, the origin of modern *Homo sapiens*, an event dated to between 137 and 250 thousand years ago that occurred somewhere in East Africa.

A second question can be asked of the findings of the WHO study: who (apart from sufferers themselves) carries the schizophrenia predisposition? This question is relevant to genetic linkage studies (that attempt to locate a gene or genes) but has also been asked, in a eugenic context, by those who have thought that it might be possible to eliminate this predisposition from the population. As the forerunner to the Nazi policy of genocide during the Second World War, this view has an unfortunate historical precedent.

The WHO study casts light on this issue. There can be no simple sense in which there is a fraction of the population that carries a gene that is absent from the remainder of the population, because if such a fraction existed there is no reason why it should remain constant in populations that are separate for significant periods of time. Variation between populations, either as a result of differential selection or genetic drift, would be expected. The conclusion to be drawn is that the variation of which predisposition to schizophrenia forms a part is not confined to a subfraction of the population – it must cross the population as a whole.

Next to population distribution, age of onset is a peculiar and unexplained characteristic. Onsets of psychosis occur (a mean two to three years earlier in males than females) throughout the reproductive phase of life. As this is also the healthiest phase, in which the expectation of physical disease is lowest, these facts again draw attention to the singularity of psychotic illness. Given that the illness is associated with a procreative disadvantage (sufferers are less likely than the population in general to have children), this fact points a finger at the central paradox: if the disease is genetic in origin why are these genes not selected out of the population?

Language and psychosis: common evolutionary origins?

An evolutionary theory, drawing on natural selection, that is, a theory of the origins of the genetic variation and its associated advantage, is required. To what function might such variation relate? What advantage might balance the disadvantage associated with schizophrenia? Clearly the advantage is not present in sufferers themselves, nor from the arguments given above can it be confined to the first-degree relatives. If the predisposition to schizophrenia is a part of variation that crosses the population as a whole, and if it can be traced back to the origin of modern *Homo sapiens*, it is difficult to resist the conclusion that this genetic variation is associated with the function that characterizes the species, that is, language.

As communication, language has characteristics that distinguish it from precursor primate systems. The linguist Saussure emphasized that the relation between the sign (word) and the thing to which it refers is arbitrary. Words can be made to mean what we want them to mean. Vervet monkeys have a system that communicates 'eagle', 'leopard' or 'snake' to other vervet monkeys, but the signs which they use are fixed. In human language, as Chomsky has pointed out, the number of possible sentences is infinite, but each properly formed sentence can be recognized as such by a competent speaker of that language at first hearing. The capacity for language is the identifying feature of *Homo sapiens*, but it is one for which there is limited archaeological documentation. Evidence for representational capacity, for example as shown by rock art, goes back no more than 50 thousand years, but it is widespread across the populated regions of the world. Like the complexity of language itself, the capacity to represent appears to be intrinsic to *Homo sapiens*, and relatively constant across populations. The two abilities reflect different aspects of a single genetic change that underlies the communicative potential of the human brain. Language, it seems, must have its origin in the change (the 'speciation event') that gave rise to modern *Homo sapiens*; it must be the reason why this species, unlike any preceding primate or hominid species, has spread across the world, increased in population size, and so changed the environment that the existence of thousands of other species is threatened.

Neoteny in human evolution

In the 1920s, Bolk first suggested that *Homo sapiens* evolved by a process of neoteny: the prolongation into adult life of what in precursor species are features of infancy. In this way one can explain the resemblance of the skull and facial characteristics of humans to those of the infant rather than of the adult chimpanzee. What has to be accounted for in humans is the progressive delay in maturation relative to earlier primate species. When the increase in brain growth relative to body growth is compared in macaque, chimpanzee and humans, the trajectories are remarkably similar. What differs between the species is the point of the plateau, this being progressively later in humans compared to the chimpanzee, and in the chimpanzee compared to the macaque. Some selective factor has delayed the point of maturation, with the result that the brain is bigger in the human. Perhaps the plasticity of the infant brain also persists longer. Whatever cerebral characteristic is under selection, the physical effect is the retention into adult life of the physiognomy of the infant.

Selection acting on the relatively simple genetic mechanisms underlying the point of maturation could account for the rapid increase in brain size in the hominid species. Underlying this process, 'proto-language' could have developed; the evolution of natural language, including the use of arbitrary symbols and infinite recombinational capacity, came late in the sequence. Some relatively abrupt change appears to be required to explain the transition. It is plausible that this change constituted the speciation event for modern *Homo sapiens*.

Asymmetry

Since the observations of Paul Broca and Marc Dax in the 1860s, it has been known that language or some component of language is located in one, usually the left, side of the brain. Language is the

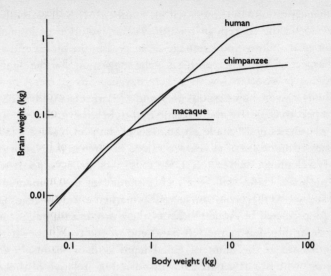

Figure 1. Increase in brain weight with body weight in macaque, chimpanzee and human. (After Holt et al., *1975, In:* Fetal and Post-natal Cellular Growth Hormones and Nutrition *(ed. D. B. Cheek), pp. 23–44. John Wiley.*

pre-eminent function for which the human brain is lateralized. But it is a function for which there is a population polymorphism. Whereas for a substantial majority language is located in the left hemisphere, for some individuals (a majority of whom are left-handed) it is in the right. If the balance between the two sides of the human brain is a critical factor in its functional capacity, a single gene that influenced the relative rates of development of the two hemispheres played a central role in its evolution.

In 1978 Marian Annett proposed the 'right-shift factor' as a single gene of additive effect which, when present in a single dose (rs +/− genotype), biases the left hemisphere to be dominant for speech and the individual to be right-handed. When absent (rs −/− genotype) handedness and cerebral dominance are determined at random, and when present in a double dose (rs +/+) the individual is likely to be strongly right-handed. This theory accounts well for the transmission of handedness within families. Michael Corballis has developed the concept in relation to the evolution of human psychological abilities and language capacity. But the most controversial aspect of Annett's hypothesis is the suggestion that the right-shift factor is associated with a heterozygote advantage – that individuals who are homozygous (+/+ and −/−) are at a disadvantage with respect to cognitive ability compared to heterozygotes (+/−).

My colleagues and I made an analysis of data on relative hand skill assessed at the age of 11 years in 12,000 children in the National Child Development Survey (NCDS). This gives strong support to the hypothesis. Hand skill is a highly significant determinant of verbal and non-verbal behaviour as well as mathematical and reading skills. As predicted by Annett's theory there are disadvantages for strong dextrality, but at the left-hand end of the continuum it is those who are at the point of equal hand skill or 'hemispheric indecision' who are at a particular disadvantage relative to those who are unequivocally left-handed or anywhere to the right of the point of equal hand skill.

Annett's hypothesis and the above findings point to the following conclusions:

(i) A single hypothetical gene (the 'right-shift factor') is a powerful determinant of cognitive ability.

(ii) This gene is probably under continuing evolutionary selection.

Twenty-two individuals in the NCDS sample who (by the presence of nuclear symptoms) later developed schizophrenia completed the test of hand skill at the age of 11 years. They differed from the rest of the population in being closer to the point of hemispheric indecision. Predisposition to schizophrenia, it seems, is associated with inadequacy or delay in establishing dominance in one or other hemisphere. Parallel to this loss of functional asymmetry is evidence for loss or failure of development of the anatomical asymmetries (e.g. of brain width) that are present in the brains of most individuals. Risk of schizophrenic symptoms, I believe, is associated with a brain that is less clearly lateralized in anatomy and physiology.

Nuclear symptoms as anomalies of hemispheric specialization

The concept of psychosis as a failure of hemispheric differentiation has a number of precedents running back through the nineteenth century. In his book *A New View of Insanity: The Duality of Mind*, published in 1844, A. L. Wigan put forward the view that 'a separate and distinct process of thinking . . . may be carried out in each cerebrum simultaneously' and that 'each cerebrum is capable of a distinct and separate volition, and that these are very often opposing volitions'. He considered that the interaction of the two functionally separate hemispheres was at the root of the symptoms of insanity. Medical scientists like Crichton Browne (1879) and Southard (1915), influenced by evolutionary considerations, entertained the concept of serious mental illness as a disorder of the dominant or left hemisphere. Flor-Henry, on the basis of his observations on the psychoses associated with epilepsy, also supported this view. But the findings from the NCDS study are consistent with the hypothesis that schizophrenia is not a disorder of one or the other hemisphere, but of the interaction between them, and specifically that there is a failure to establish unequivocal dominance. Julian Jaynes, in his book *The Origins of Consciousness in the Breakdown of the Bicameral Mind*, first published in the 1970s, relates how schizophrenia might represent a regression to an earlier state of consciousness (the 'bicameral mind') in which the two hemispheres were less differentiated and the interaction between them (representing the 'will' of the social group) was experienced as 'voices'.

Henry Nasrallah proposed that a normal component of interhemispheric integration is 'inhibition of any awareness by the verbally expressive hemispheric consciousness (usually the left) that it actually receives and sends thoughts, intentions and feelings from and to another (the right) consciousness'. In schizophrenia this function is disturbed with the result that the left hemispheric consciousness becomes aware of an influence from an 'external' force, which in fact is the right hemisphere. In this way, according to Nasrallah,

Schneiderian delusions such as thought insertion and withdrawal and passivity might arise.

In the context of the hypothesis developed here – that schizophrenia and language have a common evolutionary origin in the genetic event that allowed the hemispheres to differentiate in some aspect of their function – first-rank symptoms take on a new significance. These symptoms it seems are telling us what happens when this process fails. They demonstrate the consequences of inadequate hemispheric specialization. They are clues to the cerebral organization of language, the primary function of which is to communicate with another person. Somehow this requires an interaction between the hemispheres, and the production of sentences (in which an unequivocal distinction between the 'I' and the 'other' is mandatory) and their reflection in thought (in which this distinction may not yet have been made) are a consequence of this interaction. Nuclear symptoms are telling us what happens when this mechanism goes wrong. They reflect language at the end of its tether. They are the key to the cerebral basis of the speciation characteristic.

A sex chromosomal locus

According to the above considerations the genetic predisposition to psychosis is related to that for asymmetry. Two lines of evidence are consistent with the presence of a gene for asymmetry on the X and Y chromosomes:

(i) Turner's syndrome (XO) individuals have right-hemisphere impairments while Klinefelter's (XXY) and XXX individuals have left-hemisphere deficits. This suggests a gene for the relative growth of the two hemispheres is present on the X chromosome. But since normal males (XY) have only one X but lack the deficits seen in Turner's syndrome, there must be a balancing influence on the Y chromosome.

(ii) Within sibships there is a small association between handedness and sex consistent with genetic models of handedness, such as Annett's, that postulate a substantial random element.

Such findings suggest that the asymmetry (right-shift) factor is in the recently described class of genes that are present in homologous form on both X and Y chromosomes. Such genes appear to be subject to recent evolutionary change. Because of the lack of recombination between the sex chromosomes, the copy on the Y may diverge in sequence from that on the X, a divergence which could be relevant to the sex differences in:

(a) cerebral asymmetry (greater in males);
(b) lateralization of hand skill (stronger in females);
(c) the pattern of distribution of intellectual ability (females having a greater mean verbal fluency and males greater spatial ability);
(d) mean age of onset of psychosis (earlier in males);
(e) the biological disadvantage or fecundity effect in psychosis (greater in males).

Sexual selection

Because variation in the gene sequence on the Y chromosome will be subject to selection only by females, an XY homologous gene is a target for sexual selection. But since the gene is assumed to be homologous between the chromosomes, and therefore performs the same function, quantitative differences (such as those noted above) rather than qualitative differences in function between the sexes will be expected.

There have been several studies of the role of sexual selection in humans. Differences between the sexes in preferences for a mate are constant across cultures: whereas intelligence, kindness and an exciting personality are rated highly by both sexes, males consistently rate physical attraction more highly than do females and females rate good earning capacity more highly than males. Within a socio-biological framework, such differences can be understood in terms of the difference between the sexes in their interest in procreation. On this theory, females are interested in a mate who can provide good genes and paternal investment through pregnancy and beyond, while males are interested in a female who is likely to be healthy and fertile, for which physical attractiveness may be an index. It is as though there is a debate about the optimal age of maturation –

males on average opting for an earlier and females for a later age – the debate being conducted in the medium of the speciation characteristic of language. This explanation generates the prediction that there will be a mean sex difference in age at procreation. Age at marriage does show a consistent sex difference across cultures – males being a mean 1.5 to 2 years older than females.

Such a sex difference is potentially relevant to the question of age of maturation of the brain. First, the age of selection of gene variants on the Y chromosome will be a mean 1.5 to 2 years later than those

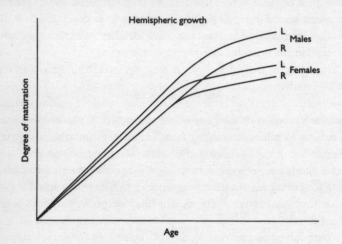

Figure 2. Hypothetical growth trajectories of the cerebral hemispheres in humans (compare with Fig. 1). The relative trajectories of hemispheric growth are assumed to be determined by the right-shift factor or cerebral dominance gene (located in homologous form on the X and Y chromosomes) acting early in development. The different genotypes acting together with a random factor as in Annett's theory are associated with different trajectories of relative growth of the left and right hemispheres. The mean difference in asymmetry is determined by the ranges of alleles on the X and Y chromosomes. These in turn are selected by mate choice; the mean point of selection on those on the Y chromosome is later than the mean for those on the X. (Adapted from T. J. Crow, 1995, British Journal of Psychiatry 167, 12–25.)

on the X as suggested by Fig. 2. Thus, if there are a number of variant alleles, one would expect the range of variation on X and Y chromosomes to differ with the effects being seen in an early influence on the relative rates of development of the hemispheres. Second, the difference between the sexes in their criteria for selecting a mate and/or the difference in age of selection will be expected to generate a dimension of variation in the normal population that is reflected in variation in brain structure (e.g. symmetry–asymmetry and brain size). This dimension is predicted to correlate with a significant dimension of variation in psychological function/personality structure (e.g. sociability/emotionality). If language competence is the function which is under selection, the variation would be expected to occur in relation to some aspect of language.

According to this hypothesis a component of this variation represents predisposition to schizophrenia, specifically that component associated with greater symmetry and failure to develop unequivocal dominance for speech in one hemisphere. If the trajectories are determined by genes acting early in foetal life but the disease only becomes apparent when some threshold (e.g. for the onset of psychosis or the appearance of premorbid precursors) is exceeded, then this point would be expected to be reached earlier in males.

Conclusions

Although psychotic illnesses are difficult to define (variation between forms of illness is continuous rather than categorical), a group of symptoms (nuclear or first-rank symptoms) can be identified with which reliable estimates of incidence can be obtained. Defined in this way, schizophrenic illnesses 'are ubiquitous, appear with similar incidence in different cultures and have clinical features that are more remarkable by their similarity across cultures than by their difference', as the WHO study conducted by Jablensky and co-workers concluded. Thus schizophrenic symptoms are a characteristic of human populations. They must be intrinsic (i.e. genetic in nature) and the origins of this variation must have preceded the 'out of Africa' diaspora of modern *Homo sapiens*. The variation is associated with a fertility disadvantage, individuals who experience such symptoms being less likely than the population as a whole to have children; it is thus under continuing evolutionary selection.

Language, without clear precedent as a communication system, is the functional capacity that distinguishes *Homo sapiens* from other primate species. Language and psychosis, it is proposed, are related both to each other and to the speciation event that gave rise to modern *Homo sapiens* 137,000 or more years ago. A genetic change allowed the two hemispheres to develop with a degree of independence. The capacity for language (for some critical component of which a dominant focus is present in one hemisphere) evolved as a result of selection acting upon this dimension of variation (that probably includes a random as well as a genetic component). Psychosis is the element of the variation associated with failure to establish dominance for language in one or other hemisphere.

The significance of nuclear symptoms – failures to distinguish between self- and other-generated linguistic signs, and between thought and spoken language – is that these reflect on the functional organization of language between the two hemispheres. The genetic mechanism underlying hemispheric specialization is thus the key to understanding the origins of language and the pathogenesis of psychosis. Evidence that the dominance ('right-shift') factor is in the class of XY homologous genes provides an explanation for sex differences in cerebral asymmetry, motor skill, verbal fluency and age of onset of psychosis. Such a gene will be subject to sexual selection, acting perhaps to determine the plateau of brain maturation in the two sexes, a mode of evolution consistent with the role for sexual selection postulated by Charles Darwin in *The Descent of Man*.

Further reading

Bickerton, D. (1995). *Language and Human Behavior*. University of Washington Press.

Corballis, M. C. (1991). *The Lop-sided Ape: Evolution of the Generative Mind*. Oxford University Press.

Crow, T. J. (1993). Sexual selection, Machiavellian intelligence and the origins of psychosis. *Lancet* 342, 594–598.

Crow, T. J. (1996). Language and psychosis: common evolutionary origins. *Endeavour* 20(3), 105–109.

Crow, T. J. (1997). Schizophrenia as a failure of hemispheric dominance for language. *Trends in Neuroscience* 20, 339–343.

Crow, T. J. (1997). Is schizophrenia the price that *Homo sapiens* pays for language? *Schizophrenia Research* 28, 127–141.

Crow, T. J., Done, D. J., and Sacker, A. (1996). Cerebral lateralisation is delayed in children who later develop schizophrenia. *Schizophrenia Research* 22, 181–185.

Jablensky, A., Sartorius, N., Ernberg, G., Anker, M., Korten, A., Cooper, J. E., Day, R., and Bertelsen, A. (1992). Schizophrenia: manifestations, incidence and course in different cultures. A WHO ten-country study. *Psychological Medicine Supplement* 20, 1–97.

Stringer, C., and McKie, R. (1996). *African Exodus: The Origins of Modern Humanity*. Cape.

9

Can a Computer Understand?

ROGER PENROSE

Understanding and computation

Is *understanding* a quality that can ever be achieved by a computer? Though few would claim that present-day computers have much or any of this quality, there are many who would argue that it is only a matter of time before computers, or computer-controlled robots, will possess genuine intelligence and, consequently, will genuinely understand what they are doing. Indeed, those who hold to the strong form of the thesis of artificial intelligence – sometimes referred to as *strong AI* – would maintain that any mental quality *whatever* must be a feature of computation in some form.[1] They would argue, after all, that it ought to be possible, eventually, to construct some form of computer-controlled robot which possessed all those essential mental qualities that are possessed by a human being. Consequently, that particular mental quality which we refer to as 'understanding' would have to be something that could, eventually, be encapsulated in terms of some aspect of computation.

I should make clear that by the term 'computation' I simply mean that activity, in mathematical idealization, that modern general-purpose computers are designed to achieve. The mathematical idealization just referred to is basically the requirement that there be no limit on the storage space available, that the machine does not make mistakes, and that it be allowed to continue to operate for as long as is necessary. Such an idealized computer is referred to as a *Turing machine*, after the mathematician Alan Turing who (with the logician Emil Post) first formalized this notion of idealized computer. There is a particular type of Turing machine referred to as a *universal Turing machine*. This is characterized by the fact that it can imitate the action of any other given Turing machine when supplied by the appropriate program. In fact, modern general-purpose computers are, in a clear sense, very good approximations to the mathematically idealized universal Turing machines. For this reason, theoretical discussions about what (universal) Turing machines can or cannot achieve are directly relevant to the question of what computers can or cannot achieve in principle.

We are now very familiar with the fact that computers can perform actions that seem to be very different from the straightforward carrying out of mathematical calculations. For example, some computers control robots that can walk about avoiding obstacles; some can catch and return balls that are thrown at them. Others can now play the game of chess so well that only a very few human players are rated more highly. In their actions, all these computational devices are, effectively, still just Turing machines, even though they may be loosely programmed in ('bottom-up') ways that enable them to learn by experience rather than their being strictly organized according to ('top-down') algorithmic procedures designed to give clear-cut solutions to particular classes of problem.

Are there limits to what Turing machines can achieve? Indeed there are such limits. There are classes of mathematical problem that are known to be insoluble by entirely computational means. However, many people – such as proponents of the (strong-AI) viewpoint that human mentality can be fully understood in terms of computational models – would claim that human mathematicians could not solve such classes of problem either. Nevertheless, there are clear mathematical arguments which show that the human quality of 'understanding' is not something of a computational nature at all. And understanding is a quality that is essential for the appreciation of any mathematical proof whatever.

It might be argued that the non-computational nature of understanding is 'obvious' to anyone involved in the actual design or use of computer programs. The quality of understanding is, in a sense, *complementary* to computation. A computation unaccompanied by understanding is of no actual value. One needs to know what a computation is *for*, and why some particular result of a computation should have any particular implication. Sometimes there is a trade-off between understanding and computation. By use of more understanding in a problem, one may be able to circumvent a large amount of computation; conversely, a lot of number-crunching or the working through of vast arrays of different possibilities may, in certain cases, act as a substitute for a deeper understanding of a problem.

Yet, strong AI supporters (and many others) would argue that whatever the quality of 'understanding' might actually be, there must surely be some way of simulating it in a computationally controlled robot. I shall be arguing very differently. Moreover, I regard understanding to be something of a test case for artificial intelligence. It seems to me to be clear that whatever it is, understanding is a quality that requires genuine *awareness*. I do not know what 'awareness' is any more than I know what 'understanding' is. Yet, it seems clear that without awareness, genuine understanding (in the usual use of that word) cannot be present. To be fully aware of a situation is, indeed, the first step towards understanding it. Thus, if we can see that the effects of understanding are not achievable purely computationally, then this strongly indicates that it may be awareness itself that is the non-computational ingredient. In any case, if the effects of understanding are beyond computation, then there is something fundamentally lacking in the purely computational model of the mind.

Can computers understand chess?

To illustrate the fact that present-day computers lack any real understanding, it is interesting to provide, as an example, the chess position given in Fig. 1 (a problem due to William Hartston and David Norwood). In this position, black has an enormous material advantage, to the extent of two rooks and a bishop. However, it is easy for white to avoid defeat, by simply moving his king around on his side of the board. The wall of pawns is impregnable to the black pieces, so there is no danger to white from the black rooks or

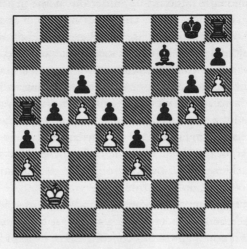

*Figure 1. White to play and draw – easy for humans, but
Deep Thought took the rook!*

bishop, provided that this barrier is left intact. This much is obvious
to any human player with a reasonable familiarity with the rules of
chess. However, when the position, with white to move, was presented to various different powerful chess computers – in particular
to the (then) most powerful of them, 'Deep Thought' (which had a
number of victories over human chess grandmasters to its credit)[2] –
they immediately blundered into taking the black rook with the
white pawn, opening up the barrier of pawns to achieve a hopelessly
lost position!

How could such wonderfully effective chess performers make
such an obviously stupid move? The answer is that all the computers
had been programmed to do, in addition to having been provided
with a considerable amount of 'book knowledge', was to calculate
move after move after move – to some considerable depth – and to
try to improve their material situation. At no stage could they have
had any actual understanding of what a pawn barrier might achieve
– nor, indeed, could they ever have any genuine understanding
whatsoever of anything at all that they did.

To anyone with sufficient appreciation of the general way in which Deep Thought or other chess-playing computer systems are constructed, it is no real surprise that they would fail on positions such as that of Fig. 1. Not only can *we* understand something about chess that the computers cannot, but we can also understand something of the (top-down) procedures according to which they have been constructed; so we can actually appreciate why they should make such a blunder, as well as understanding why they could play chess so effectively in most other circumstances. However, we may ask: is it possible that Deep Thought, or any other AI system, could *eventually* achieve any of the kind of real understandings that we can have – of chess, or of anything else?

Although this example is suggestive, and illustrative of the differences between human understanding and what computers are able to achieve, it is not by any means conclusive. For example, one might envisage a time when computers get so powerful that they can analyse chess positions, such as that illustrated in Fig. 1, right through to checkmate. Even though any real 'understanding' of what a pawn barrier could achieve might be entirely lacking, the computer could still use such brute-force calculational means to find the appropriate moves. In order to provide a more definitive argument against computer understanding, it will be necessary to turn to mathematics, where one can consider problems with a genuinely *infinite* component, so exhaustive brute-force calculations can no longer be directly used.

Unassailable reasoning

Accordingly, I shall now concentrate on certain aspects of *mathematical* understanding: basically what is involved in the notion of unassailable mathematical demonstration, or *proof*. One has got used to the idea that a mathematical 'proof' is simply a matter of following the appropriate rules. However, this turns out not to be the case. The famous mathematical logician Kurt Gödel showed, in 1930, that no matter how powerful a system of rules one might choose to adopt – provided that one accepted that the rules were incapable of being used to demonstrate the truth of some *false* arithmetical statement – then there would be arithmetical statements which must also be accepted as true, yet which lie beyond the scope of the rules. Thus human understanding, even when limited to the area of arithmetical statements, cannot be encapsulated in any system of rules that are accepted as reliable. The very acceptance of a set of rules is what enables one to transcend them.

I have not been specific about what is to be meant by 'rules' in this context. In fact, Gödel was referring to what is known as proof within some specific *formal system*, and his result shows that such a notion of 'proof' always falls short of what can actually be achieved by human understanding. Fortunately, it is not really necessary for the reader to know what a 'formal system' actually is, because Turing showed, a few years later, that the Gödel argument really applies to any system of 'rules' that can be programmed on a computer or, more precisely, carried out by a Turing machine.

It is not infrequently argued, however, that the arithmetical statements that arise by use of the Gödel procedure are very unnatural as mathematics, and can therefore be safely ignored by serious mathematicians. Thus, as far as 'ordinary' mathematics is concerned, one might as well simply ignore the Gödel problem, settle on some particular system of rules of proof and get on with the job. However, this does not enable us to avoid the problem of how it is that we know that certain mathematical propositions are actually true. How do we know that we should trust our chosen system of rules in any case? If we cannot, then we cannot trust its implications; but if we can, then we must equally trust the arithmetical proposition that Gödel comes up with, even though it is not something that can be actually derived by use of our accepted rules.

Moreover, it is not really the case that Gödel sentences – or statements equivalent to such Gödel sentences – are 'unnatural' things that can be ignored. I shall illustrate this with the wonderful example that I shall describe next (which I learned about in a lecture given by Dan Isaacson in the autumn of 1995). This is a theorem put forward by Goodstein in 1944, and it has the virtue that it can be described to people with very little mathematical background.

Goodstein's theorem

Consider any natural number (a non-negative whole number, i.e. one of 0, 1, 2, 3, 4, 5, . . .). For definiteness let us choose 1061. Write this number in binary form; so in our example we have the representation

$$1061 = 10000100101,$$

which means

$$1061 = 1024 + 32 + 4 + 1,$$

i.e.

$$1061 = 2^{10} + 2^5 + 2^2 + 1,$$

the 1's in the initial expression standing for powers of 2 that are present in the sum and the 0's for those that are absent.

We may note that there are still numerals appearing in this final expression which are not expressed in terms of powers of 2 (e.g. the '10' in 2^{10} or the '5' in 2^5) and we may choose to re-express these exponents also in such a fashion:

$$1061 = 2^{2^3 + 2} + 2^{2^2 + 1} + 2^2 + 1.$$

We are still not quite finished, because of the '3' appearing in the first exponent, so let us express this also in terms of powers of 2 to obtain the expression

$$1061 = 2^{2^{2 + 1} + 2} + 2^{2^2 + 1} + 2^2 + 1.$$

For larger starting numbers, we might have to go to third-order exponents or higher.

Now let us consider two simple operations that we can apply to numbers expressed in this way: (a) increase the base by one unit and (b) subtract 1.

The idea is to iterate these operations alternately: (a), (b), (a), (b), (a), . . . , and see what happens. We initially have our number (here

1061) expressed in terms of powers of 2, so the 'base' referred to here is 2. Therefore, in the first application of (a), we must replace this 2 by 3. In our example, application of the operation (a) thus gives us

$$3^{3^{3+1}+3} + 3^{3^3+1} + 3^3 + 1.$$

Now we apply (b) to obtain

$$3^{3^{3+1}+3} + 3^{3^3+1} + 3^3.$$

Application of (a) (now replacing 3 by 4) gives us

$$4^{4^{4+1}+4} + 4^{4^4+1} + 4^4.$$

Now the application of (b) is not quite so trivial as before, but we get

$$4^{4^{4+1}+4} + 4^{4^4+1} + 4^3 \times 3 + 4^2 \times 3 + 4 \times 3 + 3.$$

(The coefficients '3' appearing here are the analogues of the '9's that occur in the ordinary decimal notation, when we subtract 1 from 10000, for example, to get 9999.) We now apply (a) again, to obtain

$$5^{5^{5+1}+5} + 5^{5^5+1} + 5^3 \times 3 + 5^2 \times 3 + 5 \times 3 + 3.$$

(Note that the coefficients '3' and exponents '2' and '3' in our expression are undisturbed in the application of (a). There is no ambiguity here because the coefficients and these exponents are always smaller than the base and this will remain so as the base is increased in accordance with (a).) Application of (b) now yields

$$5^{5^{5+1}+5} + 5^{5^5+1} + 5^3 \times 3 + 5^2 \times 3 + 5 \times 3 + 2,$$

and so on.

It is evident, in this example, that the result of each pair of operations (a), (b) has, so far, resulted in numbers of enormously increasing size. In fact, for the example under consideration, the increase has been already extremely great:

$$1061 \rightarrow \sim 10^{40} \rightarrow \sim 10^{600} \rightarrow \sim 10^{10\,000} \rightarrow \cdots$$

very roughly, and the numbers continue to grow at a rapidly increasing rate. It is hard to avoid the strong impression that these numbers will, indeed, continue to increase indefinitely.

However, this impression is incorrect. Here is where Goodstein's remarkable theorem comes in. No matter what natural number we start with, the succession of numbers constructed in this way eventually reaches a maximum and it finally reduces all the way down to . . . *zero*! Despite the extraordinary size of the numbers that arise by the continued use of (a), it is the relentless chipping away by the modest little operation (b) that finally wins out!

How can this be? And granted the truth of Goodstein's theorem, what is its significance for the present discussion? The answer to the second question is that Goodstein's theorem is equivalent to a certain Gödel-type proposition. The theorem serves to show that Gödel propositions can be perfectly comprehensible things, and there is no way that we can simply exclude them from mathematical consideration. In fact, it is not in principle difficult to see how to prove Goodstein's theorem, but let me come back to this at the end of the next section, which will set the theorem appropriately in context.

Proof by mathematical induction

The familiar way in which the mathematical statements about natural numbers that we encounter at school are proved is by means of *mathematical induction*. Let us consider an elementary example: prove that the sum of the first n natural numbers is $\frac{1}{2}n(n + 1)$, i.e.

$$1 + 2 + 3 + 4 + \ldots + n = \tfrac{1}{2}n(n + 1),$$

which is to hold for *all* natural numbers n. (The convention for $n = 0$, of course, is that the sum on the left is simply zero, and we get the true relation $0 = 0$.)

To prove an assertion of this kind by mathematical induction we need to verify that *if* it is true for any particular value of n, then it follows that it must also be true for $n + 1$. We also need to check the particular value $n = 0$, to start it off. Thus, to prove that some proposition, depending on the natural number n – let us call this proposition $P(n)$ – holds true for *all* natural numbers n, we prove:
(i) for all n, the truth of $P(n)$ implies the truth of $P(n + 1)$; and
(ii) $P(0)$ is true.

In the present case, we simply note that the algebraic identity

$$\tfrac{1}{2} n(n + 1) + (n + 1) = \tfrac{1}{2} (n + 1)(n + 2)$$

establishes the needed relation.

Now consider Goodstein's theorem. How would one prove this using ordinary mathematical induction? In fact this turns out to be impossible! It was shown by Kirby and Paris in 1982 that Goodstein's theorem is equivalent to the Gödel proposition that arises from the rules of mathematical induction.[3] Thus, Goodstein's theorem is both true and not provable merely by means of ordinary mathematical induction!

One might think, therefore, that the 'proof' of Goodstein's theorem would be something very obscure; moreover, we might imagine that this 'theorem' is perhaps even questionable as a valid mathematical truth. Perhaps, as some might try to argue, its very validity is indeed a matter of opinion – depending upon which mathematical system one might arbitrarily choose to adopt. Yet, all these things are very far from the truth. The proof of Goodstein's theorem is immediately understood by any mathematician with a standard background in the appropriate notion of infinite set theory (called *transfinite induction*).[4] In fact, it is not at all necessary to present things in this particular way. Anyone who spends a sufficient time familiarizing herself/himself with what is involved in the procedures (a) and (b), as applied to ordinary natural numbers, and who is able to appreciate fully the essentials of what is going on, will come to the same conclusion: eventually (b) wins out and the procedure terminates with 0. (For the interested reader, I recommend starting with the 4. The numbers increase until they reach

$3 \times 2^{26 + 3 \times 2^{27}}$, before eventually reducing to zero!) The essential fact is that all the towers of exponents will eventually get eaten into, their defences of smaller towers being ultimately chipped away one by one by the relentless operation of (b), no matter how large the base gets in accordance with (a). (The use of transfinite induction is merely a beautifully convenient way of organizing all this understanding into a single principle.)

Understanding and natural selection

How is it that creatures can have evolved on this planet who can actually *understand* mathematics, following correct reasoning about potentially infinite procedures to arrive at valid results concerning the infinitude of natural numbers? I would certainly not dispute the standard scientific answer to this kind of question: Darwinian natural selection. However, the key issue is not whether or not natural selection operates, but what does it have to operate *with*?

For beings who inhabit an entirely computational universe, there is indeed a problem. Many would try to claim that an 'understanding' of numbers could come about in an entirely computationally describable way. Accordingly, it was the computer-like response of our remote ancestors to their environment that produced 'understanding'. In their experiences, they would have come across small numbers of objects, and then larger and larger collections, finding that it is to their advantage (and to their evolutionary 'fitness') to be able to count them consistently, and then to add and subtract them. Rather than having the need to refer always to the specific entities – stones, berries, days, species – which the numbers might quantify, it would be found useful, and therefore selectively advantageous to these ancestral creatures, to be able to 'abstract' the notion of natural number from these various instances so that it can be applied in diverse circumstances.

However, no matter how broad the experiences of these ancestral creatures may have been, they would have encountered instances of only a vanishingly small proportion of the natural numbers. Perhaps they found it convenient to idealize, and then to postulate that the 'numbers' that they encounter in direct experience actually belong to an infinite family: the natural numbers themselves. Such ancestral beings might have evolved who could reason effectively and with precision about these ideal objects. But if the physical principles upon which they and their surroundings are constructed can be described entirely in *computational* terms, then the precise and effective rules upon which their reasoning depends would also have to be of a computational nature. Eventually, consciously or unconsciously, these ancestral creatures might conceivably, stimulated by their direct experiences, contemplate the notion of mathematical induction. One could imagine that those creatures who found the principle of induction to represent an obvious and necessary truth concerning the nature of the natural numbers were favoured by natural selection. This feeling could be reinforced by its unfailing validity in special cases and by its acceptance within the community at large.

Basically, mathematical induction is indeed a computational procedure, and it does not seem to be inconsistent that entirely computational creatures might come to 'believe' securely in the validity of this procedure entirely through the pressures of natural selection. But how would such creatures cope with Goodstein's theorem? That particular mathematical assertion is something entirely outside direct experience. Moreover, the actual numbers that arise in the repeated application of the procedures (a) and (b) are far beyond those that could conceivably have been directly encountered. Yet, our mathematical understanding can cope with Goodstein's theorem without excessive difficulty. How can this be? Clearly our understanding of the natural numbers is *not* limited so as to be in accordance merely with the computational rules of ordinary mathematical induction. Our direct experiences of individual instances of natural numbers and of the relations between them might conceivably have provided us with certain computational rules that we have come to regard as 'intuitive' (such as that of mathematical induction) – because those individuals with inclinations towards those rules were selectively favoured – but these experiences did not include anything of the nature of Goodstein's theorem.

Moreover, as Gödel's theorem tells us, this understanding of the

Figure 2. For our remote ancestors, a specific ability to do sophisticated mathematics can hardly have been a selective advantage, but a general ability to understand *could well have.*

natural numbers cannot be encapsulated by any knowable set of rules *whatever*, if 'knowable' entails 'trustable' and 'set of rules' means something of an entirely computational character. Mathematical rules that purport to ensure unassailable mathematical truth ought surely to be trustable. If the nature of mathematical understanding can be encapsulated by rules, then those rules cannot be computational.

It seems to me to be clear that there is a fundamental conflict, as revealed by the Gödel(–Turing) theorem, between mathematical understanding and purely computational processes. There is no obstruction to our mathematical understanding being the product of evolution provided that the physical laws with which natural selection operates are *not* of an entirely computational nature.

It is, however, most unlikely that natural selection would have called upon some subtle non-computational ingredient hidden in physical laws merely so as to evolve *mathematical* beings. I have illustrated the absurdity of this possibility in Fig. 2, which is taken from my book *Shadows of the Mind* (p. 148). It was (and probably still is!) of no selective advantage whatever to be in possession of computational rules powerful enough to cope with mathematical propositions of the particular nature of Goodstein's theorem. However, the general quality of *understanding* would have been of a distinct and obvious selective advantage to our ancestors. (The cousins of the ill-fated mathematician in Fig. 2 are much more selectively favoured than he is, their understandings being put to far more effective use.)

Provided that 'understanding' is something non-specific and of a non-computational nature – so that it is flexible and subtle enough to handle the proof of Goodstein's theorem as well as other Gödel-type theorems whenever they arise – then it could indeed have been a quality that was favoured by natural selection. There appears to be no essential dividing line between mathematical and other forms of human understanding. The understanding that is involved in the proof of Goodstein's theorem is, in effect, just organized common sense. Perhaps that is what is involved, at root, in *all* mathematical arguments, though the 'organization' that is needed may sometimes be very considerable indeed.

Where is there scope for a non-computational physics?

It would seem to be a clear conclusion of the above arguments that this 'common sense' that underlies understanding in general – and mathematical understanding in particular – is something outside any computational description, and consequently it could not arise, by natural selection processes or otherwise, in an entirely computational universe. If we are to grant this, we must ask what kind of physical action could indeed lie outside computation, and how might such physical action be actually relevant to the behaviour of our brains?

First, we must ask whether those physical laws that have been revealed to us by physicists do actually contain any scope for non-computational action. Or shall we need to look outside these presently accepted physical laws if we are to find an essentially non-computational behaviour? The issue is a somewhat delicate one, particularly because physical laws, as they are presently understood, employ continuous quantities rather than just the discrete ones upon which the standard notions of Turing computability depend. That is to say, these laws operate with *real numbers* (including numbers such as π or $\sqrt{2}$ which may require infinitely many digits in their decimal representations) and not just the natural numbers (or integers or fractions) to which the standard notions of computability apply. For example, real numbers are used for the conventional descriptions of time, space and energy.

The usual view on this issue – which Turing himself strongly argued for (as recounted by Andrew Hodges) – is that the continuous quantities of standard physical theory can indeed be adequately approximated by discrete ones. Accordingly, there is no bar to an effective computational simulation of physical behaviour merely on account of its continuous rather than discrete nature. For myself, I would tend to concur with this view, although I believe that the issue is not yet altogether clear.

Let us grant, for the purposes of discussion, that the use of continuous variables in current physical theory is indeed an inessential issue here. Moreover, the nature of current theory (which is given in terms of certain differential equations – equations that permit future behaviour to be determined from appropriate initial data) strongly suggests that an adequate computational simulation of any process in accordance with that theory should always in principle be possible. (Genuinely random elements can also be present, but these do not allow the system to evade an effective computational description.)[5] The complication that can be involved in such a simulation is frequently enormous, in any particular case, but we are here concerned with what can be achieved in principle, not just in practice, so the complication is also an inessential feature.[6]

It would thus appear to be a consequence of the foregoing discussion that we must seek something outside current physics if we are to find a physical action that could underlie our conscious behaviour and conscious understanding. If we are to take the view (as I do) that consciousness must indeed have a physical basis, then we seem driven to ask: what scope is there for a non-computational physics, of relevance to brain action, lying *outside* the presently known laws?

Before I attempt to address this question directly, it is important that I make some remarks about quantum mechanics – that profoundly accurate physical theory which describes the behaviour of physical particles, atoms, molecules, chemical bonds, superconductors, lasers and innumerable other physical phenomena. Although phrases like 'Heisenberg's uncertainty principle' are frequently invoked to suggest that there is a certain vagueness or even irrationality of behaviour at the quantum level of activity, this is, in fact, highly misleading. There is a mathematically very precise description of quantum-level behaviour whereby the quantum description, called the *state vector*, or *wavefunction*, evolves in a completely deterministic – and indeed *computable* – way, in accordance with a well-defined equation, the famous Schrödinger equation. The lack of determinism comes in only when a 'measurement' is made, which normally involves the magnification of a quantum-level event to the large-scale *classical* level (such as with the 'click' of a Geiger counter, a mark on a photographic plate or a track in a cloud chamber). At this stage, the rules are changed, and a probabilistic element is introduced – involving the strange notion of 'wavefunction collapse', which I shall refer to here as *state-vector reduction*. But at the quantum level itself, determinism and computability hold true – according to the standard procedures of the quantum theory.

It may seem odd that one seems to have to change the rules when one passes from the quantum to classical levels of physical behaviour. Indeed, it *is* odd, and the correct attitude to take concerning this is a highly controversial matter amongst physicists. There are many different schools of thought, and this is not the place to attempt to enter into a detailed discussion of them. I can only present my own opinion here (which is also the opinion of an increasingly sizeable minority of physicists concerned with the foundations of physical understanding) that there is indeed a major gap in the scope of presently accepted physical laws. This gap concerns the nature of the so-called 'measurement problem' of quantum mechanics, which is concerned with the issue of what is actually going on when a quantum event gets magnified from the quantum to classical level, and the procedure of state-vector reduction must be applied.

Let me elaborate a little. As present-day physics is presented, irrespective of one's view as to the *actuality* involved, there are indeed two quite different levels of physical description. On the macroscopic scale, we have *classical* physics – the physics of Newton, Maxwell and Einstein. It is a deterministic physics and is (as far as can be told, with the above provisos) computable. On the submicroscopic level of molecules, atoms and particles, on the other hand, another completely different-looking description takes over, namely *quantum* physics. Quantum physics is characterized by the fact that different alternative histories of behaviour seem to coexist in some strange kind of superposition, this being what constitutes the state vector or wavefunction. These superpositions of alternatives remain superposed, so long as the system stays at the quantum level, and the evolution of the system is again deterministic and computable, taking place in accordance with Schrödinger's equation. The non-determinism of standard quantum theory occurs only when effects get magnified from the quantum to the classical level, at which point the state-vector reduction is deemed to take place, whereby the state vector is considered to jump discontinuously from one state to another.

There are many different attitudes to this curious state of affairs. Some physicists (such as Niels Bohr) regard the state vector not as describing any kind of quantum-level *reality* but as being merely a mathematical convenience useful for making predictions. Others would take the state vector as actually describing a quantum-level physical reality, but would regard the reduction phenomenon as some kind of approximation or illusion. Yet others are driven to the logical conclusion that the superposed alternatives must still exist at the macroscopic level, but for some reason we are not aware of them, there being 'parallel universes' in which all these superposed alternatives (including copies of ourselves) are supposed to coexist. Finally, there is the viewpoint to which I myself subscribe, that the Schrödinger equation is only an approximation to some yet largely unknown physical theory which straddles both the quantum and classical levels. My own position is that it is *here* that non-computable physics must enter the scene.

The gap between the two levels is a genuine one, I am contending, and not just an apparent effect due to our incomplete understanding of quantum-level physics. There are strong grounds for believing that the nature of this gap in physical theory is closely connected with the problems that are encountered in attempts to combine the rules of quantum theory with the principles of Einstein's general relativity (the theory of gravitation which involves the notion of curved space-time). In fact, this kind of viewpoint is now commonly favoured by those who believe that an essential modification of the rules of quantum mechanics is indeed needed before it fully makes sense at the quantum/classical borderline (Károlyházy and the Budapest school, Diósi, Ghirardi and co-workers, Percival, Pearle, Gisin, Bell, myself and others, have all expressed sentiments in this direction). According to this view, it is with *gravitational* effects that state-vector reduction indeed occurs as a *real* phenomenon (and not just an imagined or approximate one). I use the acronym OR for this phenomenon – standing for *objective reduction* – which is handy because it stands for a process whereby a quantum superposition between two (classical) alternatives becomes one *or* the other.

How could OR physics influence brains?

One thing that is valuable about the gravitational viewpoint, with regard to state-vector reduction, is that it enables some calculations to be performed according to which estimates can be made as to the mass/distance/timescales at which such a theory should become relevant. For example, a quantum superposition of two distinct mass distributions, each of which is clearly defined, ought to be *unstable*, according to a specific version of this view, with a lifetime which is roughly Planck's constant (divided by 2π) times the gravitational self-energy of the difference between the two mass distributions. My arguments require that there is an essential non-computability in physical laws occurring with this OR phenomenon. Accordingly, the choice that Nature makes as to which of two (or more) quantum-superposed states enters the classical level is *not* simply random, as is dictated by the procedures of standard quantum mechanics, but is governed by some (presently unknown) non-computable process. We must ask whether the time scales predicted by this theory could be of relevance to those brain processes responsible for consciousness.

There are various experiments (Kornhuber, Libet, etc.) which indicate that conscious processes normally take place in accordance with timescales of the order of about half a second. If we are to take the view that consciousness is associated with some appropriately organized OR processes, then, according to the above gravitational view, coherent quantum-superposed displacements of differing mass distributions must occur in the brain, of a magnitude that would give an OR decay time of about half a second in the above scheme.

Before considering this in detail, there is an important point that I must make clear. In the above gravitational scheme, there would be many OR processes taking place all the time, whenever the quantum/classical borderline is breached in any physical process. However, in almost all of these, the quantum system would be inextricably entangled with its random environment. In almost all cases, the most significant mass displacement occurs in this environment and not in the system itself. This has the effect that, whatever the details of the (non-computable) OR process might be, these would normally be entirely masked by this randomness. Indeed, it would be for this reason that the standard (random) procedures of ordinary quantum mechanics – as is manifested in the procedures adopted in the measurement process – actually give the correct answers. Despite the somewhat unconventional view that I am presenting with regard to the quantum state-reduction procedure, this is very close to what is argued for in the conventional 'environmental decoherence' attitude to quantum mechanics.

Thus, in order to see any difference, in the OR theory, from that which is anticipated according to the conventional viewpoint, we require a 'large' quantum system, very well isolated from its random environment, which is *coherent* in the sense that superconductors (or other Bose–Einstein condensates) are 'coherent', so that the

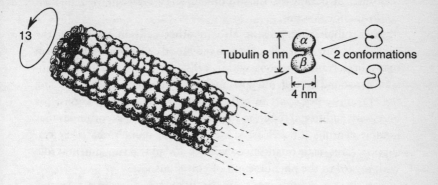

Figure 3. The structure of microtubules.

quantum-mechanical state-vector description applies on a macroscopic scale, with large numbers of constituent particles all acting in concert. The conventional viewpoint would be that such things are exceedingly improbable in biological systems because the temperature is far too high. Indeed, under normal circumstances, the ambient temperature of biological systems is such that quantum coherence would be destroyed almost instantaneously, with no chance of it persisting for up to half a second. In particular, it is quite unreasonable to expect that nerve transmission could be of such a quantum-coherent character. The electric fields that accompany a nerve signal would strongly influence its 'noisy' environment and any quantum coherence would be instantly destroyed.

However, there are other structures present in nerve cells which are much more promising in this regard. Most particularly, there is a system of tiny tubes, known as *microtubules*, which are especially prevalent within nerve cells. Microtubules are composed of large collections of peanut-shaped proteins called *tubulin*, each of which is a dimer consisting of two protein monomers: the α- and β-tubulins (see Fig. 3). Each tubulin monomer is about 4 nanometres in diameter. According to Stuart Hameroff and his associates, microtubules should be capable of information processing and of supporting signals transmitted along the tubes. These would involve the continual switching of the tubulin dimers between two distinct conformational states.

Microtubules are present also in other cells in the body (the exception being their absence from red blood cells), and they perform many important functions within cells, such as transporting substances around the cell, influencing the cell's movements, and guiding the chromosomes apart in cell division. What is being argued for here is an additional function for those particular microtubules that inhabit neurons (or at least some neurons), namely that they can support large-scale quantum coherence and play a fundamental role with regard to the phenomenon of consciousness.

For this, it would appear to be necessary that (the relevant) neuronal microtubules have a different structure or different organization from those which inhabit other cells, although it would not be impossible that there is a more minor role for quantum coherence (or even conceivably a very low level consciousness) in other types of cell – such as one-celled animals, which can behave in quite sophisticated ways. One distinctive property of neuronal microtubules seems to be that they have a parallel organization, rather than the radial one that is the usual situation for microtubules in cells. Perhaps more significant is that whereas the microtubules within ordinary cells are continually growing and shrinking (by polymerization and depolymerization of tubulin), there is a network of microtubules within neurons that appears to be *stable* in this respect.

An important and possibly related issue is that according to Tuszńyski and his colleagues, Hameroff-type information processing can take place along microtubules only if they have the lattice structure known as an *A-lattice*, which is what is illustrated in Fig. 3. However, there is another very similar-looking arrangement of the tubulins in which the α- and β-tubulins are displaced by one unit along alternate columns from that depicted in Fig. 3, referred to as a *B-lattice*. Since the number of columns is an odd number (13), this leads to the presence of a 'seam' between two of the columns in which the lattice structure is different from elsewhere. Experimental evidence seems to point to the prevalence of B-lattices in ordinary cells and suggests that B-lattices are probably primarily involved in the transport of materials around cells. It would seem to be an important requirement for the specific ideas that I am putting forward here (in conjunction with Stuart Hameroff) that there should indeed be a prevalence of A-lattice microtubules in (cerebral) neurons.

What is the role of the OR criterion in this picture? The proposal that Hameroff and I have been developing requires, first, that there be a large-scale quantum-coherent state involving many microtubules in many different neurons globally across the cerebrum (and perhaps other parts of the brain). There are various possibilities for this, but the most promising seems to be some kind of electromagnetic activity involving ordered water molecules inside the microtubule tubes, as has been suggested by Jibu, Yasue and co-workers. Other possibilities for large-scale quantum activity have been suggested by Fröhlich (an early pioneer in the theoretical explanation of superconductivity). The microtubules themselves could offer some kind of shielding from the 'noisy' environment within the rest of the cell, but this, in itself, would not be enough.

The analogy with superconductivity may be suggestive. For many years, this was thought to be a phenomenon which could take place only at temperatures very close to absolute zero, but in recent years, *high-temperature superconductivity* has been discovered. While the temperature at which this is known to occur is still far from the 'body temperature' that we require, the temperature at which these superconductors operate is something like half-way to what is needed. Moreover, according to present-day (albeit inadequate) understanding, there seems to be no bar to high-temperature super-conductors which operate at the required body temperatures. The lattice-like nature of microtubules (and of some other structures associated with synapses) might be favourable to the possibility of some kind of high-temperature superconductivity, but there remains a great deal of speculation in these suggestions.

There is a feature of quantum coherence that is important to mention here: there is no requirement that the different parts of the quantum system be connected to each other. A coherent quantum system might well consist of a large number of parts, all physically separated from one another, but where their quantum states involved in the various parts are all *entangled*, so that they behave as a single system. To set the state up in the first place requires some form of physical connection, but thereafter the different parts can remain separated. Thus there is the possibility of a single quantum state permeating the microtubules of large numbers of neurons all at once.

The second ingredient of our model is the requirement that, at a certain stage, the tubulins themselves become involved in this quantum-coherent state. Quantum superpositions of different arrangements of tubulin conformations could then occur and, when there is a large enough mass displacement between these differing arrangements, OR would take place – where we must assume that there is still sufficient shielding from the noisy environment within the cell that the actual details of the OR process are important to the outcome – i.e. it is non-computational rather than merely random. Accordingly, one pattern of tubulin conformations is selected by the OR process rather than another, in a non-computational way. At this stage, according to our model, a conscious event takes place!

Finally, this selected choice of tubulin conformations would have to influence (collectively) the strengths of a whole pattern of synapses and the brain's detailed organization would, accordingly, be slightly altered. There are, indeed, various ways that microtubules are able to influence synapses, and our model is not, at this stage, specific as to which of these is to be preferred.

Rather surprisingly, one finds that the *gravitational* OR criterion described in this section actually gives a timescale for the relevant OR process – of the general order of half a second – that is broadly consistent with the timescale for a conscious event. This is assuming that some 10^4–10^5 neurons, acting coherently, are involved in a single conscious event. These numbers are compatible with present-day knowledge on this issue.

According to the viewpoint that I have been expressing here, conscious actions and conscious perceptions – and, in particular, the conscious phenomenon of *understanding* – will find no proper explanation within the present-day picture of a material universe, but require our going outside this conventional framework to a new physical picture (involving OR physics) whose mathematical structure is very largely unknown. Of course, there is a good measure of speculation in the detailed development of this viewpoint, but this is also the case with any other proposal for the scientific nature of consciousness.

Notes

1 See: Igor Aleksander's chapter in this book.

2 This same chess position was presented to 'Deep Blue', the computer that defeated Gary Kasparov, and it made precisely the same blunder as the other chess computers!

3 To make it clear to the experts, what I mean by 'the rules of mathematical induction' is 'first-order Peano arithmetic'.

4 For readers familiar with transfinite induction, the proof proceeds as follows. Imagine the steps all written out, starting from some given natural number. Then replace each occurrence of the 'base' by Cantor's first transfinite ordinal ω. Now, the operation (a) does nothing, but (b) provides us with a descending sequence of ordinals. From the fundamental property of ordinal numbers, this must have a least member. This can only be 0, proving the result.

5 Although the strict notion of Turing computability does not incorporate the possibility of genuinely random elements, *effectively* random elements (called *pseudo-random*) are, in practice, frequently incorporated into computations. The essential conclusion is that there is nothing to be gained in practical terms from the introduction of genuine randomness into a computer's operation. For a more complete discussion, see Chapter 3 of my book *Shadows of the Mind*.

6 The issue of the extreme complication in the (supposed) computational action of a human brain is frequently brought up as a way of evading the Gödel-type obstructions to an entirely computational simulation of human mental activity. But if one believes that it is the mere immense *complication* in a supposed algorithm, unconsciously underlying a mathematician's conscious reasoning powers, that enables Gödel's theorem to be circumvented, then one must address the issue of how such an extremely complicated, essentially unfathomable algorithm could actually have come about. The two basic possibilities are natural selection (in an environment which is not favourable to the development of mathematical thought processes

able to achieve far more than is required for Goodstein's theorem) or deliberate AI construction. In either case, it is not anticipated that the underlying *principles* for the development of the required unfathomable algorithm are themselves unfathomable, and the Gödel theorem can be applied to those principles directly, rather than to the algorithm itself, so long as these principles are (as is normally assumed) of a computational nature. Details of these arguments against mere complication being a satisfactory answer to the Gödel conundrum are given in Chapter 3 of my book *Shadows of the Mind*.

Further reading

Burkhill, J. C. (1962). *A First Course in Mathematical Analysis*. Cambridge University Press.

Goodstein, R. L. (1944). On the restricted ordinal theorem. *Journal of Symbolic Logic* 9, 33–41.

Hameroff, S. R., and Penrose, R. (1996). Orchestrated reduction of quantum coherence in brain microtubules – a model for consciousness. In: *Toward a Science of Consciousness: Contributions from the 1994 Tucson Conference* (ed. S. Hameroff, A. Kaszniak and A. Scott). MIT Press.

Hameroff, S. R., and Penrose, R. (1996). Conscious events as orchestrated space-time selections. *Journal of Consciousness Studies* 3, 36–53.

Hodges, A. P. (1983). *Alan Turing: The Enigma*. Burnett Books and Hutchinson (UK), Simon and Schuster (USA).

Hodges, A. P. (1988). Alan Turing and the Turing machine. In: *The Universal Turing Machine: A Half-Century Survey* (ed. R. Herken). Kammerer & Unverzagt.

Jibu, M., Hagan, S., Hameroff, S. R., Pribram, K. H., Yasue, K. (1994). Quantum optical coherence in cytoskeletal microtubules: implications for brain function. *BioSystems* 32, 195–209.

Károlyházy, F. (1966). Gravitation and quantum mechanics of macroscopic bodies. *Nuovo Cimento* A 42, 390.

Kirby, L. A. S., and Paris, J. B. (1982). Accessible independence results for Peano arithmetic. *Bulletin of the London Mathematical Society* 14, 285–293.

Lucas, J. R. (1961). Minds, Machines and Gödel. *Philosophy* 36, 120–124. Reprinted in: Alan Ross Anderson (ed.) (1964). *Minds and Machines*. Prentice-Hall.

Lucas, J. R. (1970). *The Freedom of the Will*. Oxford University Press.

Penrose, R. (1989). *The Emperor's New Mind: Concerning Computers, Minds, and the Laws of Physics*. Oxford University Press.

Penrose, R. (1994). *Shadows of the Mind: An Approach to the Missing Science of Consciousness*. Oxford University Press.

Penrose, R. (1996). Beyond the doubting of a shadow. *Psyche* 2(1), 89–129.

Penrose, R. (1997). *The Large, the Small and the Human Mind*. Cambridge University Press.

Tuszński, J., Hameroff, S. R., Satarić, M. V., Trpisová, B., and Nip, M. L. A. (1995). Ferroelectric behavior in microtubule dipole lattices: implications for information processing, signalling and assembly/disassembly. *Journal of Theoretical Biology* 174, 371–380.

10

A Neurocomputational View
of Consciousness

IGOR ALEKSANDER

Consciousness seems to me to be such an important phenomenon that I simply cannot believe that it is something just 'accidentally' conjured up by a complicated computation.

R. Penrose, *The Emperor's New Mind*, Conclusion: a child's view

The computer-like classically interconnected system of neurons would be influenced by this cytoskeletal activity [i.e. quantum-gravitational effects in microtubules] *as the manifestation of whatever it is we call 'free will'. The role of neurons is more like a magnifying device . . . A key requirement is that some non-computability should be a feature . . .*

R. Penrose, *Shadows of the Mind*

Artificial consciousness must appear to be the mother of all oxymorons. At least I thought so until a peculiar thing happened to me on a hot day in July 1991. I was facing the cameras during the filming of a programme on the artificial neural nets in our laboratory. These nets do not just learn to recognize patterns, but they learn to form 'mental images' of what they 'see' with their artificial eyes. 'Do they sleep?' asked the interviewer. 'Yes,' I said, 'they have states which do and states which do not relate to their previous experience. When their eyes are shut they eventually drift off and kind of relax into meaningless states. But when their eyes are open again, they snap into some representation of what they are seeing. They can also "think" of their previous experience with their eyes closed. They even have states which could be described as dreaming.' 'So,' went on the interviewer, 'they actually appear to be conscious at times and not at others.'

My instinct made me rebel against this thought – consciousness must have something to do with being biological, with being alive. But in some way, the interviewer was right: what I had described is close to a psychological definition of consciousness. This distinguishes between being awake and alert to sensory input, thinking with one's sensors inactive, and being unconscious during sleep or anaesthesia. Rolling cameras don't allow confused explanations, so I said, 'Yes, but they are conscious in some artificial way, they are artificially conscious.'

That was the beginning of an 'artificial consciousness' programme in the laboratory. I saw this as an opportunity of contributing to the currently fashionable attempts by the great and the good at explaining consciousness. There is also not much agreement among the great and the good and the battle for capturing the high ground is fierce and acrimonious. My hope is that, as engineers, my colleagues and I can develop a different perspective on explaining consciousness, one that is based on structuring and design rather than analysis and speculation. What would have to be done were one to design a machine which could be said to be conscious?

A lack of definition, but much history

The first rule of design – the need for a proper specification – has immediately to be broken. There is no specification for consciousness, there is no definition. Consciousness is not one thing which you either have or do not have. Even the dictionaries either refer to consciousness as just to being awake or develop definitions using words such as 'all the thoughts contained in a person's mind' without defining 'thought' and 'mind'. So how does the engineer begin the design? By boning up on the history of the topic was part of the answer to this question. Consciousness may not have a definition but certainly has a genealogy. While the philosophy of mind may be traced back nearly two millennia to Aristotle and Plato, my personal interpretation is that the word *consciousness* was introduced into language (the English language, at that) by John Locke in 1690 in *An Essay On Human Understanding*. He spoke of '. . . the original of those ideas, notions, or whatever else you please to call them, which a man observes and is *conscious* to himself he has in his mind . . .' (my italics). This was a clear shift away from earlier dualist philosophy which Locke saw as pointless meddling with 'the physical consideration of the mind . . . [by what] alterations of our bodies we come to have any sensation . . .' It seemed to me that Hume, Kant and Hegel continued refining a taxonomy of the fascinating differences between the sorts of ideas we can have in our mind – see my book *Impossible Minds* (1996) for references to and discussion of the work of these philosophers. The distinction between what Kant calls analytic concepts (an upturned tumbler is still a tumbler), synthetic *empirical* propositions (there is a horse in the stable) and synthetic *a priori* propositions (two plus two is four) is vital in the design of a conscious machine. Coming into the current century, Wittgenstein's concerns, expressed in *Philosophical Investigations* (published posthumously in 1953), with the 'non-essentialism of language' (we cannot think of, say, 'dog' in the abstract, we can only think of dogs we have experienced) are also pertinent. This concern distinguishes between a machine which relies on its experience and one which is programmed in great detail to perform logical operations. The latter could never be sufficiently complete to qualify in a search for artificial consciousness.

The scientific hijack

It is curious that we are approaching the end of this millennium with scientists competing to explain consciousness making only scant reference to this defining genealogy. Penrose, for example, in *Shadows of the Mind* (1994) shows a fondness for Plato's ideas about the lack of contact between perfect thought and physical objects and discomfort with Kant's taxonomy of ideas. He seems not to worry about Wittgenstein or Locke. Many other contemporary scientists dismiss the entire philosophical enterprise as being less than rigorous. I do not side with this – for me the notion of consciousness is not only deeply rooted in philosophy but also a product of it. Despite the distaste modern philosophers may have for the notion of a conscious machine, such a machine should not be designed in ignorance of the last three hundred years of philosophical thought. As philosopher David Papineau pointed out in a recent review of David Chalmers' *The Conscious Mind*, modern approaches based on cognitive science and mathematics merely reopen the debate on dualism. Chalmers, a philosopher well versed in the rigour of mathematics, argues that most current scientific concern (such as Francis Crick's, in the *Astonishing Hypothesis*) only relates to the easy side of the problem, that is, how the firing of neurons correlates with conscious experience, but avoids the hard problem of how neural firing *causes* the personal sensation. This is good old dualism, and this is precisely where the conscious machine may be able to clarify things.

The artificial domain: why neurons?

What is a 'sensation' or a feeling? Can an artificial system have sensations and feelings? Like 'consciousness', the word 'sensation' is one for which we develop a meaning based entirely on experience. Looking around me gives me the sensation of knowing where I am. But sensations are in the past and the future too. I can think of the pleasant company I experienced last night, that special farm holiday I had with my parents at the age of nine, or what is likely to happen when I get to work later this morning. These are all sensations, as are pain and pleasure. Some of these phenomena are given the label 'memory' and others 'knowledge', but it is the sum total of these and the continuity between them that make up much of what we attribute to being conscious.

Because these sensations are such a valuable property to each of us, sometimes it is hard to believe that they can be conjured up just by some strange firing of neurons either in our heads or in a machine. But it is here that building machines can suggest how the firing of artificial neurons could become just as meaningful to the machine as our own sensations are to us. I shall show later that the key to this meaning lies in something we call an iconic transfer. But studying the firing patterns of neurons in brains is an incredibly difficult task, mainly because if done in detail, by invasive techniques, it can only be done for a few neurons (out of at least 100 billion) at a time, while if done in bulk, as through scanning techniques (PET and fMRI scans), the results are interesting but, as yet, too inaccurate to confirm or deny mathematical predictions.

This is the reason that the method of operating in the domain of *artificial* neurons may be of interest, despite the need this creates for having to be very persuasive to overcome the contempt that some have for the artificial or 'inanimate' as opposed to the real or 'animate'. Indeed, these very words give some of the game away. Animate and inanimate imply the presence or otherwise of a 'soul'. This, when confused with consciousness, debars artificial devices from having either. But soul and consciousness should be kept well apart. Belief in the soul implies the existence of a substance which survives the body after death, implying its dualist existence during life. It falls into the realm of theological dicta such as Heaven and Hell or the Holy Trinity. It belongs to an area of human thought where mysteries have a place and scientific explanation is inappropriate. Consciousness, on the other hand, is in need of scientific inquiry. For example, as Susan Greenfield points out, we know that consciousness is altered by drugs, so it is important to know by what mechanism this happens. Consciousness supports communication between various forms of organism, but how? Precisely because consciousness is a rich and varied compendium of many forms of mental activity, it is important to know how such concepts support one another and to study the properties of the widest group of organisms (real or artificial) which might acquire and sustain them.

So, why use artificial neural nets as opposed to just some healthy computational models designed by a programmer? The answer has to do with that primary facet of consciousness: the *self*. Self is that which enables the organism to know what it can and cannot do, knowing where it has been, and building a mental image of what the world is like. The key part of all this is knowing *how* this knowledge is acquired, how acquisition strategies are developed. This has two characteristics which make it difficult for a programmer to carry out. The first, and the weaker, implies working out ahead of time the detailed contingencies which might occur during the lifetime of an organism. The second, and the stronger difficulty, is that the organism must own and recognize its knowledge-building processes. Putting a programmer in the loop removes the sense of control and ownership which the organism needs to possess. Without these, its consciousness would be a rum thing. It would leave the organism bereft of the security that it can anticipate events and survive them.

The domain of neural networks has come to the fore because it does not require detailed planning by a programmer or design by a designer. Learning is the primary property of neural systems. But, as Penrose correctly points out, many learning neural networks simply learn to obey their trainer's wishes. This is tantamount to programming, as the trainer would have to teach the net everything it would ever need to know. However, it is wrong to believe that this is *all* that a neural net can do. To approach consciousness, one needs to study the properties of a neural net which enable it to be a dynamic artificial organism whose learned states are a meaningful representation of the world and its own existence in this world. I shall argue that a method of neural learning called 'iconic' could be the key to the creation of an artificial consciousness and may be an important factor in the understanding of real consciousness.

Neural nets and iconic learning

Artificial neurons are devices which have many inputs (called synapses in the living version) and one output (the axon in the real thing). Neurons receive their inputs both from the senses and from one another. Each neuron fires with a probability which becomes tied by learning to the pattern of input messages it receives. A well-known result is that for a given overall sensory input to a network of such neurons the network will enter a repeating sequence of internal states after passing through some intermediate states called transients. This is known as the response cycle for a particular sensory input. It is also known that the response cycle is dependent not only on the sensory input but also on the state of the net when the sensory input changes. It is the latter property which makes this internal representation sensitive not only to the current sensory input but also the past history of the input. Without this sort of property there would be no concept of time and sequence in the organism, so that language could never be understood, or images of a world seen through darting eyes.

Without learning, these internal response states would be merely incoherent internal reactions to the sensory world. To be useful, learning must be a process whereby final response cycles are selected to label the sensory input (either single inputs or sequences) into classes. The position where a programmer selects these patterns of firing (as labels or symbols) has already been dismissed. Certainly, in living beings no programmer has privileged access to the inner brain cells to tell them what to learn. An alternative is to leave these state cycle responses as arbitrary representations and have a learning scheme which simply ensures that the sensory input for any object in a given class ('cat', say) is represented by the same arbitrary representation. This too would not work as these representations are required to acquire meaning in terms of their features. When thinking of a cat without seeing one, I can say things like: 'it has pointed ears, four paws, whiskers . . .'. This would be impossible unless the representation contained the hierarchy of features possessed by the object being represented, a property that arbitrary representations clearly do not have. The third possibility is iconic learning.

The key to this is that input sensory patterns not only provide the input to which neurons learn to respond but they also select the neurons which will fire and those which will not. Once made to fire, the neurons continue learning the patterns created by other neurons, with the result that an unchanging or stable representation of the sensory stimulus is created in the inner parts of the net. In Fig. 1 the roughly horizontal shape selects neurons to fire retinotopically: that is, in a roughly horizontal shape. Of course, these neurons need not be horizontal in any geometrical sense, they merely need to sample the input in such a way that when the same shape appears on the input, the related group of neurons will fire and preserve some

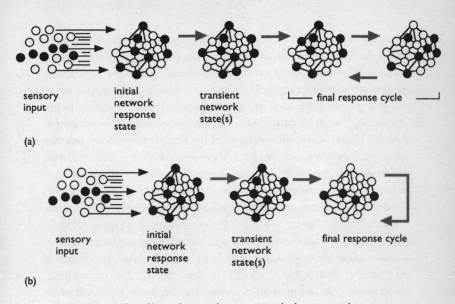

Figure 1. *The effect of iconic learning: (a) before iconic learning;*
(b) after iconic learning.

geometrical properties of the sensory stimulus. The figure actually
shows what happens once learning has taken place. With the inner
net in some arbitrary state, exposure to a horizontal stimulus causes
the net to go through some arbitrary states and head for the learned
iconic representation, which is the only stable firing configuration
that satisfies the constraint imposed by the input.

But this is just a beginning: before asking some of the more
peripheral questions about the modelling of consciousness, three
focal phenomena arising from iconic learning need to be briefly
explored. These are iconic memory (mental imagery), representations of self, and free will.

Iconic memory

What has been described so far is a learning process which creates 'echo-like' internal representations of what may be sensed by sensory neurons. But how could such representations exist in the absence of the sensory input? I can think of my cat with no cat being there or retain a pleasant memory of my last holiday in the Aegean. I can 'almost see' the brilliant ink-blue sea with cotton-white wind-swept wavetops and Turkish mountains in the background. Not only do these images exist in my head but they create feelings of pleasure at the thought or even sadness at no longer being there. These feelings are precisely what some philosophers see as the vital ingredients of consciousness. They are sometimes called 'qualia': the qualities of a mental event. Some, such as the philosopher Thomas Nagel, argue that this is the essence of what cannot be explained about consciousness. Other philosophers, like Daniel Dennett, are adamant that 'qualia' do not exist, which, in view of what I have just said about the Aegean, seems a bit extreme. The key issue here is whether these magical feelings could be conjured up by the firing of neurons. I shall argue that the principles for this being so are all in place.

As with much of this material, inspiration comes from living systems. Living sensory cells are subject to habituation. Continuous stimulation of a cell can lead to a decaying response in the firing in that cell. In Fig. 2a a mechanism is shown whereby an external stimulus causes sensory cells to fire. Iconic learning transfers a representation of this image into the firing of the inner neurons.

If one postulates that the persistence (i.e. resistance to habituation) of the inner neurons is greater than that of the sensory ones, the inner neurons learn to sustain the recently created image. Clearly much more needs to be said here about the mechanisms of long-term as opposed to short-term memories, but this is not the aim of the current discussion. The important fact is that long-term memories of experience which retain the features of that experience may be created by the simple process of iconic neural learning.

A branch of computational mathematics which is particularly well suited to the formulation of these concepts is called automata

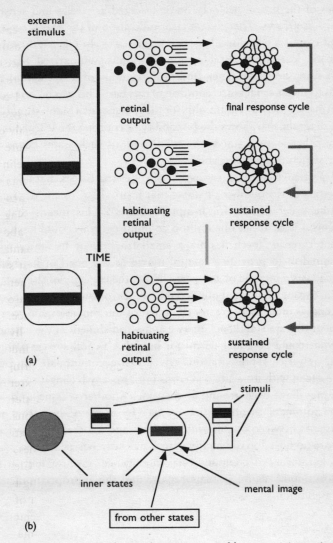

Figure 2. *The creation of mental imagery as stable states: (a) creation of a stable state; (b) state diagram or state-space representation of the mental image.*

theory. Part of this is concerned with 'state spaces', where the inner states of the neural net may be represented as circles and sensory inputs as arrows. This gives a clear indication of the way a sensory input causes a transition between inner states. In Fig. 2b the effect of iconic learning and stable state creation is summarized. Starting with some arbitrary inner state, the stimulus of a horizontal bar leads to the internal representation of this bar. This can be sustained even in the absence of a stimulus (or the presence of a blank stimulus). The diagram also shows the possibility of entering the learned state from other learned states, the totality of all such states being the state structure of the organism.

A particularly reassuring aspect of state structure is that it is very generous in the number of states that it provides for the organism (of the order of $2^n/2$ for n-input neurons). This means that an organism with about one million 30-input neurons could have sufficient capacity (even if only a small fraction of its states were meaningful) to provide a mental movie in the head of its owner which lasts a lifetime of 100 years. Now, the capacity of the human brain, through having about 100 billion neurons with n up to about 100,000, is immensely greater than that of our movie-organism. No wonder that we stand back in awe and astonishment at the vastness of what could be going on in our heads! A neural system affords amazingly rich representations which can accommodate not only the Aegean with its white wavetops but also any feelings (see later) that may have been around at the time. Another reassuring result from automata theory is that it may be used to show that the transients between one meaningful state and another are short, so there is no question of lengthy exhaustive searches as are necessary in other forms of computational intelligence: given a hint at its sensory input, neural systems rapidly find the appropriate mental representation.

Representations of self

The organism described so far is merely capable of observation and recognition. It has no way of behaving. To behave, it needs to have the ability to perform outward actions. As a simple example, imagine that the only action of which it is capable is to move its input window up with the horizontal bar in view, down, or leave it where it is. Also, the environment in which it operates does not allow movements which take the bar out of the field of view (i.e. there are walls in place). This is shown in Fig. 3a.

Initially it performs these actions at random as in Fig. 3b, where the action of the output neurons is shown at the bottom of the state circle. Most organisms have not only neuronal connections (motor neurons) to muscles which cause them to act but also return connections (proprioceptive feedback through motorsensory neurons). So, as learning takes place, not only can the effect of the actions be represented iconically in the neural net, but so can the actions themselves, as sketched in Fig. 3c. Finally, in Fig. 3d there is a sketch of the way in which the main net could enter states of 'thought' about the effect of its own actions without actually taking the actions. Theory shows that if the connections from the main net to the output net are weak and one-directional, then this freedom to think about one own's actions would come about. Indeed, the *wish* to execute an action, shown by transitions such as 'a', would have to be learned and could be contingent on other events in the main net.

It is this representation of one's own actions which, in combination with iconic learning, suggests mechanisms which in artefacts would be essential to model consciousness. For example, the fact that eyes dart about and would not create representations which make sense is corrected by the fact that muscle actions may transfer into state space to coordinate the bits of what is being seen (not consciously in this case). Hearing oneself utter things and forming iconic representations (used in this case for sounds as well as pictures) is crucial in the development of linguistic competence.

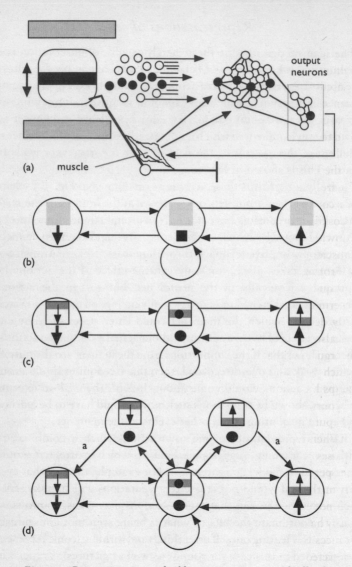

Figure 3. Representations of self: (a) proprioceptive feedback; (b) before iconic learning; (c) iconic learning of one's own actions; (d) thought and action.

Free will

The idea of freedom of the will is deeply ingrained in Western culture. Christianity, in particular, teaches that it is a feature of consciousness which is jealously guarded as a human property: it is seen as a gift from God, a gift which if well used will lead to the pleasure of the Deity and Heaven, but one which if badly used will lead to its disapproval and Hell. Despite this cultural character, free will enters the scientific discourse on consciousness. Indeed, as shown in the quote from Roger Penrose at the beginning of this chapter, the freedom of will resides, according to his principles, well below the computational activity of neurons, but in quantum effects in cytoskeletal microtubules. So even if neurons do store some lifetime knowledge and help with perception, the basic driving force of consciousness, free will, is not accessible at this level of computation.

From Penrose's point of view, stemming as it does from physics, the question of free will is bound up with determinism. For a deterministic system, once its state is known its future behaviour is fully determined (in theory), and hence it has no freedom of will. He also equates the algorithmic with the purely deterministic. So, he argues, an organism with free will has to rely on a physical process which is not deterministic and hence not computable. Quantum jumps have such properties, and from this flows much of Penrose's discourse which focuses on quantum jump phenomena and non-computability.

When looking for free will in a neural state machine, the issue focuses on choice. The machine, given a state of the input stimulus (the perceptually available state of the world), can mentally imagine (as in the above paragraphs) the effect of available actions. What has not been discussed in detail is that the imagined states could easily have quality factors associated with them: putting on a sweater reduces the feeling of cold on a cold day, so being warm may be a predicted mental state which the organism will choose to act on as satisfying a need which is also represented in its imagined states. So, if the net could speak, it would say: 'I feel cold so I *want* to put on a sweater.' This is an act of need-driven will. But when does this demonstrate its *freedom*? In theory it is possible to assume that when the automaton reaches a point when several courses of action are within its range it will make an arbitrary decision based on the state of some noise generator in the system. Penrose would argue that such a noise generator, relying on computation as it might do, is not perfect, and hence the will of the organism is not perfectly free. But this is a perfectionist's argument.

In living organisms there is plenty of 'noise': neurons fire in a probabilistic fashion and inner events synchronize badly with each other and world events. In practice, any organism facing an imperfect world will find plenty of non-determinism. Indeed, the state space of a neural machine is full of 'attractors' and 'repellers'. The former are states, like troughs on a billiard table, to which the system moves from other states, while the latter are states, like hills on a billiard table, from which the system flees to other states and the result of this is not easily predicted. The point is that there is sufficient non-determinism in a normally functioning neural system to make the organism itself 'feel' that it can take freely arbitrary decisions.

Indeed, it may even be erroneous to assume that an individual's knowledge of its own free will comes from *actually* making unpredictable decisions. Figure 3d shows that it is possible for the organism to enter mental states which define what choice of outward actions is available. That is, it can 'think' of moving the window up or moving the window down freely, in the sense that there is no representation of any constraints which cause one or the other states to be favoured. It is this neurocomputable mental representation of choice which may be responsible for the millennia of discussion on the freedom of the will rather than the action of non-computable cytoskeletal generators of uncertainty.

Conscious machinery: questions with answers

The approach to consciousness through iconically adapted neural state machines appears to deal with some focal issues, as discussed above. However, there are many other elements of consciousness which need to be addressed, as well as some problems which are as yet unresolved and are topics of current research. Much of the content of this section summarizes the discussion in my own recent book.

Is a conscious organism aware of the firing of all *its neurons?*
No, is the answer to this. The iconic learning argument suggests that only those neurons selected by sensory inputs create iconic forms of which the organism is aware. In living beings this may be quite a small proportion of the totality of the neural processing power which the organism possesses. Much neural circuitry must be involved in keeping the organism alive and active (e.g. in controlling heartbeat, temperature, locomotion, etc.). There is a subtler activity which is closer to conscious sensation and this has to do with time, sequentiality and disambiguation between identical events. In artificial neural systems, so-called *auxiliary* neurons are used to perform these functions. They are responsible for differentiating between the same experience at different times or the order in which things happen. So, while I can say 'Yes, I remember coming to work today, and this is different from my memory of coming to work yesterday', I may not be able to describe accurately what actually causes the difference. This may be due to different firing patterns in some of my (auxiliary) neurons, impinging on awareness but not in as vivid a way as the iconic firing patterns of what is being remembered.

Among the neurons which act in an iconic way, do all the states *lead to conscious sensations?*
Again the answer is negative. In fact, at least three kinds of states could be defined in the artificial system and probably in the living system as well. The first is that which is active during perception, that is, occasions when the iconic patterns are at their most vivid as they are directly driven from the activity of sensors. The second are the 'eyes closed' patterns, that is, everything that has to do with mental acts which are not directly driven from the senses but were originally created by them during learning. Interestingly, it is possible to note situations where the internal patterns develop even while perception is active, but are not related to it. The third is not part

of conscious experience. While 'dreaming' may be due to the firing of iconic neurons in strange juxtapositions of states related to experience, there are periods of sleep and anaesthesia during which no recognizable sensation would be reported. In the artificial system these correspond to a very large number of possible network states which are not related to the iconically learned ones, but could be entered when the links between neurons are weakened through mechanisms such as high noise levels.

Can machines have an 'unconscious'?

Curiously, artificial neural machinery could have states which have the characteristics of what we would call 'the unconscious' in human beings. There are mental states which we cannot describe or account for which, nevertheless, have an effect on our moods and possibly influence our dreams. In an artificial neural net, iconic state structures are formed both in terms of the states and the transitions between them. It can happen that transitions to certain areas of state space are broken through a process of overwriting, leaving these areas isolated with no means of being explored during waking life. They remain, however, legitimate representations of some experience. During 'sleep', or sometimes by accident, they could be entered due to noise in the system. On exiting them, the experience is lost, but it could have an effect on the direction taken by the system in the conscious state space, an effect which could be felt but not explained. Of course, theories of the repression of unpleasant memories could be explained in terms of this model.

Can artificially conscious organisms have personality?

As the state structure developed by two different organisms through their own actions and choices is likely to be different, their behaviour is likely to be different and this could be expressed as a difference in their personalities.

Is language necessary to conscious beings?

Much of my recent book is devoted to showing that iconic neural mechanisms have a natural propensity for supporting meaningful communication between organisms which, at the most advanced level, takes the form of a human language. Curiously, this opens the possibility of creating artificial organisms which do not fit on a linear scale of sophistication in forms of consciousness from the amoeba to *Homo sapiens*. Objects could be created which use language to build up their conscious state structures and are therefore close to *Homo sapiens*, but have less than the physical dexterity or the instincts of a slug.

Can the artificially conscious organism be logical?
Iconic learning does support logical thinking, but not as well as preprogrammed artificially intelligent machines. The logic built up by a neural machine is based on the logic of experience. If it says 'all men', it will refer to all the men it knows. In this sense it uses linguistic logic in Wittgenstein's non-essentialist sense, that is, it is a bit fallible like people rather than coldly rigorous like the programmed computer.

Can a neural machine have iconic representations for abstractions such as 'love' or 'beauty'?
Much of the meaning of abstraction comes from a competent use of language. So a machine may be able to have representations of abstractions which come mainly from linguistic definitions. Through this it may be shown that logically correct representations of sentences such as 'Fred knows that Bill loves Sally who is a very beautiful woman' can be created; there is no requirement that personal knowledge of love and beauty should be involved in this. A subsequent question of 'What do you mean by "love"?' could provoke the answer, 'I have no experience of it, but it has to do with the wish of humans to be together in an exclusive and intimate way.' This is clearly true in human modes of abstraction.

What are emotions, feelings and qualia in a machine?
As in the last question above, care must be taken to distinguish real feelings that a robot might acquire in the satisfying of some of its needs and those acquired by humans in the satisfying of theirs. It is the relation between sensation and need that is at stake, not the detailed nature of the sensations. There is no reason why an artificial

neural organism should not have sensations related to its needs (for fuel or heat, etc.). Having acquired language with which to communicate with humans, there is also no further reason that it should not form representations for abstract feelings felt by humans as was suggested in the previous paragraph. Of course, the question of 'qualia' is almost as vexed as that of consciousness itself. At the simplest level, there is no technical difficulty in explaining 'the redness of red'. Colour receptors in sensory neurons ensure that iconically derived neural firing patterns will be spatially differentiated and therefore give rise to differentiated sensations. At the level of Nagel's question 'What is it like to be a bat?', one needs to admit that no amount of knowledge of automata theory or neurophysiology will enable anyone to get into the bat's skin and give an answer to the question. However, it is sufficient to ask what mechanism a bat needs in order to know what it is to be that bat, and the answer may well be an iconically adaptable neural state machine.

Conclusion: another child's view

Like Penrose's 'A child's view' quoted at the beginning of this chapter, I too have a child's view. I have no doubt that consciousness is important and special. It defies definition and yet nobody will deny having it and being intimately comfortable with it. It angers the great and the good when their view of the topic is contradicted. It makes scientists seem mystics and gives mystics a scientific platform. It fools some into thinking that they are competing for a great shining prize awarded for unravelling its mystery, possibly through some as yet ungraspable and non-computable equation. This does not show the emperor in his naked state as he appeared in the fable, but regales him with the richest clothes of material so fine that it makes an industry out of the race to discover the secret of its manufacture.

My child's view is that consciousness draws its astonishing importance through being something rather simple, not something that escapes computation, but something that is the ultimate masterpiece of iconically adapted firing patterns of parts of the brain, something which the advances of neural computation allow us to approach, study and imitate, something which is just too important to be smothered by an assumed complexity engendered by taboos rather than science.

Further reading

Aleksander, I. (1996). *Impossible Minds: My Neurons, My Consciousness*. Imperial College Press.

Aleksander, I., and Morton, H. B. (1993). *Neurons and Symbols: The Stuff that Mind is Made of*. Chapman & Hall.

Chalmers, D. (1996). *The Conscious Mind*. Oxford University Press.

Crick, F. (1994). *The Astonishing Hypothesis*. Charles Scribner.

Dennett, D. C. (1991). *Consciousness Explained*. Allen Lane.

Greenfield, S. A. (1995). *Journey to the Centers of the Mind*. Freeman.

Karmiloff-Smith, A. (1992). *Beyond Modularity*. MIT Press.

Locke, J. (1690). *Essay Concerning Human Understanding*, 1975 edn. Oxford University Press.

Nagel, T. (1974). What is it like to be a bat? *Philosophical Review* 83, 435–450.

Papineau, D. (1996). The consciousness of zombies. *Times Literary Supplement*, 21 July 1996.

Penrose, R. (1989). *The Emperor's New Mind*. Oxford University Press.

Penrose, R. (1994). *Shadows of the Mind*. Oxford University Press.

Wittgenstein, L. (1953). *Philosophical Investigations*. Oxford University Press.

II

Flagging the Present with Qualia

RICHARD GREGORY

Recent work on processes of visual perception by brains and machines concentrates on signal processing 'bottom-up', from eyes or cameras, most influentially by David Marr. It has, however, been suggested that sophisticated object perception depends very largely on 'top-down' knowledge, derived from the past, and that perceptions in many ways are like predictive hypotheses of science. Both predict unsensed properties of objects, fill gaps in data, and both have limited prediction into future time.

For describing visual perception, it is usual to distinguish between real-time 'bottom-up' signals from the senses and 'top-down' knowledge stored from the past. Here we may add 'sideways' general rules, in a scheme something like Fig. 1 (developed in Fig. 4).

As envisaged over a century ago by the German physiologist, physicist and psychologist Hermann von Helmholtz, who introduced the notion that human perceptions are unconscious inferences, top-down contributions from knowledge are far greater than have generally been realized and may be considerably more than the bottom-up contributions of signals from the eyes and perhaps the other senses. It is now known that such a large knowledge contribution to vision is anatomically possible, as there is a remarkable richness of downgoing pathways in the primate brain to the lateral geniculate nuclei (LGN) relay stations, which receive at least 60 per cent of their input fibres downwards from the visual cortex and only 10–20 per cent from the retinas.

Knowledge of the world is needed, top-down, for intelligent visually guided behaviour to be appropriate to hidden and to non-

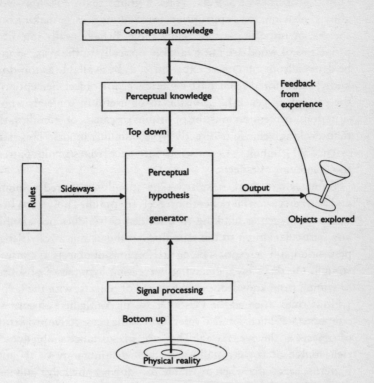

*Figure 1. Speculative flat box of vision. Bottom-up signals from the eyes
are processed, by many channels, to be interpreted with top-down
knowledge and sideways rules, to produce predictive hypotheses –
perceptions of objects and situations – for intelligent predictive
behaviour from limited sensory data. As phenomena of illusion are
experienced though their origins are understood, conceptual and
perceptual knowledge are largely separate. They work on different
time-scales: perception must be fast and, to be useful, must operate in
real time. Conceptual imagination is essentially timeless.*

optical properties of objects. Thus, a grainy texture seen as wood allows behaviour to be appropriate for kindling fires, or making book shelves, or respecting a mahogany table. Behaviourally important properties of wood are not available optically to the eyes, so must be derived from interactive experience, to be available as top-down knowledge, stored from past experience, for object perception in the present. In general, for vision to be useful in somewhat novel situations, perception must be of origins or causes of stimuli, rather than evoking behaviour directly from stimulus inputs. This is the essence of Helmholtz's unconscious inference from stimulus patterns to perceptions of objects.

Primates have both primitive-type stimulus-triggered responses and also perception far richer than received stimuli. Thus, responding by a reflex, such as blinking to a sudden noise, does not attribute any particular origin to the stimulus; so this is not a fully fledged perception, full perception being attributions of objects as causes of stimuli. On this view, perceiving is creating hypotheses of sources of stimuli from knowledge of the world of objects, with the help of various rules, such as the Gestalt laws of contiguity, closure and common fate. There are also rules for reading perspective projections of objects at the eye, though they are size-distance ambiguous. A rich source of cognitive illusions is such ambiguity of stimulus patterns, especially when available top-down knowledge and sideways rules are inadequate, or not appropriate for reading sensory signals in terms of objects lying in external space. Applying this backwards, phenomena of illusion are useful for discovering knowledge and rules used by the brain for perception.

Figure 2. Probabilities affecting selection of perceptual hypotheses. A depth-reversed face is so unlikely, it is impossible to see without very strong stereoscopic signals from the two eyes. When rotated, this hollow mask goes through bizarre transformations, changing direction of rotation as the outside becomes the actually hollow, though apparently normal, face inside.

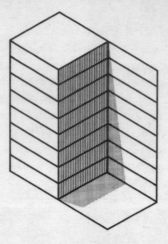

Figure 3. Mach's corner. When this figure (or a real corner with a shadow) flips in depth, the dark region changes brightness, though there is no change of sensory input. It appears darker when seen as a mark on the wall, and lighter when flipped in, when it is a likely shadow. This indicates effects of the prevailing perceptual hypothesis on early processing. (This is consistent with the large proportion of downgoing fibres from the cortex to the LGN, shown as a loop in Fig. 4.)

Perceptual hypotheses

The notion that perceptions are predictive hypotheses removes them from the apparently direct perception of the object world. It is this separateness from physical reality that allows the richness of illusions which provide evidence of many kinds of physiological and cognitive processing. Particularly revealing are phenomena of ambiguity, when perception switches between alternatives, though sensory inputs remain unchanged. Effects of probability are seen clearly in such unlikely depth-reversed objects as the hollow face in Fig. 2.

Ambiguous figures and objects can show modifications of apparently simple sensations, qualia, with switches of perceptual hypotheses, as in Mach's corner, dating from the nineteenth century, shown in Fig. 3.

Signalling the present

The evident importance of top-down knowledge and sideways rules for object perception raises a curious question: if perceptions are hypotheses, based largely on memory from the past, why are perceptions generally appropriate to the present moment, and recognized as belonging to the present rather than to memories of the past? In short: why are perceptions but seldom confused with memory or imagination? This identification of the present is clearly important for behaviour to be appropriate to present situations, for hypotheses are generally timeless or, at best, provide inexact time prediction. So how does heavily top-down knowledge-based vision identify the present, for controlling behaviour in real time? For primitive vision there is no such problem, as reflexes and tropisms are triggered directly by real-time sensory inputs. For sophisticated perception, we may suppose that real-time afferent inputs continue to signal the present, though they are inadequate for controlling novel intelligent behaviour.

Flagging the present

A striking difference between hypotheses of science and perceptual hypotheses is that only perceptions have consciousness – *qualia* – such as sensations of red, sound or pain. It seems that qualia are generally associated with the present moment. Could it be that qualia serve to flag the present?

A simple experiment is to look carefully at an object, or a scene, then shut the eyes. Note carefully what happens when the eyes are closed. Surely the vivid qualia of perception disappear. One remembers the object, or the scene, but without vivid qualia. In general, it seems that qualia are associated with afferent signals, normally occurring in real time, and so signalling the present. The further speculation is that real-time afferent signals trigger qualia, in order to flag the present in consciousness to avoid confusion with the past.

Some exceptions

Qualia can sometimes occur without sensory stimuli. In visual after-images, from a bright flash of light, the initial qualia linger for several seconds following the stimulus. This is due to maintained signals from the eyes after they are shut, so this is hardly an exception to stimuli triggering qualia, though these are displaced in time.

It is a common experience for memories of emotions to be accompanied with qualia, for example of embarrassment, from situations recalled years after the humiliating event. If the James–Lange theory has some truth (that emotions are afferent sensations of bodily changes, associated with embarrassment, fear, rage, or whatever), then there could be memory-induced afferent signals from the body (such as blushing at the memory) much as for the original situation, though delayed in time. On this account, we should expect remembered emotions but not other memories to be rich in qualia, which seems to be generally true.

Fortunately, the present is seldom confused with memory from the past, or with imagination such as anticipated futures. Exceptions are rare cases such as 'Mr S', described by the Soviet neuropsychologist Alexander Luria, whose memories were so vivid they were not separated from real-time reality; so he was confused, for example, by remembered hands of his alarm clock, and dangerously so by remembered or imagined colours of traffic lights, which for Mr S might be red (or green) in the present or in his remembered past or imagined future. Such cases stand out as highly unusual; but vivid dreams and hallucinations of schizophrenia are further exceptions, where vivid qualia appear without related afferent stimuli and can be confused with present perception. We may suppose that normal qualia-flagging breaks down in these situations, as also with hallucinogenic drugs.

The neurological situation is illuminated by experiments with PET brain scans, showing that brain processes of perception aroused by afferent signals are also active in vivid dreams, and with hallucinogenic drugs, when the system may be fooled into experiencing a non-existent present as though it is real. Visual images normally lack vivid qualia, although brain regions of primary visual cortex are active during imagery. We may conjecture that under such special conditions as dreaming, schizophrenia or hallucinogenic drugs, the normal mechanism demanding afferent inputs to trigger qualia breaks down. This seems a promising area for further brain scan experiments.

Elaborating on the tentative scheme of Fig. 1, we may add as in Fig. 4:

(i)   The prevailing task – to select knowledge and rules appropriate to needs in the given situation;

(ii) a downgoing loop from the prevailing perceptual hypothesis to early processing (as evidenced by, for example, the brightness change with switched depth in Mach's corner, of Fig. 3);

(iii) qualia of consciousness, normally triggered by real-time afferent signals (modified by the prevailing perceptual hypothesis), conjectured to flag the present to avoid confusing perception with memory.

To suppose that consciousness has causal effects implies that explanations of behaviour in terms only of physics and physiology-based psychology are inadequate. If causal consciousness emerges through evolution, we might suppose that evidence of increasing consciousness-endowed perception might be available in behaviour developments through species, and conceivably in fossil records of extinct behaviour with necessary structures preserved in fossil records.

The notion that qualia serve to flag the present does not begin to explain how qualia are produced by brain processes, though much has been discovered recently and especially for vision. If indeed qualia are normally triggered by afferent signals, modified by cognitive processing associated with object hypotheses, it would seem that consciousness results from cognitive processing rather than more directly from the support physiology of the brain.

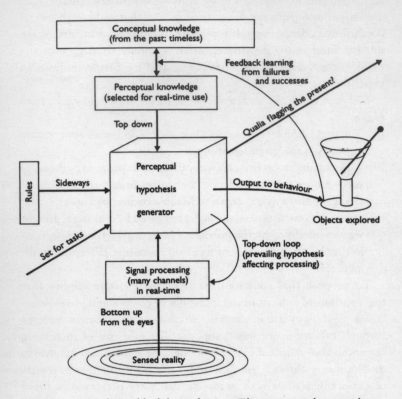

*Figure 4. Speculative black box of vision. The current task may select
'top-down' knowledge and 'sideways' rules (though they may not be
altogether appropriate or adequate, so generating cognitive illusions).
Real-time 'bottom-up' afferent signals are essential for signalling the
present. It is further suggested that real-time afferent signals trigger
qualia of sensation, in order to flag the present with vivid consciousness,
to avoid confusion with memory and imagination.*

Further reading

Gregory, R. L. (1968). Perceptual illusions and brain models. *Proceedings of the Royal Society* B 171, 279–296.

Gregory, R. L. (1970). *The Intelligent Eye*. Weidenfeld & Nicolson.

Gregory, R. L. (1980). Perceptions as hypotheses. *Philosophical Transactions of the Royal Society* B 290, 181–197.

Gregory, R. L. (1997). *Eye and Brain: The Psychology of Seeing*, 5th edn. Oxford University Press.

James, W. (1890). *Principles of Psychology*. Macmillan.

Kosslyn, S. M., Thompson, W. L., Kim, I. J., and Alpert, N. M. (1995). Topographical representations of mental images in primary visual cortex. *Nature* 378, 496–498.

Luria, A. (1969). *The Mind of a Mnemonist: A Little Book about a Vast Memory*. Cape.

Posner, M. I., and Raichle, M. E. (1994). *Images of Mind*. Freeman.

Silbersweig, D. A., Stern, E., and Frith, C. (1995). A functional neuroanatomy of hallucinations in schizophrenia. *Nature* 378, 176–179.

12

How Might the Brain Generate Consciousness?

SUSAN GREENFIELD

Anyone contemplating consciousness might well have some sympathy with a wasp, attempting sortie after sortie against an impenetrable glass window. What is the survival value of consciousness? How did it evolve? Could a machine be conscious? How can we even define the term? But perhaps the most tantalizing question of all, and indeed one that might help elucidate this host of other problems, is: what is the physical basis of consciousness? The brain is an organ of the body like any other, but somehow it must, in addition, have some sort of seemingly magic ingredient that enables billions of its banal-seeming cells to provide the pivot and inspiration of a person's outlook and personality. The issue of how a 'mind' might emerge from a brain is hardly new. Yet still we have no idea what type of answer to expect that would be unequivocally acceptable. There are those, for the most part scientists, who believe that the solution lies in a 'special' physiological mechanism that could act as a magic bullet; an alternative, more sophisticated approach, favoured by some philosophers, is to frame reasons to devalue the question. In this chapter I would like to suggest a different strategy.

I need to start with two disclaimers that could be discussed at length, but which, for our purposes, can be summarily put to one side. First, consciousness is impossible to define. However, I know that I am conscious and I assume that people would agree that they were conscious. Perhaps, then, it is simply best to give a hazy description of the phenomenon, something like consciousness being 'your first-person, personal world', and leave it at that. Second, let us assume that the brain generates consciousness and that it is not beamed in from outside. Rather, the physical brain is the only starting point. From a Yorick-like position then, almost holding the brain in one's hand, I would like to explore here how far scientists, in particular neuroscientists, can make a contribution to understanding consciousness.

The problem for me arose twenty-five years ago now. I remember wondering: if I got a bit of human brain tissue underneath my fingernail, would that have been the bit that someone loved with? Would that be the bit that made someone fidget when they spoke? Would it be the memory of a hot summer day? How would the boring-looking, banal stuff relate to my special fantastic, personal and unique character?

Consciousness and the brain

The most obvious feature of the brain is that it is not homogenous, but composed of different regions. There are no intrinsic moving parts, no obvious way of knowing where to start to understand what is actually happening, or what functions are taking place. Some scientists who are interested in consciousness have nonetheless looked at the workings of different brain regions, and if they found some novel mechanism they have then effectively said: 'Aha! This is a novel mechanism not found before. Consciousness is novel. Therefore, one must relate to the other.' Although, by following this path, one might be acting as a good scientist and looking at different aspects of the way the brain is functioning, one would nonetheless be ignoring – and this is why philosophers are often so dismissive of scientific approaches – so-called 'qualia', the feel of the first-person experience to you.

Any scientific explanation of consciousness must be objective and embrace physical properties of the brain: but at the same time it must, nonetheless, somehow take account of the subjective. This is why consciousness has been such an anathema to scientists, because the whole essence of science is objectivity. And yet we are going to deal with a phenomenon that is subjective, so how can we proceed?

The approach that I favour is to develop a means for looking at various events in the brain that somehow marry up with subjective feelings. But before we start at the science, we should look at what we expect of consciousness. Are there any properties that we could try and work out, which we could then use to go back to the brain and see if we can accommodate them?

Properties of consciousness

As an initial step, I shall try to develop some possible properties of consciousness. The first might be location; if we concede that the brain is the physical basis of consciousness, then it must occur somewhere within it. So where might such a 'consciousness centre' be? One of the recurring problems in neuroscience in general is the difficulty of 'location of function'. Researchers have for a long time tried to relate events in the outside world directly to certain brain structures. However, brain and mind functions, such as memory, vision or movement, seem almost certainly not to be related in a modular way to single respective brain regions. Many different brain regions play parallel roles, analysing the outside world in a variety of ways and reintegrating it so as to generate a connected whole. So may it be too for consciousness. Since there is no committed brain tissue, it seems more likely that non-committed neuronal populations in some way contribute to the final process. Hence, one property of consciousness could be that it is spatially multiple. On the other hand, one is normally only conscious of any one state at a time. The first possible property of consciousness might be then that it is spatially multiple, but temporally unitary. What about a second property?

If a dog is trained to put its paws to its ears at the sound of a violin, does that mean that it is having the same consciousness as a human being would who exhibited the same behaviour, putting hands over the ears: or would the dog have been trained like some Pavlovian automaton? What kind of consciousness, if any, would a dog be experiencing? And while we are thinking about dogs, let us also turn to rats. Rats are masters of survival. In potentially hostile conditions they are chillingly efficient. For example, they will be very cautious about eating unfamiliar foods: instead, they will wait and see if a small sample has deleterious effects, and then go back only after three or four hours, once no gastrointestinal mishap has occurred. It is very hard to think of rats, therefore, as little automata. But is a rat *really* conscious in the same way that a dog is or, indeed, in the same way as a primate? It is very easy and dangerous to anthropomorphize, but anyone looking at enchanting pictures of a chimpanzee staring at itself in a mirror would be hard pressed to say that such an animal (who has only a 1 per cent difference in its DNA from ours) is a computer or an automaton. But is this consciousness the same as that of someone like George Bernard Shaw? How do we handle animal consciousness therefore, particularly when compared to our own?

In my view an unnecessary problem arises here, because consciousness is often thought of as all or none: either you are conscious or you are not. A more plausible scenario, however, is that consciousness is more like a light on a dimmer switch that grows as the brain does. The more complex the brain, the greater the consciousness. If you go along with that idea, it circumvents many of the problems we normally have with animal consciousness. Think of a continuum of consciousness, ranging from minimal through to very profound, and that in turn will be reflected in the sophistication of the brain. Such a continuum of consciousness would help us understand child consciousness, and indeed potentially that of the foetus.

Foetal consciousness has in the past posed quite a conundrum. If a foetus is not conscious, then that suggests that a baby suddenly becomes conscious as soon as it is born, even though the brain does not undergo any such sudden, conspicuous changes at all at birth. Alternatively, we have to assume a baby is conscious only at two or three months, say, or at an even older age. Try telling any mother that her new-born child is not actually conscious. The only alternative is that a foetus would have to be conscious in the womb, in which case we would have to imagine what it might be conscious of. I think one can get round this riddle by saying that consciousness is emerging or growing as the brain is growing in the womb.

Consciousness is continuously variable: it is a continuum. It follows that it is not only with apparent dichotomies – animals versus humans, children versus adults – where consciousness is variable: adults too will have moments when they are more conscious than at other times. We are, of course, already used to talking in everyday parlance about 'raising' our consciousness, with drugs, religious experiences, or simply by listening to music.

A third property of consciousness derives from the fact that one is always conscious of *something*. One is not always conscious of everything, but it is paradoxical to say one is conscious of nothing. One is always conscious of some kind of focus, epicentre or trigger: consciousness thus derives from a specific stimulus.

These are three fundamental properties of consciousness that, if we are to posit any kind of physical basis of consciousness, we will have to somehow accommodate in the physical brain. But first, we need to bring them together. Here then is a formal description of consciousness, incorporating the three properties:

Consciousness is spatially multiple, yet effectively single at any one time. It is an emergent property of non-specialized groups of neurons that are continuously variable with respect to an epicentre.

We will take an 'emergent property' to signify a property of a group of components that is not attributable to any individual component. For example, the sound of a symphony is not directly attributable to any one instrument; the flavour of a curry could not be attributable to any one single ingredient. Both emerge collectively. Simply, the whole is more than the sum of its parts. If consciousness is somehow an emergent property of a transiently recruited group of neurons that are not specialized (because after all we know there is no consciousness centre), its extent will depend on how many neurons are entrained around some kind of epicentre. Imagine a stone thrown in a puddle, and the rings that would spread out over the surface of the water. The extent of these neuronal 'ripples' would determine the degree of consciousness at any one time. What grounds are there to justify such a scenario?

Epicentres

Instead of thinking straight away about the whole neural assembly, let us turn first of all to the simpler idea, that of an 'epicentre', the stone in the puddle, the focus of consciousness. It is a simpler concept because in itself this epicentre is not going to generate any consciousness at all. On the other hand, we need to assign it some neural correlate since it plays an important part in initiating the steps that will lead eventually to a conscious state. The most obvious candidates for such an epicentre are neurons themselves. So is it the case that one particular neuron becomes active when a person's brain receives a visual signal relating to their grandmother, for example? Although the starkness of this idea renders it attractive, neurophysiological studies show that it is not the case that individual neurons represent single objects in the outside world. After all, it would be a rather precarious state of affairs since there is some, admittedly contested, evidence that one loses neurons throughout one's adult life: how sad for one to lose the cell that registered one's grandmother.

Instead, it seems it is not so much the single neuron that relates to a specific object in the outside world, but, rather, circuits of neurons. By far the most striking feature of brain tissue is the extremely dense network of synaptic connections, providing an awesome number of permutations and combinations of different neurons that results in the greatest possible flexibility and versatility. The same cell, which according to the simple model would have just slavishly been activated only at the sight of one's grandmother, can as a result participate in all number of circuits responsible for representing different objects.

Neuronal connectivity is a very important feature of the brain. Such circuitry is plastic, changing with development and learning. It is the connections, rather than the neurons themselves, that are established as a result of postnatal experience. This plasticity is particularly marked in humans. One can argue that such experience-related connections account, to a certain measure, for a person's individuality, particular fantasies, hopes and prejudices. Once established, connections are not necessarily fixed, but are subject to change over a fairly rapid period of time. For example, it has proved possible to take time-lapse photographs of neurons, cultured in a dish, with their axons growing out to make connections, eventually, with other neurons. When the neurotransmitter acetylcholine is introduced into the culture, there is a rapid, clear divergence of the axon from its original path, towards the site from which the acetylcholine is diffusing. Within as little as 90 seconds the presence of the acetylcholine has changed the destiny of the future neuronal connection. This sort of event, in itself, has nothing to do with consciousness, of course, but simply shows how plastic the brain is during development, how it can be modified by the availability of certain chemicals, how it is not necessarily pre-ordained or intransigently 'hard-wired'.

Neuronal plasticity

Even in adulthood, the brain remains adaptable and sensitive to the experiences of life, as seen clearly in a particularly elegant study with adult owl monkeys. In these animals, Michael Merzenich and his team in San Francisco recorded from different groups of brain cells responsible for each digit of the hand. The hands and mouths of all primates are very sensitive; both these parts of the body are exquisitely controlled in the brain. The hand has a very extensive representation in the brain in terms of numbers of neurons that serve each digit. Merzenich mapped out how many neurons were allocated in each case; he then asked the monkey to repeatedly manipulate a small disc using only two of the digits. Then he looked again, some months later, to see if the situation in the brain had changed. In the area of the brain associated with hand movements, there was an enlargement of the territory of the neurons representing the two digits that had manipulated the disc. Experience changes the connectivity of neurons according to whatever circuits are the most stimulated and thus the most active.

What is the relevance of this sort of finding to consciousness? I suggest that the epicentre, the stone in the puddle, which is going to trigger consciousness at any one moment, is mediated by a group of neurons with relatively long-lasting connections between them. It takes a while to establish such contacts – seconds or so, if not longer – but once they are there, then they are fairly robust. Such adaptive events will occur too slowly to be directly relevant to consciousness, but they do enable associations to be built up during experience, forming the neural substrate for certain objects derived from sensory perceptions. If grandmother comes into view, that hub of neurons will become activated, although this will not mean in itself that one is as yet actually *conscious* of grandmother. That is, such circuits are not the centre of consciousness, but they are going to trigger it.

What we really need to do now is to see how the activated hub of neurons could generate the ripples in the brain that I argue constitute consciousness. How might this epicentre, once stimulated, corral up, transiently and temporarily, a much larger group of neurons that is going, in turn, to determine the moment-by-moment degree of consciousness? Here the task is much harder because we have to think in a timescale of subseconds during which groups of neurons can be recruited and then disbanded. The neurophysiologist Ad Aertson sums up the situation as follows:

Instead, we should distinguish between structural and anatomical connectivity on the one hand and functional or effective connectivity on the other. The former can be described as quasi-stationery, whereas the latter may be highly dynamic with time constants of modulation in the range of tens to hundreds of milliseconds. It appears that dynamic co-operativity is an emergent property of neuronal assembly organisation in the brain which could not be inferred from single neuron observation.

Recruiting neuronal assemblies

The task then is to try to work out exactly how groups of neurons can be swiftly and temporarily recruited into an extensive congress. But first, perhaps we need to be convinced that it occurs. Let's consider an experiment first performed by Robert Frostig and colleagues in Israel in the 1980s, which made use of a powerful experimental tool (that cannot be used in humans): voltage sensitive dyes. When a brain cell is active, its voltage will transiently change. Certain dyes are sensitive to this phenomenon, in that they fluoresce when the neurons become excited. Instead of looking at simply one cell, as in conventional electrophysiological studies, a whole group of cells can be monitored. Using this technique, Frostig flashed a light into a frog's eye and then studied the number of neurons in the brain that responded to the flash. Instead of all the neurons responding at once, which might have been expected, Frostig showed that, over a period of 500 milliseconds (which is quite a long time in terms of brain operations), there was a gradual enhancement in the activity of large numbers of cells. It is not after all a simple matter of light on, brain response, end of story, but, rather, a gradual recruitment of neurons occurs over about half a second.

A different type of experiment, with human subjects, has been done by Benjamin Libet in California. Libet gently pricked the skin of these volunteers and recorded the activity of large parts of the surface of the brain via electrodes on the scalp (that is, an electro-encephalogram: EEG). He found that there was a huge amount of activity in the area of the brain associated with the sense of touch. The experience, however, was not reported as consciousness. The subjects did not feel anything, although their brain was registering signals of the touch to the skin via the spinal cord. It is this early component in the response that I would suggest is the equivalent of the 'epicentre' in my model. But then over some 500 milliseconds, the activity evoked by the prick spread away from the committed area (the somatosensory cortex) to much larger areas of the brain. It is only at this stage, after 500 milliseconds, once the activity has spread extensively, that the person says, 'I am feeling a tingle.'

If we consider these two experiments together, the slow lighting up of the frog's brain and the late dawn of consciousness in the human, it supports the view of consciousness in terms of growing populations of neurons – the relatively gradual recruitment of neurons over about half a second that will only be linked to appreciable consciousness when they have reached a certain quantity.

However, this scheme as it stands presents a problem. One could easily argue that if such an event occurs consistently all the time, then we would have the same consciousness every time. But we never have the same consciousness on two separate occasions, apart perhaps from very rare cases of *déjà vu*. It is possible to overcome this objection, but to do so we will find it easier to take recourse to yet another metaphor.

Instead of a stone in the puddle, imagine the epicentre as the director of a company who only has power via the number of managers he can contact on a telephone network. Such a director would need to be powerful enough to sustain conversations with many managers and the managers to telephone submanagers and therefore establish a strong network. The current model would be represented by a rather static arrangement of the same director and managers all behaving in the same stereotypic way, like a sequence on video repeated over and over. More realistic, however, would be the idea that, although the director is trying to make phone calls, some of the managers are chatting, some have a hangover, some cannot be bothered to answer the phone, some are very keen to get a pay rise and so pick the call up quickly: in general, there is a variability in the extent to which these managers and submanagers will respond to the corralling, recruiting signals of the director. This seems a more plausible model, because on no two occasions would the same number of neurons be corralled to exactly the same extent in exactly the same way. How might we then go back and accommodate such a varying arrangement in the brain? Is there any neuronal mechanism which responds that fast, which can somehow modulate the activity of vast banks of brain cells?

The role of neuromodulation

In the traditional view of neuronal communication, electrical signals pass from one cell to another one at a time, a little like a baton changing hands in a relay race. What we need is to have an increasing number of batons changing hands all at once, over an ever larger group. We need something, let's say a chemical, that can bias a large number of neurons to be activated simultaneously. Such a chemical will not in itself make neurons excited, but it will make cells more receptive to the recruiting signals of the stimulus epicentre, as these spread progressively out in all directions. And indeed there might be the brain machinery for just that scenario. Some neurotransmitters signal merely across the synapse to an adjacent cell; others have a fountain-like distribution in the brain, so that they are very well equipped to access large target areas and intercept other messages. It would, therefore, be appropriate for our purposes if just these transmitters were somehow able to bias or modulate neuronal activity. Indeed, many electrophysiological experiments have shown that they can. When such neuromodulators are present, the response of a neuron to a given stimulation is far greater than when the same stimulation is given alone. Drugs such as Prozac, amphetamine and LSD, which are well known to modify consciousness, all target neurotransmitters and their receptors, as described in Chapter 3. Could it be that neurotransmitters and neuromodulators affect consciousness by helping determine the degree of neuronal corralling that will finally determine the depth of awareness at any one time?

To summarize the model so far: an epicentre, the hard hub of cells that are more long-lasting in their connectivity, is activated by, let us say, one of the senses – a prick on the skin, or looking at something – that in itself will not generate consciousness. But if, at the same time, arousal levels are such that neuromodulators affect a large group of cells, these target cells will be more sensitive transiently to the corralling signal from the epicentre. If enough neurons are recruited, consciousness will ensue for that moment. In my view, therefore, the critical factor is not *qualitative*; it is much more sensible to think in terms of *quantity* of neurons engaged. I cannot at this stage describe exactly how a large number of neurons has the emergent property of consciousness. On the other hand the model offers an appropriate framework for marrying up these two sides of the coin, the physiological nuts and bolts of the brain and one's subjective experience of being conscious.

The physiology of consciousness

Let us see how far we can go with this model in extrapolating from the physiology of the brain to subjective sensations. We can then go back again, taking a particular experience, and see how we might explain it once more in terms of physiology. A good approach, as always in science, is to start with caricatures. So instead of trying to think simply of a 'typical' consciousness, let us think of what kind of consciousness one might have if, for whatever reason, one's neuronal assemblies (which reflect the extent of consciousness) were abnormally small.

Starting with the physiology, the following factors would be important. First, the actual strength of the epicentre. One reason for a small assembly would be if the epicentre was weak. Is there any situation when we could be almost sure that it would not be very strongly driven? Common sense has it that when one is asleep one is not conscious, but that is not quite true. There is indeed a certain form of sleep when one is not conscious, when the EEG discharges as synchronous 'slow waves'. But what is exciting, and perhaps unexpected, is that during dreaming the EEG reverts to being identical to the fully awake state. Hence dreaming, although we traditionally think of it as a form of sleep, appears instead to be a form of consciousness. We all know that when we dream we are certainly experiencing something; it can sometimes be extremely vivid and realistic. So could it be that dreams would be an example of the activity of a minuscule neuronal assembly? If we are talking of a continuum, could it be that dreams – because they have only a very weak hub, because in turn there is no strong external stimulus to drive or to excite a large group of neurons – exemplify the lower end of the continuum of consciousness?

This is an attractive idea, if only because, despite much speculation, no-one has really come up with a very satisfactory concept to date of what dreaming is. On the type of model I am proposing here, however, it would seem that during dreaming there is a kind of meandering over the brain where, because there is no strong drive from outside, there are rather flimsy, fragile little bits of consciousness. This explanation would account for how somehow one can be on a beach and then suddenly in a house; suddenly one's mother is there and suddenly she is somewhere else. At the time, this all seems very real, but is not like the consciousness of reality, of being awake, when there is a continuity provided by the sobering input of sense-data flooding in from the external world.

So much for when a neuronal assembly is small because of weak neuronal recruitment. What about if it was small because connectivity was modest? We saw earlier that the new-born brain has very modest connectivity. Childhood would thus be a good example of the presence of only small neuronal assemblies. For a very young child a toy placed in front of it will be the centre of attention, the epicentre. But as soon as the toy is hidden, it no longer 'exists' for that child, whereas a child only a little older with a more sophisticated or mature brain would have been able to internalize and have a name for the toy and continue thinking about it. It is a relatively easy matter to distract an upset child by pointing out a bird, or offering a bar of chocolate. But it is harder to stop an adult being miserable simply by saying 'Look at that bird' or 'Have some chocolate.' I would suggest that less mature brains have smaller potential for large assemblies and therefore are much more dominated by whatever epicentre is triggered from the outside.

The common physiological base of a small neuronal assembly would suggest that in a sense, although dreaming and childhood are of course very different, they might nonetheless after all be similar in some regards because the connectivity is modest in one scenario and underactivated in the other. Interestingly enough, at about 26 weeks *in utero*, the foetus spends all its time in dreaming: this generous allocation gradually decreases in the early stages of post-natal life. Such an observation would suggest that the immature brain in the first year of life, and to a certain extent in the further nine years, is very different from our adult waking brains.

Could there be any further causes of abnormally small assemblies? We have seen the consequences of a weak epicentre or sparse connectivity. The other factor that we have not mentioned yet is how many of the modulatory neurotransmitters are being released at any given time. It is well known that these chemicals are related to arousal levels: therefore, perhaps if one is highly aroused and/or moving around a lot, then there are so many potential epicentres that one does not have time to form an extensive neuronal assembly. Any nascent assembly would be competed for, elbowed out of the way by other assemblies: so although the connectivity is present and although the stimuli are very strong, they do not have time to form. The sort of scenarios one can imagine fitting into this category are downhill skiing or bungee jumping. In such activities, very powerful sensations are bombarding the brain in rapid succession and giving very little time for reflection on anything else. Perhaps this scenario is an extreme example of small neuronal assemblies, due to very high turnover.

One might start to draw up a profile of neuronal assemblies that were abnormally small. I would suggest that the kind of consciousness that would dominate would be raw phenomenal consciousness – that is to say, an absorbing awareness of the outside world. This outside world would impinge very heavily, one would be very much at its mercy. One would not have a lot of 'internal resources' of reflection and memories and thoughts; rather, one would just be very reactive to whatever crossed one's path, a passive victim of one's senses. In a way this is the situation in dreams, when one is very much at the receiving end of experiences, for instance in nightmares where one is being chased. Things happen, one observes all manner of happenings, but one isn't really in control. When one is in such a state, one cannot reflect, think or rationalize away the fear.

Interestingly enough, such a profile also could be applied to another condition: schizophrenia. Schizophrenia can be characterized by abrupt shifts in logic, often by the person thinking themselves divine because the outside world appears glowing and special. People suffering from schizophrenia are dominated by external events and images. Frequently, they will feel at the mercy of outside forces, completely out of control, mere victims. Here too, then, the underlying consciousness might be one of abnormally small neuronal assemblies. Indeed, it has been suggested that in schizophrenia certain neurotransmitters, such as dopamine, may be functioning abnormally, by inference from the efficacy of drugs which interact with dopamine in affecting schizophrenic symptoms.

It would follow that abnormally large neuronal assemblies have the opposite effect. Here the outside world would be more remote, in extreme examples it might appear very grey, very distant, the opposite of the glowing bright colours of the child's perspective and indeed that of the schizophrenic. There would be a strong continuity, a certain logic to what was happening, or a perseveration in what one was thinking about, and finally reduced movement because there would be less competition from many epicentres. Perhaps most of our normal lives are lived with a mix between small assemblies and large assemblies. One is walking home from work, plotting revenge against someone who has offended you and then suddenly a car screeches around the corner and one is thrown back into the immediate world again, and so on. But if we are thinking of caricatures, is there a scenario we can think of where overly large neuronal assemblies would dominate? Perhaps clinical depression offers a good example, when often patients will indeed say that the world seems grey, remote, and people a long way off.

In general, there will be no single factor in determining the neuronal assembly size and, hence, degree of consciousness. Rather, consciousness is always varying, because it is controlled by a combination at any one moment of the available neuronal connectivity, the strength of the epicentre, how many neurons are wired up together, how strongly they are stimulated, your arousal levels and therefore how quickly these neuronal assemblies are turning over, resulting in the particular size they have time to achieve.

The consciousness of pain

So much for the physiology. But if the model is valid we should be able to use it in the other direction. Can we take some common conscious experience, and cater for it by explaining it in terms of a neuronal assembly? One such experience is pain. A very interesting aspect of pain is revealed by an experiment in which at different periods of the day subjects had a cold stimulus or electrical stimulation applied to their teeth, either for different periods of time or, in the case of the electrical current, at different intensities, until they said it hurt: this is called 'the pain threshold'. What is really interesting, apart from the fact that individuals exist who would volunteer for such an unpleasant experience, is that the pain threshold varies enormously. What subjects thought of as painful in the early hours of the morning or the middle of the night was very different from what they would recognize as painful in the middle of the day. Pain fibres do not change, they are still conducting pain signals into the brain in the same way. Rather, consciousness is changing to this seemingly straightforward stimulation, perhaps as a result of changing biorhythms and neuromodulators. Perhaps variable pain thresholds could be something to do with the differential recruitment of neurons at different times of the day.

There are a number of relevant aspects of the experience of pain. First, we have just seen that it is variable. Second, quite often we refer to pain in metaphorical terms. We talk about it as 'burning', 'pricking' or 'stabbing' – always in terms of something else. Another interesting feature is that pain is usually absent in dreams. One can see things happening, can *fear* pain, but never actually feel it. The actions of the analgesic morphine are also very interesting. People taking morphine do not necessarily claim that the pain goes away: they are still aware of it, but it does not matter any more to them. Finally, there are the well-known cases of phantom limb pain, when amputees will still feel the pain of their absent limb. To a certain extent, all these phenomena fit with the idea that the extent of pain could be related to the extent of available neuronal assemblies. Could it be that morphine, for example, modifies how easily neurons can be corralled in the brain and therefore would give a subjective sensation of a reduction in its importance? Similarly, in dreams, if one has a small neuronal assembly, could that account for why it is not of sufficient size to be associated with pain?

Conclusions

In conclusion, I suggest that there is no magic ingredient in the brain that mediates consciousness. A critical factor could be the number of neurons that are corralled at any one time and it is the extent of these assemblies that will determine consciousness. The most valuable approach would lie in brain imaging in conscious volunteer subjects as they were undergoing different tests that one could predict would modify their neuronal assemblies in certain ways. But at the moment the time and space resolution, although awesome in what has been developed over the past ten years, is still not sufficient. At the moment, only voltage-sensitive dyes showing up areas of activity in response to an epicentre can be used – and then only in experimental animals. By virtue of the fine temporal resolution available from their use, such studies can show, for example, that a second assembly will not form because the first is acting as a rival. That is the kind of precision, the sort of timing we are going to need to characterize how neuronal assemblies relate to consciousness. We are also going to need a very much finer spatial resolution of defined groups of cells, before we could really look at consciousness and its regulation in human subjects. However, there is no conceptual reason why the time and space resolution of brain imaging should not improve over the next few years. By using models such as that suggested here, we might then have some purchase on a true science of consciousness.

Further reading

Greenfield, S. A. (1995). *Journey to the Centers of the Mind*. W. H. Freeman.

Grinvald, A., Lieke, E. E., Frostig, R. D., and Hildesheim, R. (1994). Cortical point spread function and long range lateral interactions revealed by real time optical imaging of macaque monkey primary visual cortex. *Journal of Neuroscience* 14, 2545–2568.

Hobson, A. (1994). *The Chemistry of Conscious States: How the Brain Changes Its Mind*. Little, Brown.

Kolb, B. (1995). *Brain Plasticity and Behavior*. Addison-Wesley.

Strange, P. (1992). *Brain Biochemistry and Brain Disorders*. Oxford University Press.

Woolf, N. J. (1996). Global and serial neurons form a hierarchically arranged interface proposed to underlie memory and cognition. *Neuroscience* 74, 625–651.

13

Consciousness from a
Neurobiological Perspective

WOLF SINGER

Despite the rapidly expanding literature on consciousness, the phenomenon remains ill defined. I shall not attempt to add yet another definition that is likely to fall short of covering the complexity of the phenomenon. Rather, I shall take the stance that consciousness has several different connotations, some of which are amenable to treatment within neurobiological description systems while others are not.

I shall first exemplify some of the aspects of consciousness in order to facilitate agreement on terminology. In essence, these examples illustrate that most facets of consciousness are intimately related to perception, or in more general terms, to cognitive processes such as perception, attention, declarative memory and decision-making. I shall use visual perception as a paradigmatic case to illustrate the nature of explanations that neurobiology can offer and to point to some of the unresolved problems in cognitive neuroscience. In particular, I shall address the question of how the brain constructs from the sparse and diverse signals of its sensors coherent models of its environment. I shall then discuss the possibility that iteration of the very same cognitive operations when applied in a reflexive way to processes within the brain itself might explain one important aspect of consciousness, the ability to be aware of one's own cognitive functions. Subsequently, I shall defend the position that those aspects of consciousness that give rise to the so-called hard problems in the philosophy of consciousness, the experience of self-awareness and the notion of the privacy of one's subjective sensations, transcend the reach of reductionistic neurobiological explanations, because these aspects are social phenomena and products of cultural evolution.

Perception and awareness

When we say that we are conscious, we usually mean that we perceive and remember in a way that makes it possible to report about the perceived or remembered content or to make that content the object of internal deliberations. This aspect of consciousness is closely related to awareness and allows us to distinguish between sensory processes that give rise to conscious experience and those that do not. If we become aware of events, this awareness can occur at different levels of abstraction. We can be aware of the presence of particular objects in the outer world, we can be aware of there being other organisms around us, we can be aware of the fact that we are capable of moving autonomously and interacting with the world in which we are embedded, thus being able to perceive ourselves as segregated and independent entities. We can also become aware of signals generated within our body, for example if we experience pain or thirst. We have receptor systems for pain, for the position of joints and muscles, for the osmotic conditions of the blood, and for the state of most of our organs. These signals are processed in very much the same way as signals from the outer world. Some of these signals are in principle excluded from reaching the level of consciousness, others have facultative access to consciousness and then give rise to sensations in very much the same way as signals from the outside world. The only difference is that it is more difficult to exchange views on these sensations of internal origin because the physical or chemical stimuli that cause these sensations are imperceptible for others.

For a brain to be able to be aware of something, it has to be in a particular, well-defined state. The brain needs to be aroused in order to perform the cognitive functions required for awareness, and there are well-defined electrophysiological correlates that allow one to distinguish from outside whether the brain is in a state where it can be aware of things or not. But even arousal is only a necessary and not a sufficient condition for awareness. Cognitive processes may fail to convey their contents to the level of conscious experience even if executed by a fully aroused brain. There are many instances when our brain processes sensory signals and translates them into adaptive behaviour without us being aware of this. When driving along a familiar route, we may engage in a conversation and not notice that we perform a sequence of highly complex cognitive operations while we get the car safely home. We may even be unable to recapitulate any details of the journey when we try to remember. In fact, evidence from psychological experiments indicates that sensory signals only reach the level of consciousness if they become the target of selective attention. This is the case only for a small fraction of the plethora of sensory stimuli that continuously flood our sense organs, get processed by the brain, and are used for the control of adaptive behaviour. Thus, processing of sensory signals is not necessarily associated with being aware of the result of the respective computations. We become only aware of those events to which we pay attention, and only these find their way into declarative memory, the memory that stores souvenirs about past events and episodes.

Awareness in non-humans

Evidence from animal experiments indicates that at least the large-brained mammals have attentional mechanisms very similar to those of primates and humans. This suggests that animals, too, process sensory information at different levels, one being independent of attention and the other requiring selection of contents by attention. At least to the observer it appears as if such animals were in some way aware of sensory events to which they have paid attention and also remember these events in a different way as events to which they may have reacted but not paid attention.

Much is known already about the neuronal mechanisms of selective attention and it will not be too long before we will have a detailed account of the neuronal conditions that need to be fulfilled for awareness to manifest itself. Still, we would have learnt little about the nature of awareness or consciousness. All we would have defined are the neuronal prerequisites that need to be fulfilled in order to allow a brain to be conscious. What is needed in addition is a comprehensive understanding of how perceptual processes are organized, of how the brain generates representations of sensory objects at different levels of abstraction.

Comparison of the structural and functional organization of the brains of different species indicates that the low-level cognitive functions that allow for the perception of signals from the outer world and from within the organism are similar across species, including primates and humans. It appears further that these primary cognitive functions are readily amenable to neurobiological explanations. In principle it should be possible to provide a complete description in neurobiological terms of the processes that enable an organism to classify and to interpret sensory signals, to direct attention to selected items, to store these items in memory, and to generate appropriate responses.

But how about higher cognitive functions? We know from introspection and observation of other human beings that we can be aware of the fact that we perceive, that we are aware of our own cognitive abilities, that we have a sort of meta-awareness of our primary cognitive functions. We can be aware of being aware and we can even be aware of others being aware of their experience and of others being aware of us being aware. The metaphor of the inner eye refers to this subjective but collectively shared experience. I propose that this meta-awareness results from an iteration of the very same processes that support primary cognitive functions, except that they are not applied to the signals arriving from the sense organs but to the computational results of the primary cognitive operations. The idea is that there are second-order processes that treat the output of the first-order processes in the same way as these treat sensory signals and that the results of these secondary, higher-order cognitive processes should also have access to effector systems and contribute to the control of behaviour just as is the case for the primary processes. Because the results of the second-order processes contain descriptions not only of the outer world and the internal state of the organism but, in addition, of the primary cognitive processes within the brain itself, organisms endowed with brains that possess such secondary cognitive structures can communicate to others what they perceive and what their sensations are.

To a limited extent, primates such as chimpanzees seem to possess such an internal eye. Because the results of the primary cognitive processes are already encoded in the language of neurons, no specialized sense organ is required in order to read the results of the first-order computations. All that is necessary to implement the function of an inner eye are additional processing centres that treat the results of first-order processes in exactly the same way as the latter treat signals from the sense organs. Hence, in terms of neuronal hardware, no qualitative changes appear to be necessary in order to accomplish the evolutionary step from simple brains that are only able to process signals arriving from the outer world and from within the organism to the complex brains that are capable of perceiving their own functions.

Since the computations that underlie primary cognitive functions are carried out in the neocortex, one has to conclude that also the operations leading to meta-awareness, the awareness of perceiving, are due to cortical operations. All that is needed then in order to implement cognitive functions of higher order is the addition of new cortical areas. These new areas would have to receive their input primarily from lower-order cortical areas which process signals arriving from outside the brain. This postulate agrees with the evidence that the evolution of higher cognitive functions, including meta-awareness in chimpanzees and humans, is paralleled by the addition of new areas of neocortex that no longer receive direct input from sense organs but process mainly the output of other cortical areas.

So far then, it appears as if it should, at least in principle, be possible also to identify the neuronal correlates of those computational operations that underlie the higher cognitive functions which lead to awareness of being aware, or, in other terms, generate awareness of one's own mental states. It would seem that if we understand how the brain processes and interprets signals arriving from the outer world and from within the body, we should also be able to understand by extrapolation how complex brains monitor their own functions. The reason is that this meta-cognition appears to be the result of the iteration of the same basic processing algorithm that mediates primary perception.

The visual system as a model for awareness

In the next part of this chapter I shall attempt a brief outline of what we believe we know about the way in which signals are processed in the neocortex when the brain perceives visual objects, and I shall point in particular to unresolved problems and propose solutions to some of them. However, before entering the discussion of neurophysiological facts, I wish to emphasize that, even if we had explained in neuronal terms how the brain perceives the outer world and the organism in which it resides and how it comes to perceive and monitor its own functions, we would have explained only some but not all connotations of consciousness. The hard problem in the philosophy of consciousness that results from our perception of sensations and awareness as subjective, immaterial phenomena would still remain unresolved. There would still be no answer to the question of how it comes that we experience ourselves as freely acting selves who are able to decide how to go about with our sensations and how to react to them. It would remain unexplained why we experience this self as immaterial and somehow opposed to the neuronal processes in the brain, why we feel that this seemingly immaterial self can control what happens in the brain. I shall return to this problem after the following, brief excursion into the mechanistic world of neurons.

A basic requirement in sensory processing is the detection of consistent relations among incoming signals and the representation of these relations by responses of neurons. The iteration of this process is thought to lead eventually to descriptions of the consistent constellations of elementary features that characterize individual perceptual objects. Because the number of possible feature constellations that need to be examined and eventually represented is astronomical, it is essential that the relevant processing algorithms be capable of coping with combinatorial problems.

The neurons of the visual cortex

I propose that these functions take place essentially in the neocortex and that the neocortex exploits two complementary strategies to cope with these combinatorial problems. First, hard-wired neurons are used to detect and represent relations that are particularly frequent and important. Second, dynamic grouping mechanisms, allowing for a flexible recombination of responses from hard-wired neurons, enable different, higher-order relations to be analysed and represented successively within the same hardware.

Any attempt to provide a brief description of cortical circuitry, either graphically or with words, is bound to fall short because of the immense complexity of this structure. In essence, a cortical area consists of a sheet of six layers of densely packed neurons. Inputs from sense organs or cortical areas of lower order typically terminate in the middle layers. From there, signals are relayed to the more superficial layers and then, bypassing the middle layers, down to the deep layers. These distribute output activity to a number of different targets: back to where the input came from, forward to cortical areas of higher order, or directly to effector organs. Feedback signals from higher cortical areas are sent mainly to superficial layers and these layers are also the main termination site of reciprocal connections that link cortical areas occupying the same level in the processing hierarchy. If one records from neurons along trajectories extending orthogonal to the lamination from the surface to the deep layers, one encounters similar response properties while one observes a gradual change of response properties if one analyses neurons along trajectories tangential to the lamination. A particular feature is thus represented by a column of neurons extending vertically throughout the cortical sheet; different but closely related features tend to be represented in nearby columns and very different features in more remote columns. It is commonly held that the feature selectivity of the neurons within a particular column is due to selective convergence of different input connections on individual target cells in the middle layers. If such a cell receives selective input from a linear array of ganglion cells in the retina, it will respond best to the elongated contours which activate simultaneously a maximum number of ganglion cells in this array. This is the case when the orientation of the contour matches the orientation of the array of ganglion cells in the retina. Hence, the respective cortical cells will come to respond best to a particular orientation, or, in other words, their responses signal the presence of a particular feature, in this case, of a particular orientation. It is obvious that more complex constellations of features can be represented if this process of selectively recombining convergent inputs is iterated from one cortical processing stage to the next. However, such a strategy cannot be applied to represent the virtually infinite number of possible constellations of features that characterize perceptual objects, as it would require an equally large number of hard-wired representational units.

For this reason, there is an additional principle of organization in cortical networks that allows for a complementary representational strategy. Columns representing different elementary features are massively interconnected by far-reaching association connections that run tangentially to the cortical lamination. These connections allow for dynamic interactions which have the effect of temporarily associating neurons representing different features into functionally coherent assemblies. This allows representation of a particular constellation of features by the joint activity of a temporarily associated assembly of cells. The constellation of features defining the letter T can thus be represented by dynamically associating cells representing a horizontal and a vertical contour at the appropriate location. The great advantage of this dynamic representational mechanism is that subsets of the same cells can be used again in different combinations to represent different perceptual objects, and this greatly economizes the number of required neurons. To represent the letter L, for example, it suffices to form a new assembly, comprising the same set of cells coding for vertical contours and another set of cells coding for horizontal contours at a different location.

Among the features extracted by input recombination in primary visual cortex are the location, orientation and polarity of luminance gradients, their direction of motion, their spectral composition, and their interocular disparity, reflecting viewing distance. This strategy of evaluating and representing relations by selective combination of input connections is repeated several times on the way from primary visual cortex to higher areas. As suggested by the substantial divergence of projections beyond primary visual cortex and by the functional specialization of neurons in prestriate areas, many of these operations appear to be performed in parallel, each of the areas evaluating particular subsets of higher-order relations in feature space.

In agreement with the notion of ensemble coding, this strategy of recombining inputs and generating cells with selective response properties is not pursued to exhaustive descriptions, either of the elementary features represented in primary visual cortex or of the immensely more complex constellations of features of natural objects. At all processing stages neurons remain responsive to variations of stimulus parameters along different feature dimensions (as discussed in Greenfield's chapter in the context of putative grandmother cells). The responses of individual cells are ambiguous, and a full description of a particular constellation of features can be obtained only by evaluating jointly the responses of a population of neurons.

However, there is a serious problem with such assembly codes. Natural visual scenes usually contain many image components that are adjacent or overlapping in cartesian and in feature space, thus evoking simultaneous responses in overlapping populations of feature sensitive cells. In order to exploit the advantage of assembly coding, the responses related to a particular object must be identified and labelled in a way that assures their joint evaluation at subsequent processing stages and prevents false conjunctions with responses evoked by other unrelated objects.

Dynamic selection processes

A dynamic selection process is required that permits the grouping of distributed neuronal responses in ever-changing constellations. With such dynamic grouping, signals can then be selected at one level and reassociated in a flexible and context-dependent way at the next level via feed-forward connections. This allows for dynamic rerouting of signals within a fixed hardware configuration and circumvents the combinatorial explosion of representational units that would result if every possible feature or constellation of features required analysis by selective recombination of feed-forward connections and was represented by sharply tuned neurons. Dynamic grouping can therefore be iterated over successive processing stages to analyse and represent in a versatile way relations of ever-increasing complexity up to the level where the represented relations describe whole perceptual objects. The problem is, however, that the responses of neurons that have become temporarily associated into an assembly need to be labelled in a way that defines them for subsequent processing stages as belonging together and protects them reliably from getting confounded with responses of cells that belong to other simultaneously active assemblies.

Such dynamic selection and association of responses for further joint processing is best accomplished by enhancing their saliency. In principle there are two strategies to raise the saliency of distributed responses. The selected neurons can be made to discharge more vigorously or they can be made to discharge in precise temporal synchrony. Both mechanisms enhance the impact of the selected responses, the first profiting from temporal and the second from spatial summation of synaptic potentials in the target cells. Grouping through synchronization has the additional advantage that it can operate at a fast time scale because no temporal integration is required and selection can occur at the level of individual action potentials. This permits grouping operations to be multiplexed and may be beneficial when several groups need to be established simultaneously within the same cortical area.

Available evidence suggests that both strategies are used. It has been shown that cells in the visual cortex responding to the features of a perceptual figure discharge more vigorously than cells which respond to similar features that are not part of a figure but belong to the background in which the figure is embedded. This supports the notion that response selection can be achieved by modulation of discharge rate. Experiments on response selection by attentional mechanisms also indicate that responses are selected by enhancing their amplitude.

Synchrony

It is now firmly established that cortical cells can synchronize their discharges with a precision in the range of milliseconds. Cells preferentially synchronize their responses if activated by contours of the same object and can rapidly switch the partners with which they synchronize when stimulus configurations change. Evidence is also available that synchronization probability is related to behaviour. In strabismic cats (that is, animals with squint), for instance, neurons driven by different eyes no longer synchronize their responses. This may reflect the inability of strabismic subjects to jointly process the signals arising from the two eyes and to fuse the images seen by the two eyes. When strabismus leads in addition to amblyopia – a developmental process that leads to permanently impaired vision in the deviating eye – perceptual deficits are associated with disturbances in the synchronization patterns of cortical neurons rather than with abnormalities in the response properties of individual cells. In animals trained to perform sensory–motor tasks synchronicity was seen to increase both within and across areas in relation with problem-solving. These episodes of precisely synchronized activity were confined to those behavioural epochs during which the animals had to focus their attention and they were particularly pronounced among those areas of the cerebral cortex that had to cooperate in order to accomplish the task. Upon completion of the task, when the food reward was made available, this highly organized pattern of synchrony collapsed and gave way to low-frequency oscillatory activity that exhibited variable and unsystematic phase relations.

When the two eyes are presented with different visual patterns that cannot be fused into a single percept, one does not perceive a superposition image of the two patterns but instead either the pattern seen by the right or the pattern seen by the left eye. These two percepts alternate despite constant stimulation conditions because of internal selection of the inputs arriving from the two eyes. This paradigm, called binocular rivalry, is thus ideally suited to investigate how neuronal activity that is perceived differs from activity that is not perceived. Analysis of the responses of neurons in the cat visual cortex recorded simultaneously revealed that at this early level of processing responses to the perceived and the non-perceived patterns were of equal size. Hence, selection among the inputs from the two eyes does not seem to be achieved by suppressing the responses to the pattern that lost in the competition between them and is thus not perceived, nor is selection associated with an enhancement of responses to the pattern that is perceived. Rather, the data show that the differences between the responses from the two eyes lie in their degree of synchrony. Responses of neurons conveying signals evoked by the perceived pattern exhibit strong and precise synchrony, while responses from neurons conveying signals referring to the suppressed pattern exhibit only weak synchronization, if any. This is strong and rather direct support for the hypothesis that the selection of neuronal responses and their grouping together for further joint processing can be achieved not only by selectively enhancing or inhibiting subsets of responses but also by synchronizing or desynchronizing the respective groups of neurons. What makes this case particularly interesting is the fact that here the degree of synchronicity predicts with great reliability whether activity will give rise to conscious experience or not.

It is likely that such selection mechanisms operate also at other levels of processing, because the structural and functional organization of the neocortex is strikingly similar across the different areas. If so, this would imply that only those activation patterns that succeed in becoming sufficiently coherent eventually reach the threshold of conscious experience. In other words, only coherent activity should be recognizable by the 'inner eye' as the representation of a perceptual object that can be described in explicit terms and stored in declarative memory. This conjecture is also attractive for another reason. It is well established that synchronized input to neurons is a particularly favourable condition for the induction of long-lasting modifications of synaptic efficacy, the latter being regarded as a likely mechanism for the inscription of memory traces (see Chapters 4 and 5). There is thus some – admittedly still indirect – support for the hypothesis that signals need to be sufficiently coherent in order to be perceived and to support conscious experience. The recent evidence that neuronal synchronization increases with arousal points in the same direction. If only coherent activity can reach the threshold of consciousness, it would explain why arousal and attention are required for conscious experience.

Neurobiology and self-awareness

I hope that this brief excursion into the physiology of neocortex makes it clear that it should in principle be possible eventually to understand the neuronal substrate of perception and by extrapolation also how brains can monitor the results of their cognitive computations and communicate these results to other organisms. It follows that comprehensive analysis of the activation patterns of large numbers of neurons should eventually allow us to predict with high reliability which patterns correlate with conscious experience and which patterns do not. But this is probably as far as we can get. The question remains as to whether we are prepared to accept this as a neurobiological explanation of consciousness. According to our present view, a particular state of neurons and the subjective experience of being conscious belong to different ontological categories. The former is the prerequisite for the latter, but the two phenomena are defined within different description systems.

How, then, should we deal with the subjective connotations of consciousness that are associated with self-awareness or self-consciousness, connotations that result from the fact that we experience ourselves as individuals with private feelings, sensations and thoughts, that we experience our self as an agent who controls functions such as directing attention, reaching decisions, assigning value, initiating a motor act, allowing a feeling to take over or to repress it? This perceiving and acting self appears to us as ontologically different from the functions that it seems to control and which we consider amenable to neurobiological explanations. These connotations of consciousness are experienced as immaterial, mental entities, and our intuition suggests that they cannot be explained in a satisfactory way by material processes, by chemical and electrical interactions within the brain. This experience is at the basis of the hard problem in the discourse on consciousness and it is the incentive for dualistic positions.

The social nature of consciousness

I argue that these particular aspects of consciousness can indeed not be understood as emergent properties of individual brains in the same way as, for instance, primary sensory or motor processes. Still, I propose that one does not have to take a dualistic stance to account for the seemingly immaterial attributes of the self. The reason why I think that these attributes transcend the reach of purely neurobiological reductionism is that they come into existence only through communication among different brains. For the emergence of these attributes as perceivable entities, as something that can be felt and experienced as real, two prerequisites have to be fulfilled: first, brains must interact with one another in a reciprocal dialogue, and, second, these interacting brains must have cognitive abilities that allow them to generate a theory of mind; each of the communicating brains must be able to generate models of the presumed states of the other brains with which it is communicating. They must be able to monitor – or to perceive – their internal states and to communicate the result of this monitoring to other brains via signalling systems that are sufficiently differentiated to allow other brains to decode and interpret the reports about the sending brain's state – and this communication must be reciprocal. In brief, the brains must be sufficiently differentiated in order to enter a dialogue of the kind 'I know that you know that I know' or 'I know that you know how I feel'. It is my proposition that only once brains can enter such a dialogue can they experience what we associate with being conscious of one's self and of one's own feelings, and only then can the experience of self-awareness and subjectivity develop. Without such a dialogue, these phenomena would simply not exist and hence also not be perceivable.

Considered in this way, the phenomenon of self-awareness – the experience of one's own individuality, the ability to experience oneself as an autonomous individual with subjective feelings – is to be seen as the result of social interactions, and hence of cultural evolution. Only because communication with others allowed us to extrapolate from our own unarticulated awareness of mental states to that of others and in turn to receive their respective reflection do these subjective attributes of consciousness come into existence. They are the result of communication, and just as information requires a sender and receiver to be definable, the subjective attributes of consciousness would not exist without these reflexive interactions. I propose, therefore, that the subjective connotations of consciousness that give rise to the hard problems in the philosophy of mind have the ontological status of social realities, of realities that only come into existence through communication among brains. In this sense they go beyond the functions that individual, isolated brains would be capable of realizing, and this is the reason why purely neurobiological explanations fall short. So far neurobiology deals only with processes within a single brain and hence cannot encompass in its description system phenomena that result from collective interactions among different brains, even if these phenomena ultimately depend on the cognitive abilities of individual brains. There are obviously other phenomena which come into existence only through social interactions that are perceived as less cryptic than the subjective connotations of consciousness such as value systems or beliefs. Much of the difficulty, I think, that we have with the allocation of the mental phenomena related to consciousness comes from the fact that the critical dialogue between brains that generates the awareness of one's self occurs during an early phase of postnatal development and that we have no explicit memory of this phase. While our brains develop, our care-takers force us into an intensive dialogue during which we – our brains – acquire awareness of ourselves and realize that we are different from others, but we do not remember that this learning process took place. It seems quite natural then that the contents installed by this early imprinting process are experienced as being different from the contents of primary perception. The inner eye – which implies nothing mystical, as I made clear above – sees no cause, no history, of these early acquired perceptions and sensations, and hence the awareness of one's self is perceived as detached from any causation. In conclusion, then, I propose two causes for the mysterious aspect of the phenomenon of self-awareness: first, its social origin, and, second, the amnesia for the acquisition process.

The development of consciousness

Human babies are immature at birth and acquire their cognitive abilities only slowly and over several years. Throughout that time they are exposed not only to the world of objects but to care-takers whose cognitive abilities are extremely well tuned to entertain an intensive dialogue with the slowly maturing baby brain. By the time this brain is sufficiently developed to keep track of its experience by building and recalling episodic memories, the experience of individuality and self is likely to be already deeply imprinted in its architecture. But there is no record of the installation process and, unlike conventional sensory experience, these early imprinting processes are not repeatable, because they influence directly the developmental expression of the processing architecture. Hence, it is not at all surprising that the cognitive categories acquired by early social interactions assume qualities that differ from those of other brain processes and seem to transcend neurobiological descriptions.

Another but closely related reason for the particular status of self-awareness is that the contents installed during early development have a historical dimension. The early experience of one's self is mediated by interactions with brains that are themselves primed by education. Hence, the contents transmitted by this early learning process reflect notions that have been acquired during cultural evolution. As a consequence, the specific human connotations of consciousness are likely to be the product of cultural evolution. This in turn implies that they are not invariant but must have changed over the centuries. The proposal is that these connotations have evolved and have become increasingly differentiated since humans first exchanged signals about their internal states, feelings, emotions, intentions and thoughts, since humans drew pictures on the walls of caves and communicated with each other through signs and simple languages. The genetically determined architecture of our brains cannot be too different from that of our ancestors, but most probably we experience ourselves not in the same way as we would had we grown up in a community of cave-dwellers or, as Rudyard Kipling's Mowgli, in a community of animals. If this hypothesis is correct, if the enigmatic aspects of consciousness, its subjective mental attributes, are indeed the result of a social learning process in which brains experience a class of mental phenomena that emerge only from mutual reflection, then one should be able to witness the gradual emergence of these aspects of consciousness during ontogenesis. This is not the place to pursue this prediction further, but it might be rewarding to consider such developmental aspects in discussions on the nature of consciousness.

Consciousness and history

There is common consensus that the way in which we perceive the outer world depends very much on *a priori* knowledge. This knowledge resides in the specific processing architectures of our brains and has been installed both by genetic instructions and by early developmental learning. The same dependence of the perceivable on the known holds with all likelihood for the internal monitoring of brain processes, for the inner eye. Hence, it is perhaps not too far-fetched to assume that knowledge acquired about the nature of mental states can be passed on through education to the next generation and influence substantially the way in which humans become aware of themselves and perceive their internal states. Thus, while awareness is of course due to neuronal processes within one's own brain, the frame of reference within which this perception occurs transcends the limits of the individual brain and assumes a social and, by that also, a historical dimension.

Still, my proposition is that self-awareness and the subjective connotations of qualia can be understood as emergent properties of brains without having to take a dualistic position. They belong to our world but because they have a social or cultural origin, and hence both a historical and interpersonal dimension, they cannot be understood simply as an emergent property of an isolated brain, and therefore they transcend the reach of conventional neurobiological approaches.

Further reading

Engel, A. K., Roelfsema, P. R., Fries, P., Brecht, M., and Singer, W. (1997). Role of the temporal domain for response selection and perceptual binding. *Cerebral Cortex* 7, 571–582.

Fries, P., Roelfsema, P. R., Engel, A. K., König, P. K., and Singer, W. (1997). Sychronization of oscillatory responses in visual cortex correlates with perception in interocular rivalry. *Proceedings of the National Academy of Sciences of the USA* 94, 12699–12704.

Roelfsema, P. R., Engel, A. K., König, P., and Singer, W. (1997). The role of neuronal synchronization in response selection: a biologically plausible theory of structured representations in the visual cortex. *Journal of Cognitive Neuroscience* 8, 603–625.

Roelfsema, P. R., Engel, A. K., König, P., and Singer, W. (1997). Visuomotor integration is associated with zero time-lag synchronization among cortical areas. *Nature* 385, 157–161.

Singer, W. (1994). Putative functions of temporal correlations in neocortical processing. In: *Large-Scale Neuronal Theories of the Brain* (ed. C. Koch and J. L. Davis), pp. 201–237, MIT Press.

Singer, W. (1995). Development and plasticity of cortical processing architectures. *Science* 270, 758–764, MIT Press.

Singer, W., and Gray, C. M. (1995). Visual feature integration and the temporal correlation hypothesis. *Annual Review of Neuroscience* 18, 555–586.

Singer, W., Engel, A. K., Kreiter, A. K., Munk, M. H. J., Neuenschwander, S., and Roelfsema, P. R. (1997). Neuronal assemblies: necessity, signature, detectability. *Trends in Cognitive Science* 1, 252–261.

14

One World, but a Big One*

MARY MIDGLEY

The importance of social facts

Is matter somehow more real than mind? Is physical explanation always more fundamental than other kinds of explanation? These odd questions surely lurk in the background of current debates about consciousness. But can reality be the kind of thing that has degrees? Or again, does it make sense to talk of one enquiry as more fundamental than another until one has explained 'fundamental for what?'

I want to approach these large issues by looking at the admirably clear discussion which opens John Searle's book *The Construction of Social Reality*. Searle sets out a manifesto that lights up sharply the troubles that have lately distorted this topic. He writes: 'We live in exactly one world, not two or three or seventeen.' That is surely right. But then comes the difficulty. Searle goes on:

As far as we know, the *fundamental* features of that world are as described by physics, chemistry and the other natural sciences. But the existence of phenomena that are not in any obvious way physical or chemical gives rise to puzzlement ... How does a mental reality, a world of consciousness, intentionality and other mental phenomena, fit into *a world consisting entirely of physical particles in fields of force*? (Emphases mine.)

So far, that will sound familiar for those who have been following this controversy. What is new is that Searle goes on to point out strongly that this question is not an isolated one dealing only with hidden, private experiences – aches and images and qualia. It opens

---

* An earlier version of this chapter appeared in the *Journal of Consciousness Studies*, 3(5/6).

issues of a quite different order of magnitude, namely, the whole extent of social phenomena. We must go on to ask:

How can there be an objective world of money, property, marriage, governments, elections, football games, cocktail parties and law-courts in a world that consists entirely of physical particles in fields of force, and in which some of these particles are organized into systems that are conscious biological beasts, such as ourselves? (p. 1)

As he shows, in order to deal with these topics we have to be objective – that is, fair, honest and methodical – about the whole range of the subjective. We have to treat seriously, not just a few detached aspects of our consciousness, but the whole range where subjective experience affects objective facts – facts which are a real part of our single world. Since much of our subjective life is unconscious, this greatly enlarges the ground to be covered, though the conscious part, the lit centre, is still a crucial aspect of it.

Institutions such as money, government and football, which have played little part in debates on this matter so far, are forms of practice shaped and engaged in by conscious, active subjects through acts performed in pursuit of their aims and intentions. They can therefore only be understood in terms framed to express those subjects' points of view. Physical analysis of the material objects involved may be quite irrelevant.

Money, for instance, notoriously cannot be defined as a particular material thing or stuff. It gets made out of many kinds of stuff or even – as seems to happen at present – out of mere credit. Money is whatever people agree to use as a medium for exchanging goods. This has radical consequences for the project of explaining it. Someone who asks what money is, or who wants to understand its workings better, needs to know about the wishes and intentions of people wanting to exchange goods. This is the only way of explaining money. No physical analysis of coins or notes, or of the neurons of the people using money, need form any part of this explanation.

Explanations vary

Explanation, then, is not always of a single kind. It is whatever information or reasoning will solve the particular problem that is causing trouble at the time. This is a central point for the project of 'explaining consciousness' because many people discussing this assume that asking for an explanation of it is simply asking for its cause – for a physical condition that produces it. They therefore look for these antecedents – usually either in evolution or in neurology – and they are mystified to see why anybody should look anywhere else.

The approach which looks always for the cause is of course very often the right one. It is suitable when we are trying to 'explain' some phenomenon such as global warming, where we are already confident that we grasp an effect adequately and the cause is then the next thing that we want to find. But the project of *explaining money*, or *elections*, or *time*, or *marriage*, or *football*, or *grammar*, or *art*, or *laughter*, or *gambling*, or *the Mafia*, or *post-structuralism*, or *differential calculus* is not like this at all. Here, what we need is to know more about the thing itself.

Similarly, it is often said that DNA 'explains life' because it fills an important gap in the causal story about how life is reproduced. This gap-filling is indeed welcome. It is needed because it eliminates vitalist speculations about a special quasi-physical force or stuff-of-life which might have done this particular job. But the discovery of DNA tells us nothing about the peculiarity of life itself while it is actually being lived. And this peculiarity is often what puzzles us.

It is interesting that biologists are at present just as frightened of attempts to analyse the concept of *life* as psychologists were, until lately, by any similar attention to the concept of consciousness. Standard dictionaries of biology simply do not have an entry for this word. Writers who occasionally mention it usually either say that it is indefinable or refer briefly to a few formal properties such as homeostasis, replication and complexity. But what sort of complexity? And how would we get on if we confined our understanding of money to a similar set of formal properties?

Category problems

The reason why words like life and consciousness are awkward is that they lie at the peculiar level of generality where we have to change gear at the boundary of a category. They mark the frontier of a whole logical type. The same kind of trouble arises over terms like *time, necessity, chance, matter, space* and *reality*. For these large items, dictionaries notoriously start to revolve in a circle of near-synonyms, dodging the philosophical problems. Even *game* is a much harder word to define than *football*, since the idea of *play* is itself a distinctive and somewhat puzzling category of thought.

'Consciousness' is not one among a class of parallel instances as football is one among games. It is a term used to indicate the centre of the subjective aspect of life. Understanding such a word means relating that aspect fully to the other aspects. And this business of relating is – like medicine – inevitably an art rather than a science, though, of course, sciences can sometimes form a very important part of it.

Of course, when these awkward words which signal category-boundaries have to be used in a particular science, they can be given sharp, limited definitions to suit immediate purposes. Thus, a science which only wants to account causally for the physical conditions of consciousness can perfectly properly do this by using a vague, min-imal definition of consciousness, thereby investigating what David Chalmers has called 'the easy problems'. But the results may have little relevance to the wider difficulty of fitting together the various aspects of our world. The problem here is the vast one that each of us has in trying to relate our own individual experience sensibly to that of others and to the official views of our society. This problem is a central concern of serious literature and also of philosophy. It has often been held not to concern physical science. The pioneers of modern science deliberately withdrew from it in the seventeenth century, confining their attention to physical matters, and the sub-sequent success of the physical sciences is generally thought to have owed much to this traffic regulation.

However, once consciousness is admitted to be real, the brute causal regularities studied by a narrower perspective do not satisfy all scientific enquirers. The scientific spirit looks also for an understandable connection, a reason why the effect is suitable to the cause. If this can be found at all in the case of consciousness – which is still not clear – the search for it must certainly involve reference to a much wider context which takes both aspects seriously as a whole. This kind of wider reference is something that current specialization makes extremely difficult for scientists. For a start, it is surely going to include the social context which Searle mentions and also, beyond that, the context of life.

As for life, I suspect that, twenty years hence, biologists may be concerning themselves with 'the question of life' just as vigorously as the rest of us now are with problems about consciousness. As Lynn Margulis and Dorion Sagan have lately pointed out, it really does not pay to neglect one's central concepts. In both these cases, one question that enquirers often have in mind is what kind of *importance* or *significance* these things have, what makes them matter so much? The weight that we attach to the difference between being alive or dead, conscious or unconscious, for others as well as ourselves, is not just a chance matter of our individual fancy but a part of the concept.

Importance affects selection, so science cannot be 'value-free' in the sense of neglecting it. The assumption that consciousness was unimportant was what led the behaviourist psychologists to their bizarre and unworkable conclusions. If we now decide to take the matter seriously we shall have to use different methods. We must, I think, be led into much larger philosophical problems such as free will and personal identity – problems which deeply affect our view of the kind of creatures that we ourselves are. These questions are primarily about finding the best way to think rather than about strictly factual matters. Though, therefore, they concern scientists and raise many scientific questions, they do not seem to be in the narrow contemporary sense purely scientific questions. I am not sure whether the current idea of 'a science of consciousness' is meant to define a territory parallel to that of, for instance, 'a science of digestion', but if it is, I doubt whether the notion will work.

Mapping the background

What sort of explanation, then, is needed here? In the case of the social items which I listed such as money and football, explanation involves mapping the structure of each and showing how that structure connects it with the surrounding conceptual areas of life as a whole. Among those areas the participants' aims and intentions form a crucial core. We always need to ask: 'What are these people trying to do and why?' This gives us, not a causal story in the sense now expected in physical science, but a historical story. B. F. Skinner dismissed 'those collections of personal experiences called history' as amateurish and inadequate because they did not use the methods of a physical science. History in fact works by the disciplined use of multiple analogies and the careful scrutiny of evidence. These methods are not antiscientific. They are as rigorous, as necessary, as important and as reputable as the methods of the sciences. Indeed, they are needed and used in important areas of science itself, such as cosmology and the study of evolution, because those areas deal with single, unrepeatable historical processes, exactly as the study of past human life does.

The need for new conceptual plumbing

We must surely accept, then, that the kinds of explanation we need vary according to the nature and state of our topic. Different kinds of concept need to be explained in different ways, ways which vary according to the current gaps in our ability to handle this particular subject-matter. Like explorers in a territory where few places are yet known, we try to find connections between our existing insights. And, like those explorers, we often see reason to distrust the maps which have been used so far.

The enterprise of relating different aspects of life is, however, trickier than that of relating lakes and mountains because there are more ways in which they might be related. It is sometimes very hard to be clear about just what it is that we have got right and what it is that we still do not understand. That is the kind of trouble we are presently having about consciousness. We really need new concepts that will bring into focus again the whole person. We need to correct the unrealistic division which has long distorted our thought, and which is now being constantly widened by the image of the mind as a computer program, carrying the sharp, simple dualism of software and hardware.

This need for different concepts is always hard to grasp while we are in the grip of it. It becomes plain by hindsight when new and needed concepts are finally invented, as happened with the modern concept of tolerance. Towards the end of the seventeenth century, people all over Europe were looking for a way of thinking that would allow them to drop the habit of fighting wars of religion, without their simply ceasing to care about the important issues which had underlain those conflicts. They had more difficulty in finding that path than we can now imagine. At that point, however, John Locke and others hammered out ways of thinking about tolerance which made it possible to move steadily in that direction. They did not, of course, fully solve the problem. We still have sharp difficulties about what to tolerate and in what spirit to tolerate it. But they did provide a most useful conceptual tool – a tool which we now take completely for granted – for avoiding a whole set of (previously popular) disastrous answers to such problems.

The roots of dualism

This claim about variation, this declaration that kinds of explanation differ and new ones must be found, is not a shocking manifesto for irrationalism. It does not mean that just anything can count as an explanation. It merely means that the one world in which we all live is complex and that our powers of thought are, luckily, suppler and more versatile in dealing with it than some philosophers have supposed. The many ways of thinking that we possess, and are always developing, are not rival alternatives. They form a potentially coherent set of tools which we always learn to use harmoniously to some extent (as carpenters do) and whose various capacities we can come to understand better with careful practice.

However, ever since the time of Descartes – who so mistakenly amputated minds from bodies and was so certain that the world was basically simple – the ambition to simplify thought by reducing it to one great underlying form has been terribly strong in Western philosophy. His faith that the world itself is built on a single, fundamentally simple pattern has only lately begun to be questioned.

Descartes's dilemma still deserves our attention because it is essentially the same one that has cropped up again today. It has done so now because we can no longer live with the inadequacies of his simple solution to it. Descartes was the first great thinker who was struck by the peculiarity of inner experience, the full, strange specialness of the subjective viewpoint. He was too honest and clear-headed to try to sweep this specialness under the carpet by saying that experience was somehow unreal, or was not important enough to be taken seriously in our understanding of the world. He saw that this personal experience was in a way the centre of all importance. He therefore made it the starting-point of his enquiry, remarking *Je pense, donc je suis* – I think, therefore I am.

But what sort of a thing is this I? (This is where the real difficulty starts.) Descartes was (again) too honest and clear-headed to think that it could be tucked in somewhere among the subject-matter of physical science – as many people apparently want to do today. Ahead of his time, Descartes fully appreciated the dawning science of people like Galileo and Harvey. He was eager to display its importance. But he understood that the success of this modern science was due precisely to its sharply limiting its subject-matter and excluding from it concepts such as purpose which presuppose a particular point of view – concepts which (as he saw) had blocked and confused earlier physical theorizing.

That is why Descartes divided mind from body in the most radical manner, ontologically – by declaring that they were unrelated kinds of substance, linked only by God's external mediation in a perpetual miracle. In this way reason, which thinks about both items, could still be viewed as a single faculty although it used different methods for these two different purposes, because the difference of concepts was due to the difference between the two subject-matters. It was, then, possible to hope that, on both sides of this gap, reason would soon produce beautifully simple explanations.

This drastic piece of world-splitting surgery did, of course, work well for a time. It allowed various real and important simplicities to be discovered, especially on the physical side. By using the extreme resource of ontology, Descartes succeeded in laying out a safe enclosure for modern science, isolating it from interference by other forms of reasoning. So this notion of a deep split in reality was the background that was taken for granted in the first days of that science.

The failure of unification by conquest

Many people, however, always suspected that the idea of such a radical division was unworkable for just the reasons that are now bringing forward the 'problem of consciousness'. People saw that it is not really possible to keep up a reason-proof barrier between subjects and objects, between inner and outer, between thought and things. These two elements in the world cannot be viewed as being unrelated because we continually need to think about relations between them, relations which are themselves essential sinews of our thought. Explanation cannot work without continually crossing this supposed gulf. As Searle rightly says, we live in just one world.

How then could the gap be mended? Human pugnacity saw to it that the first method which occurred to most theorists was conquest, and again this was attempted by the extreme methods of ontology, through an ambitious, sweeping metaphysical colonization of matter by mind or mind by matter. From the seventeenth to the nineteenth century, philosophers fought to establish that either Matter or Mind was the one basic substance so that the corresponding form of explanation was equally basic for all thought – a project which grew more and more contorted till it exploded and sank in its final form, the Stalinist version of the Marxist dialectic.

A *plague on both their houses*

What then were these warriors saying? To summarize crudely, on the idealist side it seemed that matter must be shown as simply a form of mind, a mere logical construction out of sense-data (Leibniz, Berkeley, Hume, Hegel, Ayer). On the materialist side, it seemed equally clear that mind was only a form of matter, that 'the brain secretes thought just as the liver secretes bile' (Hobbes, Laplace, La Mettrie, Marx, Skinner). T. H. Huxley managed to embrace both kinds of reduction at once, but this was an unusual achievement.

Unfortunately, despite some serious attempts at subtlety in both armies, this ontological warfare was always far too crude a practice to sort out the difficulty. Neither alternative can really be made to work. Both, indeed, have their strengths and both have had their epochs of success. Anyone who has not yet felt the force of the idealist position need only read Hume and Berkeley to discover that it is quite as easy to start dissolving away matter as it is to start abolishing mind. But after the first few moves both enterprises run into grave difficulties. Recently, materialism has certainly claimed the field. Many people today still think it a meaningful, reasonable doctrine. To the contrary, I want to say flatly that it is no better than its opponent and probably worse – since a world without subjects is even less conceivable than a world without objects. And if one gets rid of one alternative, one must equally get rid of the other. The whole ontological quarrel is mistaken.

The current credulity about materialism is understandable because – quite apart from the attractions of the traditional warfare against God – the way in which the dispute has lately been thought of makes it seem unavoidable. For some time, the debate has looked like one taking place within the physical sciences themselves. The combatants have tended to stay close to Descartes's idea that the two rival elements were different substances. Unless one takes the intense logical care that Aristotle used, this simply sounds like two kinds of physical stuff. Disputants – especially on the materialist side – have therefore had the impression that they were asking something close to the Presocratic question: 'What physical stuff is the world made of ?'

From this position, Mind naturally evaporates because it looks like a kind of gas, a gas which is certainly not recognized by modern chemistry or physics. Nor do things get better if, instead of a substance, mind is treated as a force closely comparable to physical forces. Again, there is simply no room for such an extra force on the physical table or anywhere near it. This is just the mistake which the nineteenth-century vitalists made when they tried to insert a quasi-physical force or entity called 'life' as a factor on a par with those already considered by physics and biology, instead of pointing out that the extreme complexity of living things called for quite different forms of explanation.

Consciousness as an honorary physical entity

The current wish to take consciousness seriously has, however, led people to hope that they can manage to legitimate it by finding it a place on the borders of physical science, without repeating the vitalists' mistake of trying to locate such an item inside it. Thus Gregg Rosenberg suggests that 'the irreducible character of experience implies that fundamental natural laws are governing it, laws on the same level as those governing properties such as mass, motion and gravity'. This is a variant of David Chalmers's suggestion that we should avoid reductionism by taking 'experience itself as a fundamental feature of the world, alongside mass, charge and space-time'. Chalmers remarks with satisfaction that, if his view is right,

then in some ways a theory of consciousness will have more in common with a theory in physics than a theory in biology. Biological theories involve no principles that are fundamental in this way, so biological theory has a certain complexity and messiness about it; but theories in physics, insofar as they deal with fundamental principles, aspire to simplicity and elegance. The fundamental laws of nature are part of the basic furniture of the world, and physical theories are telling us that this basic furniture is remarkably simple. If a theory of consciousness also involves fundamental principles, then we should expect the same.

Physics-envy could hardly be more touchingly expressed. The trouble about this kind of proposal is an extremely interesting one. Rosenberg wants to insert his new laws 'on the same level' as those of physics. This is evidently because he thinks physics is the ground floor, the bottom line, the slot for the ultimate and most important classificatory concepts, the only place for categories. So does Chalmers. And both rightly think that 'experience' has that kind of importance because it is a category-concept, a concept too bulky to be accommodated in a mere annexe on the edge of neuroscience. They therefore want to insert it as a physical category among the largest and gravest kinds of concept that they can think of.

But *this place cannot be found by annexing it to physics, any more than to neurobiology*. Physics is an immensely specialized science. Its basic concepts are most carefully abstracted, neatly shaped to fit together and to do a quite peculiar conceptual job. They cannot accommodate an honorary member of a different kind. The meaning that concepts like 'mass' have in physics bears little relation to their everyday meaning. Trying to add a rich, unreconstructed, everyday concept such as consciousness to this family is like trying to add a playing-card to a game of chess – or perhaps more like trying to put down a real queen or knight on the chessboard. These new items are of a different logical type. They need a different type of context. They do not belong in this game at all. They can't be 'on the same level'. The category-difference is too great.

Anyone who thinks that physics could conveniently build on this kind of annexe should notice that, if it did, plenty of other concepts would have as good a claim to occupy it as consciousness does. What, for instance, about *substance, necessity, truth, knowledge, objectivity, meaning, communication, reality* and *appearance, reason* and *feeling, active* and *passive, right* and *wrong, good* and *evil*? What indeed about life, which has only been excluded because people today don't want to look at it? All these are basic categories of our thought. If physics were enlarged to accommodate all of them, it would become continuous with the philosophy of science and through this with the central areas of metaphysics. Physics has indeed been so treated in the hands of some of its greatest proponents, from Galileo to Einstein. Perhaps indeed it needs this kind of outward connection. But such a move would run quite contrary to the Popperian limitation of the scope of science which most scientists seem to accept today.

The physical 'level', then, is not the ground floor of all thought, not a set to which all really important concepts have to belong. There is no need to expect that other crucial areas of thought will turn out to be governed by universal 'natural laws' comparable with those used in physics or directly relatable to them. The quest for such quasi-physical laws governing history and the social sciences, a quest which was eagerly carried on by theorists such as Herbert Spencer, Toynbee, Spengler and Engels has turned out disastrously misleading. And it has done so largely because it was guided by blind imitation of physics rather than by attention to the needs of its subject-matter.

However, the phrase 'fundamental natural laws' is, in current usage, firmly stuck to the laws of physics. This expresses a convention which equates nature with 'the subject-matter of physics'. Rosenberg wants to unstick this phrase slightly and to widen its scope somewhat by revising the idea of nature to take in consciousness.

This widening project is surely right as far as it goes. But it has to operate on a far bolder and more drastic scale. Explaining the whole of nature is not a linear process directed downwards towards a single set of explanatory concepts. Thought is not a neat pile of bricks in which each is supported only by the one beneath it. Thought is not governed by this kind of gravitation; its connections go in all directions. The gravitational habit of explanation, now called 'foundationalism', is, as has lately been made clear, often misleading.

The vanishing subject

Chalmers's and Rosenberg's suggestions seem, then, to be further examples of the kind of mistake which has been dogging attempts to find a place for mind somewhere among the stony fields of matter ever since metaphysical materialism became the dominant fashion in the mid-nineteenth century. People have been credulous about materialism because at a deep level they still assumed that – in however sophisticated a sense – we still needed to look for a single fundamental stuff, a substrate which would provide a universal form of explanation. In spite of advances in physics which ought to have undermined this pattern, the image of matter as the *hyle* or wood out of which things are made persisted, and explanation in these terms inevitably made mind look like some kind of illusion. After all, when the brain has finished secreting thought, the product has no weight, nor does the brain itself seem to have got any lighter. And again, there is no gap in the physical forces working on the brain which might leave room for mind as an extra force. Perhaps, then, consciousness was, as J. B. Watson sometimes put it, simply a myth?

To this exciting terminus the behaviourist psychologists triumphantly drove their train at the start of the twentieth century. Life there proved, however, so strange and puzzling that nearly all the passengers (including Watson himself) quickly moved back from it and began travelling round the various neighbouring stations on this same branch line, looking for compromise positions. They are still doing so today.

Two standpoints, not two stuffs

What is needed, however, is to avoid ever going down that branch line in the first place. *These two aspects of life are not two kinds of stuff or force. They are two points of view – inside and outside, subjective and objective, the patient's point of view on his toothache and that of the dentist who studies it.* The two angles often need to be distinguished for thought. But both of them are essential and inseparable aspects of our normal experience, just as shape and size are inseparable aspects of objects. The dentist is aware of the patient's pain as an important fact in the situation he studies, and the patient, too, can to some extent think about it objectively. Indeed, patients can be dentists themselves. The only kind of item that has to exist in the world in order to accommodate these two standpoints is *the whole person*, the person who has these two aspects. Ontology has to accept this person as a single, unbroken existent thing.

Virtually all our thought integrates material taken from the two angles. As Thomas Nagel points out in an excellent discussion of these two viewpoints, we never normally take either position on its own. Instead, we constantly move to and fro between them, combining material from both:

To acquire a more objective understanding of some aspect of life or the world, we step back from our initial view of it and form a new conception which has that view and its relation to the world as its object . . . The process can be repeated, yielding a still more objective conception . . .

The distinction between more subjective and more objective views is really a matter of degree, and it covers a wide spectrum . . . The standpoint of morality is more objective than that of private life, but less objective than the standpoint of physics.

Thus we combine elements derived from the two angles in various ways that suit the different matters that we are discussing, ways that differ widely according to the purpose of our thought at the time – much, perhaps, as we combine visual and tactile data in our sense-perception.

As Nagel points out, objectivity is not always a virtue, nor is it always useful for explanation. It is only one among many ideals which we have to aim at in thinking. In many situations an increase in detachment can be a cognitive as well as a moral disaster. This is, of course, most obvious in private life, which (it should be pointed out) is not a trivial and marginal aspect of life as a whole. If we are trying to understand what is making our friends unhappy, a detached approach will at some point not only distress them but completely block our effort to find out what is wrong. Or if we want to understand a profound play or novel, withdrawing our sympathy may make our attempt impossible.

But, much more widely, this happens also about a wide range of problems concerned with the motivation of other people whom we need to know about. Indeed it is true to some extent of all our attempts to grasp the kind of social phenomena which we mentioned earlier. Some degree of empathy or sympathy with the people involved is a vitally necessary cognitive tool for understanding any of them. We have to enter into their aims and intentions. This is why the kind of 'objectivity' which B. F. Skinner aimed at in psychology – the approach which abstracts from human subjectivity altogether, treating other people as though they were simply physical objects – is a cognitive dead-end.

The peculiar status of physics

Physics, by contrast, stands, along with mathematics and logic, right at the other end of this spectrum. It is not just an immensely abstract enquiry but one which directs its abstraction specifically to shut out the peculiarities of personal experience. That is what makes it remote from ordinary thought. Its specialization is entirely justified by its success in doing its own particular work. But the idea of using it as a place from which to explain the situation of consciousness, which stands right at the other end of the spectrum, is surely somewhat wild.

This is not to say that current attempts to alter the concepts of physics in a way which can make the existence of consciousness seem less paradoxical cannot be useful. Though I have no idea whether such attempts can work, I can see that they might do so, simply by removing the crude, mechanistic idea of living organisms which at present, in many people's view, leaves no room for consciousness. But this would be an indirect kind of facilitation. It would work by altering biological concepts in a way that allowed them to mesh easily again with psychological ones. It is quite a different enterprise from fitting physics and subjective experience together directly while leaving out all the aspects of life that lie between them. A shotgun marriage with physics cannot be the right way to save the respectability of consciousness.

Subjectivity is not scandalous

This shotgun marriage – this last kind of solution to the 'problem of consciousness' – is then, I suggest, neither workable nor necessary. It won't work because wide category-differences prevent the two from fitting together. And it is not necessary because consciousness already has a much more suitable partner. It exists in a workable symbiosis with its counterpart, which is something much wider than physics – namely the whole objective viewpoint, of which physics is only one specialized department. These two counterparts are combined in a totally familiar manner over the whole range of our experience, and in a general way that range usually shows us how we had better connect them.

We are indeed often in difficulties about adjusting the details of that connection, difficulties which can sometimes be very grave. In particular, the value-questions about the relative importance of various elements in life, which I mentioned earlier, are vast and often leave us in doubt about how to balance our whole thought-structure. This is why serious literature and philosophy have plenty of work to do. *But we do not suffer from the kind of general paralysis about these problems, the depth of mutual ignorance which would be expected if current materialist dogmas were correct.* 'Consciousness' is not an isolated, peculiar phenomenon at the margin of the world, a surd item detached from the rational ways of thinking by which we make things intelligible. As Willis Harman put it:

When the conscious awareness of the scientist is conditioned by training to look outward only, the present form of science may seem to offer a reasonable world-view. But when consciousness turns back upon itself, and attention turns inward, not only is another realm of experience added to the picture, but a new order to external reality may be seen. The observer is changed in the process; never again can certainty be placed in the articulation of absolute laws that leave this factor of consciousness disregarded.

For instance, as just mentioned, dentist and patient must do business together, and they can usually do so on the basis that they have some grasp of each other's viewpoints and of the social context in which they both operate. We all know that any explanation of matters connected with pain has to take both inner and outer aspects equally seriously. In medical contexts, therefore, the need to be objective about subjective experience is quite familiar to us. Yet as soon as we move away from a science (such as medicine) with a recognized physical basis, alarm and embarrassment descend. Strange as it may seem, many educated people today do find it hard to admit that the subjective viewpoint has an important influence on the world. That embarrassment is the point from which Searle starts his argument. He himself evidently shares it. As he puts it, this problem

has puzzled me for a long time; there are portions of the real world, objective facts in the world, that are facts only by human agreement. In a sense there are things that exist only because we believe them to exist.

But how can this fact be puzzling? These alarming things are not hallucinatory or delusive objects, which it really would be odd to say 'exist only because we believe them to exist'. They are the large-scale, well-recognized social institutions that are listed above, such as laws and money, the kind of things that anthropologists and historians regularly observe and study. They are indeed arrangements *produced* by human agreement, but they are not in any way dependent on private fantasy. They are the kind of solid social fact against which (if we are not careful) we perpetually bang our shins in everyday life. Their reality becomes clear to us because we find that they can injure us. Like cities, they exist because people have made them and still 'believe *in* them' in the harmless sense that people think it worth while to maintain them. That is entirely different from saying that they exist because we believe them to exist.

It is surely odd that people should find a difficulty in counting things like this among the objective facts of the world. Has not something gone seriously wrong with the current notion of existence or reality when it is possible for such doubts to arise? But, of course,

Searle is right in supposing that they do arise. A certain kind of naïve, dogmatic materialism makes it look doubtful whether these things can properly be classed as wholly real and 'objective'. It makes these things – and the whole fact of consciousness – look like something that needs to be 'explained' in the special sense in which explaining things means justifying them, as in the phrase: 'Explain your conduct!'

What people want then is the kind of explanation that will show that – in spite of suspicious circumstances – these things do not constitute a scandal. The explainer must produce passports to prove that they are reputable parts of the world in good standing. Perhaps today this is indeed what is worrying some people most when they ask for an explanation of consciousness. Along with the two aspirations mentioned earlier – the demand for a causal account and the enquiry about importance – it may well figure among the hopes with which people embark on 'the problem of consciousness'. Taking the status of this ideological passport-inspector for granted, they ask for an argument which will convince him that their everyday experience is indeed reputable and real.

Saving the appearances

This is a job that can be done. Searle accepts the demand and produces most convincing passports. He retrieves the social facts that have slipped away through the cracks in theory. He shows how these institutions have developed in seamless continuity out of the increasing complexity of the acknowledged physical facts in the one world. He shows that no vitalism is involved. No illicit quasi-physical forces are needed. As he points out, the tendency to speak, and to crystallize accepted customs by ritual speaking, is a biologically determined characteristic of our species, an emergent property which we have developed in the natural process of evolution. Humans need to map their world by imposing meaning communally on it in this way because of their highly complex social life. This technique for fine-tuning their existence is a further stage in the development begun by other social animals. For they too use rituals to establish their own customs, but rituals of a much simpler, less explicit, less flexible and less sophisticated kind.

Social facts, then, are entirely continuous with biological facts. This shows how misleading the metaphor of 'social construction' is if it is taken in its strong sense as meaning that we are omnipotent in inventing social practices. Customs are not just an arbitrary product of our whim. Searle's central target is indeed the sense of artificiality and exaggerated power that this excessive constructivism suggests – the impression that it gives of human decisions taking place in a vacuum and dictating terms at will to the rest of the cosmos. He points out that human beings are not a separate entity detached from the natural world. Different academic disciplines, therefore, should not behave as if they each owned their own private universe. Physics, literary criticism, political theory, geology and ethics should all notice that they share a world. 'The traditional opposition that we tend to make between biology and culture is as misguided as the traditional opposition between body and mind . . . Culture is the form that biology takes' (p. 227).

This, the central theme of Searle's book, is surely dead right and very important. The Cartesian split is still rampant today. The abstractness and remoteness of much theorizing in the humanities and social sciences echoes the reductive narrowness produced by pseudo-scientific materialism among people who hope they are following the banner of science. That narrowness is what led academics in a wide range of disciplines to book tickets on the behaviourist branch line in the first place, and it is what still pulls them along it towards the futile terminus of full-scale metaphysical behaviourism. Though that terminus has in theory been renounced, it still attracts people who see that solutions half-way to it are unsatisfactory, but cannot yet nerve themselves to get off this track altogether.

'Fundamental'?

On the whole, Searle shoots with deadly even-handedness at both targets. But he is still surprisingly impressed by the materialist story. He still uses a vital part of its language, the part that privileges explanation-by-matter over explanation-by-mind. Thus, to repeat his opening fanfare, having said that we live in exactly one world, he yet goes on:

As far as we currently know, *the most fundamental features of that world* are as described by physics, chemistry and the other natural sciences.

And shortly after he asks, 'how does a mental reality . . . fit into a world *consisting entirely of physical particles in fields of force?*' (emphases mine). But in what sense is that particular way of describing and analysing the world final or magisterial? How are the features of the world which physics describes more fundamental than its other features? Fundamental to what?

If the questions you are asking are already physical questions, then of course these are the appropriate terms to use. Modern physics is the study to which the Presocratic enquiries about the basic stuff of the world finally lead if you take them – as the Presocratics themselves did not take them – in a purely physical sense. When your question is 'What are the smaller physical elements of which this consists and the forces that govern them?', you quite properly end up doing physics, which is of course a necessary, noble and rightly influential enquiry. It is, so to speak, the North Pole at the end of all those signposts 'To the North' – the terminus if that is the way that you are going. But when you reach this pole you are at a remote level of abstraction from the world we usually live in and you have gone in a direction different from that of many equally important lines of enquiry – such as, for instance, enquiries about history or human motivation. Most of life calls on us to ask and answer questions different from this one. What is so special about the atomistic quest?

An alternative – the many maps model

When we open our atlases, we find a number of diverse maps of the world. They analyse that world in different ways and answer different kinds of question about it. These maps do not need to compete for the prize of being called the most fundamental. It is just as true to say that 'the world consists' of lands and oceans, or of climatic zones, as that it consists of the territories of different nations, and so on. *It is also as true to say any of these things as to say that it consists of physical particles in fields of force.*

There is no bottom line. Our choice of terms depends on the purpose for which we want to analyse the world at the time. Indeed, the simplest atlases sometimes contain just two maps, marked respectively 'Physical' and 'Political'. What would it mean to claim that one of these maps is, in some absolute sense, less fundamental and needs to be reduced to the terms of the other? The fact that cities and national frontiers appear only on one of the maps, while mountain ranges appear only on the other, does not undermine the reality of either phenomenon.

The concession which Searle makes to dogmatic materialism in the wording of this passage (and which he repeats throughout his book) strikes me as misleading and inconsistent with his powerful central point about the full reality of social phenomena. This concession damages his thesis in a way very like the one that occurs in the plaintive title of a book by Wolfgang Köhler, *The Place of Value in a World of Facts*. One might as well ask for the place of circles in a world of squares. If you always use graph paper, and take its squares to be the fundamental units of design, you will naturally be in trouble over circles . . .

Physical and 'physical'

One source of confusion here is the systematic ambiguity of the word 'physical'. That word is often used in an everyday sense that has nothing to do with the science of physics but is simply the opposite of 'mental'. Unconscious oscillation between these two senses is widespread in this whole controversy. Thus, Searle himself often uses the word simply to divide all facts into two classes, mental and physical. At other times, however, as in the phrase 'physical particles in fields of force', he uses it to mean 'recognized by the science of physics'. At one point he even describes our perception of colour as a 'subjective illusion', saying that 'colours as such are not a part of the external world *because physics does not recognize them*' (p. 196; emphasis mine).

These meanings are radically different. In the everyday sense where physical is opposed to mental, physical things are not the entities of physics. They are ordinary, macroscopic, unreconstructed items like apples and houses, things that are coloured, solid and eatable. That is why it sounds plausible that we live in a world composed of them. But we certainly don't live in a world composed of quarks and electrons, because physics simply has no place for items such as 'we' and 'life'. Physics follows Descartes's and Galileo's advice; it entirely excludes such terms from its vocabulary. It deliberately describes an uninhabitable, life-free world.

When, therefore, Searle writes that 'we live in exactly one world', he cannot really be referring to the 'world' of physics. That world, like many other such special 'worlds' enclosed in quotes, is not the whole caboosh but an idealized abstraction from it. This becomes increasingly obvious when we remember that, since physics itself is constantly moving on, the 'ultimate particles' of which it takes the world to be composed at one time can easily be superseded and forgotten ten years later.

Neither houses nor quarks, however, are more real than mental items, as indeed Searle makes clear. Toothache is as real as teeth or electrons and debt is as real as the house that was bought with it. Everyday causality runs constantly and unhesitatingly across these borderlines all the time. The one world contains, without anomaly, all these kinds of entity – electrons and elections, apples and colours, toothaches and money and dreams, because it can legitimately be analysed in all these ways. The various explanations that we need therefore involve, quite democratically, all the various kinds of thought that are needed to deal with them. As Rom Harré has pointed out, theorists who have insisted on narrowing the language of causation in a way that seems to make these winding causal paths look impossible, end up with a picture that is as unusable for science as it is for everyday life.

Territorial problems

Thus our situation really is complex. But that complexity need not lead us into academic warfare about who owns the problem of consciousness. Such warfare is futile because, like the air, it encloses and concerns us all. This is not the only topic which is complex enough to need intellectual cooperation between different kinds of thought, and that cooperation can always be organized.

There have, however, been various trumpet-calls urging that this particular problem should be kept as a matter internal to science. Thus Jeffrey Gray defined the question as 'how to get the conscious part of our existence, which is the most important part of our existence, into the scientific framework' and insisted that this must necessarily be 'a problem for the scientists to solve', certainly not one for philosophers.

It is natural that scientists should want to keep this exciting topic to themselves. But unfortunately, even if their customs barriers managed to keep outsiders away, they would find that, in handling this matter, they themselves could not help doing philosophy. In order to make any progress at all, they would still be constantly forced to analyse concepts and to rebuild the background system of thought which connects them – a system which cannot help involving a wide range of disciplines.

There is no reason at all why scientists should not do philosophy and do it extremely well. From Galileo and Darwin to Einstein and Heisenberg, many of them have done just that. But you cannot do philosophy well by trying to do it in isolation. Protectionists who follow Gray's prescription are in fact almost bound to end up doing it badly, because – far from excluding philosophy – they are bound to be held captive by older philosophical views such as those of Descartes, which they unconsciously take for granted.

The whole project of territorial rivalry about this topic is, then, an empty one. The world we live in is indeed one world and a mixed, unreconstructed, vernacular world at that, not a world purified and quarantined to serve a specialized 'science of consciousness'. The issues that arise when we try to think about consciousness are large.

They affect the whole way in which we conceive our world. They need to be cooperatively handled because they present problems that need every sort of explanation.

Further reading

Chalmers, D. (1995). Facing up to the problem of consciousness. *Journal of Consciousness Studies* 2, 210.

Gray, J. (1995). Consciousness – what is the problem and how should it be addressed? *Journal of Consciousness Studies* 2, 5–9.

Harman, W. (1994). The scientific explanation of consciousness: towards an adequate epistemology. *Journal of Consciousness Studies* 1, 140–148.

Harré, R., and Madden, E. H. (1975). *Causal Powers: A Theory of Natural Necessity*. Blackwell.

Harré, R., Clarke, D., and de Carlo, N. (1985). *Motives and Mechanisms: An Introduction to the Psychology of Action*. Methuen.

Margulis, L., and Sagan, D. (1995). *What is Life?* Weidenfeld & Nicolson.

Midgley, M. (1981). *Heart and Mind*. Methuen; pp. 133–151.

Midgley, M. (1994). *The Ethical Primate*. Routledge; pp. 13, 66.

Nagel, T. (1986). *The View from Nowhere*. Oxford University Press; pp. 1–5.

Rosenberg, G. (1996). Rethinking nature: a hard problem within the hard problem. *Journal of Consciousness Studies* 3, 76, 210–211.

Searle, J. R. (1995). *The Construction of Social Reality*. Allen Lane.

Skinner, J. B. (1973). *Beyond Freedom and Dignity*. Penguin.

Notes on Contributors

IGOR ALEKSANDER is Professor of Electrical Engineering and Neural Systems Engineering at Imperial College, London, and has been researching cognitive models using neural networks since the 1960s. He designed an early machine for face recognition (the WISARD) in the 1970s and has recently developed the MAGNUS system, which is capable of acquiring visual and linguistic experience. Currently he is developing models of neurobiological findings of visual awareness in primates. His most recent book is *Impossible Minds: My Neurons, My Consciousness*.

RICHARD BENTALL is Professor and Head of the Department of Clinical Psychology in the University of Liverpool. His Ph.D., from the University College of North Wales, Bangor, compared learning mechanisms in children and animals. He worked in the NHS for two years before returning to the University of Liverpool. His research focuses on the classification of psychiatric disorders, psychological studies of patients who suffer from a variety of psychiatric symptoms (mainly hallucinations, delusions, mania and chronic fatigue) and the development of novel psychological treatments for people suffering from severe mental illness. His main hobby consists of imitating coma at the end of the working day, but he has recently taken up sailing in the hope that fear of drowning will take his mind off his work.

TIM BLISS is Head of the Neurosciences Group at the National Institute for Medical Research in Mill Hill, where he has worked since obtaining a Ph.D. from McGill University in 1967. The paper on synaptic plasticity in the hippocampus which he and the Norwegian physiologist Terje Lømo published in the *Journal of Physiology* in 1973 established the existence of Hebbian synapses in the mammalian brain, and provided a robust experimental model for the study of the neurophysiological basis of memory.

TIM CROW is a psychiatrist with an interest in brain mechanisms and psychosis, particularly from an evolutionary standpoint. He has worked on brain mechanisms and reward, on chemical and structural changes in the brain in schizophrenia and the mechanism of actioin of psychotic drugs. He is increasingly interested in language and the speciation of *Homo sapiens*. He is currently Director of the Prince of Wales Centre for research on schizophrenia and depression at the Warneford Hospital in Oxford.

SUSAN GREENFIELD is Professor of Pharmacology at the University of Oxford and Professor of Physic at Gresham College, London. Her primary research is on novel mechanisms in neurodegeneration, although she has developed an increasing interest in the problem of consciousness. Her work in the public understanding of science includes a fortnightly column in the *Independent on Sunday* and regular broadcasts. Her latest book is *The Human Brain: A Guided Tour*, an introduction to the brain for the general reader (Weidenfeld & Nicolson, 1997).

RICHARD GREGORY was a lecturer in Cambridge following the 1939–45 war, and moved to Edinburgh in 1967 to start the first department of artificial intelligence in Europe with Donald Michie and Christopher Longuet-Higgins. From 1970 to 1988 he directed the Brain and Perception Laboratory in the Medical School of Bristol University. In 1978 he founded the Bristol Exploratory Hands-on Science Centre, due to be expanded and rehoused with the Bristol 2000 Millennium Project. He has written or edited a dozen books on visual perception and related 'brainy' matters. He is a Fellow of the Royal Society and a CBE.

MARY MIDGLEY was born in London in 1919, and was Lecturer in Philosophy at the University of Newcastle on Tyne from 1961, retiring as Senior Lecturer in 1980. From 1978 she has published many books, including *Beast and Man*, *Science as Salvation*, *Wickedness*, *The Ethical Primate* and *Utopias, Dolphins and Computers*.

JOHN PARNAVELAS has been Professor of Neuroanatomy at University College London since 1993. His first degree was in physics, from the University of California, Los Angeles, and his Ph.D. in anatomy is from the University of Rochester, New York. The aim of his research studies is to understand the roles of genetic and environmental factors in the generation of the diverse array of nerve cells and glia that make up the cerebral cortex.

ROGER PENROSE is Rouse Ball Professor of Mathematics at the University of Oxford. His first degree was obtained at University College London and his Ph.D. in algebraic geometry is from Cambridge. His interests are largely geometrical: Einstein's general relativity, non-periodic tilings, twistor theory. He also has views on philosophy and the physics of the mind. He is author of *The Emperor's New Mind*, *Shadows of the Mind* and *The Large, the Small and the Human Mind*. He is a Fellow of the Royal Society.

TREVOR ROBBINS took his Ph.D. in Cambridge and has worked in Denmark and in Boston and San Diego in the USA. His research background is in psychopharmacology and neuropsychology. He is a Professor of Cognitive Neuroscience at Cambridge University and is currently Chair of the Medical Research Council Neurosciences Board and President of the British Association for Psychopharmacology.

STEVEN ROSE has been Professor of Biology and Director of the Brain and Behaviour Research Group at the Open University since 1969. He researches on the cellular and molecular biology of learning and memory and his most recent books are *The Making of Memory* (Bantam, 1992), winner of the Rhône Poulenc Science Book Prize for 1993, and *Lifelines* (Allen Lane, 1997).

WOLF SINGER studied medicine in Munich and Paris and then concentrated on basic neurophysiological studies on the development and functional organization of the mammalian cerebral cortex. He is Director at the Max Planck Institute for Brain Research in Frankfurt and a member of the Pontifical Academy of Sciences.

DAVID SMITH was trained at Oxford as a biochemist and pharmacologist and became Professor of Pharmacology there in 1984, and a year later Honorary Director of the MRC's Anatomical Neuropharmacology Unit. He has been awarded the Gaddum Memorial Prize of the British Pharmacological Society and is a foreign member of the Norwegian Academy of Science and Letters. He established the Oxford Project to Investigate Memory and Ageing (OPTIMA) in 1988, and Alzheimer's disease remains his main research interest.

LARRY SQUIRE is Research Career Scientist at the Veterans Affairs Medical Center, San Diego, California, and Professor of Psychiatry and Neurosciences at the University of California, San Diego. He is a member of the US National Academy of Sciences and a past president of the Society for Neuroscience. He has conducted pioneering research into the anatomy and structure of human memory and its loss through injury or disease.

Index